Beating the Odds

Beating the Odds

10 Smart Steps to Small-Business Success

Scott A. Clark

amacom

American Management Association

This publication is designed to provide accurate and authoritative
information in regard to the subject matter covered. It is sold with
the understanding that the publisher is not engaged in rendering
legal, accounting, or other professional service. If legal advice or
other expert assistance is required, the services of a competent
professional person should be sought.

Library of Congress Cataloging-in-Publication Data

Clark, Scott A.
        Beating the odds : 10 smart steps to small-business success /
Scott A. Clark.
        p.   cm.
        Includes bibliographical references and index.
        ISBN 0-8144-5023-7 (hardcover)
        ISBN 0-8144-7811-5 (pbk.)
        1. New business enterprises.   2. Small business—Finance.
3. Success in business.   I. Title.
HD62.5.C59   1991   90-56187
                                                          CIP

First AMACOM paperback edition 1992.

Printing number

10   9   8   7   6   5   4   3   2   1

To the memory of
J. Wayne Deegan,
business executive, scholar, mentor, educator, and friend,
who taught me to embrace and enjoy
the business of bettering business.

Contents

Preface

When I first decided to go into business for myself, I began reading everything about entrepreneurship that I could get my hands on. I attended government seminars and private workshops. I listened to lectures. I took copious notes and studiously applied myself to the task of launching a new business.

I left those seminars and closed the pages of those books feeling on top of the world, charged up, and confident that I had all the information I needed to go out and make my fortune. All I had to do was put together a solid business plan, present it to investors, and cash their checks at the bank.

But a funny thing happened on the way to the bank. I kept receiving polite refusals from the investors I approached. They were helpful in suggesting ways to improve my business plan. They offered some good general ideas about the company I was trying to launch. They were forthcoming with all sorts of advice. But they didn't give me a nickel.

After the umpteenth frustrating visit to the financiers, I finally realized that the approaches I'd read and been told about weren't working. So I started from scratch, developing my own specific process along the way. By the time I finally did get financing for my first company, it was clear to me that all the really important things I needed to know had never been mentioned in any of the books and workshops.

What Was Missing?

When I sat down and analyzed what had gone wrong, I reflected on what I had read and heard from all the resources that were available to me. The books I accumulated were good as reference materials, full of information about financing sources and the mechanics of developing a business plan. Some of the workshops were worthwhile too, usually because of the charisma of the leader, and I left them with a briefcase full of information about what it takes to be an entrepreneur.

What no one told me was how to go about getting all of these resources that were supposedly available to me. No one taught me the street smarts I later learned were the real key to getting investors interested in financing my business and operating my company successfully once it was funded. No one told me why the financiers were smiling politely rather than pulling out their wallets.

My experience with the books and workshops galvanized me into action. I accepted the fact that there was no specific course available to help me develop a plan for my own business. So I decided to develop one.

Over the course of two decades, while steering a successful course for my first two technology driven companies, I developed and refined a unique system for starting and operating a business. My system is called Microgenesis™ (*micro* meaning "a technique for working with small size," as in small business, and *genesis* meaning "coming into being"). It involves a logical, ten-level process beginning with the concept for a new business and continuing through managing it successfully once it's launched. Each successive level builds upon the previous one.

The Microgenesis System blends the best of the how-to books and seminars with little-known insider information to produce a specific plan of action that enables the entrepreneur to turn business ideas into a plan for success. Microgenesis works in the real world, not just the classroom.

In these pages I'll introduce you to the Microgenesis process and show you how to develop your own individualized plan for successfully launching your new company or expanding the business you've already begun. I'll share with you the proven techniques with which I successfully started and ran three small businesses during the past two decades and helped hundreds of clients realize their dreams of becoming successful entrepreneurs.

By diligently working your way through *Beating the Odds*, you

™Microgenesis is a trademark of the HTC Group.

will be in a position to sidestep many of the problems entrepreneurs frequently encounter and avoid the fatal pitfalls that lead to business failure. No matter what business you choose, you will be faced with a number of crises that are simply inevitable. My hope is that this book will help you to avoid the controllable crises and give you a realistic, workable perspective on what it takes to create and operate a business.

The odds of failure in the world of small business are high. But failures don't just happen. There are logical reasons why entrepreneurs fall short in their attempts to launch a new company—and logical reasons for the relatively few success stories. If you follow the Microgenesis process outlined in this book, you can rewrite the odds in your favor and dramatically increase your chances of turning the dream of entrepreneurship into the reality of a successful small business of your own.

How to Use This Book

This book is far more than just a reference tool. Realizing its true benefits will require a significant effort on your part. Simply reading the book will do little good; you must commit yourself to completing the creative exercises that appear throughout these pages and to diligent note-taking along the way.

Beating the Odds follows the systematic, step-by-step Microgenesis program that takes you through a ten-level process, from goal setting through successfully managing your business and marketing your products. Each chapter builds on the previous one, so it's important to work through the book sequentially rather than moving around in the text.

The book is divided into two parts: Part One, "Launching Your Business: Conception Through Financing," focuses on all of the steps leading up to securing financing for your business, including defining your market and structuring your business. Part Two, "Growing Your Business: Beyond Financing," shows you how to successfully manage your company and market your products once you've arranged funding.

Beating the Odds is designed with exercises interspersed throughout the text. To get the most out of the book, you'll want to complete these exercises as you read the book. Keep a notebook handy, using it for the exercises, key points, and any other notes you deem relevant. Please resist the temptation to skip past the exercises and move ahead in the text, telling yourself you'll return to them later. That approach will not work.

It is important that you take notes as the thoughts strike you. When you find something meaningful in the text, do not just write down the words; rather, think about the words and then write down how these words apply to your vision of your own company.

As one of my college professors used to say, "A short pencil is better than a long memory." If you write down the thoughts that strike you as you read this book, you will retain the information far better than if you try to commit it to memory without committing it to paper. And keep in mind that some points that may not seem relevant now could suddenly become quite relevant in the future.

So once again, be prepared to take lots of notes about how the ideas in these pages apply to your vision of your business. Every strategy, every tactic, every objective, every step, every component, and every formula that I introduce throughout the book must make complete sense to you for your specific goals; otherwise, it's probably wrong for your situation. But if you're not sure, write it down anyway and study it later.

It's important that you do not skip any section of the book just because you think you already know it or it may not be applicable to your business. If you have already been introduced to the material elsewhere, review it again. Consider this a refresher course, a check to make sure you are effectively applying the ideas that are presented. Because I've written this book for both novice entrepreneurs and those with established business, I'll start with the basics and then quickly advance to in-depth concepts.

So, a word to the veterans: Don't shut me off early and thereby fail to tune in for the real meat of the chapters. Even if my points are fundamental, ask yourself, "I know the point that he's making, but am I really using it to my advantage?"

Finally, for maximum concentration and productivity, make sure that you have a relatively quiet time and space set aside each time you re-enter these pages.

Introduction

Somewhere along the way, you've probably read the alarming statistics about the high failure rate of new businesses. According to one reliable source, only one out of every 100 entrepreneurs is able to secure adequate funding for his or her business. And of that lucky 1% of businesses that do finally get their money, four out of five close their doors within the first three years of operations—an 80% failure rate.*

Your Odds Are Worse Than You Think

Discouraging as that statistic sounds, it becomes even more alarming when you consider that it (and most of those other statistics you've read) doesn't include the 99 out of 100 would-be entrepreneurs who never make it to the funding stage. When those people are added in, the statistic becomes dire indeed: For every 1,000 entrepreneurs seeking money to fund their companies today, only 2 will get the money they need and still be in business three years from now—an astonishing failure rate of 99.8%!

*D&B's annual *Business Failure Record*'s data base does not currently permit cumulative multiyear tracking. Furthermore, it does not include business 'discontinuances,' where businesses cease to exist without owing any creditors, which D&B estimates to be almost two times greater than that of cited business failures. The U.S. Small Business Administration (SBA), in the 1989 *Report of the President,* using only business failures, cited a six-year failure rate of 63%. Factoring business 'discontinuities' into the equation, the SBA's oft-cited 80% three-year failure rate may be easily justified.

With those ridiculous odds, why even bother trying to start a business of your own?

Because I'm going to show you how to throw those statistics out the window and set your own odds for success. After all, here I am, a senior business executive, having worked for three Fortune 500 companies and having created three business of my own that defied the odds!

Zen and the Art of Small Business Failure

There's nothing magical or mystical about the reasons why a handful of businesses succeed or why most entrepreneurs fail in their endeavors. When you look at the reasons for failure, the vast majority of all business failures, an estimated 90%, occur because of some combination of three factors:

1. Inadequate financing
2. Poor management practices
3. Ineffective marketing techniques

The good news is that through Microgenesis you can learn how to avoid or control each of these failure factors.

But I've Already Read All Those Other Books on Entrepreneurship!

Imagine a novice mountaineer who eagerly reads all the latest books on mountain climbing tools, buys the newest mountain climbing gear, and purchases the highest-quality outfitting for the expedition. He then proceeds to lead a climbing party up the Matterhorn.

You can guess how far our novice mountaineer will get. He is really no different from the would-be entrepreneur who reads the standard how-to book on starting a business and proceeds to take that information and attempt to climb to the summit of business success. The hapless entrepreneur is likely to get no farther than will the "expert" mountaineer.

A New Approach

Unlike the reference book approach of other how-to books, *Beating the Odds* doesn't just provide you with the tools for the expedition; it takes you by the hand and leads you step-by-step to the top of the entrepreneurial mountain. It is not a typical how-to book, filled with facts that get you excited but leave you with no idea of what to do next. *Beating the Odds* takes you one step further. It gives you the information you need and shows you how to translate that information into an effective plan of action for realizing your business goals. In short, it gives you a system, a process to achieve success!

Do I claim that this is the only way to do it? No. But I do know that my system works. I've used it exclusively with many different types of business, and it has always been successful.

During your passage through these pages, I am going to show you a surefire way to turn a business idea into a viable plan that will dramatically increase your odds of avoiding the mortality statistics. Part One shows you how to set your personal and business goals, develop a sound marketing strategy, put together a strong team and business plan, and present the image of experience you'll need to sell your package to a financier. After reading Part Two, you'll be familiar with the marketing savvy and management skills that are critical to keep your business running smoothly once you've secured financing. Along the way, zero in on each of the three major reasons for business failure and make sure you know how to avoid them. I'll tell you about the fatal pitfalls that are hidden behind those horrendous statistics on business failures and show you how to take corrective action before you fall victim to them.

You'll learn street smarts, such as how to pay a fraction of the retail cost of national advertising, the behind-the-scenes information that could spell the difference between success and failure for your business. You'll read about the hot buttons that get investors interested in funding your company. I'll prepare you for the loaded questions equity financiers will inevitably ask you. You'll understand how differently bankers and professional equity financiers make their financing decisions. I'll tell you why investors may turn down your business plan, even when it's top-notch. And during all this, I'll dispel the wealth of misinformation, rumors, and bad advice that have become a part of the popular myth about what it takes to launch and operate a business.

In short, I'm going to make the business of starting a business as painless as possible for you, help you to avoid the mistakes that most entrepreneurs make, and save you a fortune in wasted time, money, and energy—energy that would be far better spent enjoying your newfound success.

Is This Book Really For You?

Now that I've whetted your appetite, are you really sure you want to read this book?

Perhaps you just plucked this volume off the bookstore shelf. Maybe you searched it out at the library, after a friend mentioned it to you. Or you might have heard about it somewhere else, and now you are glancing through the pages, trying to decide if you really want to spend the time reading it.

Browse carefully; this book is not for everyone. It was written for the dedicated entrepreneur, the person who is driven to succeed. Turn to the profile of the typical entrepreneur, at the beginning of Chapter 1. If you can't identify with many of the descriptions listed there, chances are you may not really have the stamina it takes to get a business off the ground.

But if you do think you've got what it takes, read on!

This book is meant for two types of readers:

1. Would-be entrepreneurs who have a concept for a business of their own
2. Entrepreneurs who already have an established business

Most people starting a new business have some understanding of the type of business they are entering into, but they have no clear plan for translating their product or service idea into a viable company. This book will show you every step of the way.

If you already have an established business, you may be wondering why you should be reading a book on entrepreneurship. The fact is, long-established businesses are just as likely at start-ups to fail at some point, often at the very time you would expect them to be thriving—when they are experiencing rapid growth. If you are in this position, I'll help you to identify the strengths and weaknesses of your business and show you how to take the calculated risks you need to carefully expand your operations and continue your pattern of success.

As you work your way through *Beating the Odds,* I promise that you'll find out a great deal about yourself as well as about the mechanics of running your company. This will involve some quiet introspection on your part. If you've got the guts to be honest with yourself, I guarantee that you will finish this book having learned more about your strengths, your weaknesses, and your business ability, as well as how to deal more effectively with employees, vendors, customers, and bankers. And rest assured that this information will serve you well in your personal life as well as in the business world.

ONE

Launching
Your Business

*Conception Through
Financing*

1

First Things First

Levels and Goals

Warning: *This book is not for the lethargic. If you are merely seeking a reference manual, just put this book back on the shelf. But if you are seeking a book to help you develop a personalized plan of action for your own business, then you have struck pay dirt! However, please (if you haven't already done so) read the preceding sections before continuing.*

Many people believe they would like to be entrepreneurs, when in fact they are simply disenchanted with their present jobs and see owning their own business as a way out. They long for the independence and freedom that owning a business represents to them. In their dreamy-eyed wanderings, they forget that with all of the rewards of owning a business come all of the risks and uncertainty their present employer is assuming for them. They want the glory, but they don't have what it takes to tough it out on their own.

No two people are alike, of course, and entrepreneurs are no exception. Nevertheless, certain characteristics are so common among those who start their own business that they add up to a consistent profile. If you think you've got what it takes to run your own show, read on and see if you can identify with the typical profile of the entrepreneur.

An Entrepreneur's Profile

1. Entrepreneurs are highly self-confident individuals who have established extremely high standards for themselves. They are hard-

driving, emotionally charged, overly energetic people, who will judge both themselves and their employees harshly when even minor mistakes are made that deviate from their high standards.

2. Many entrepreneurs have no college degree. If they did attend college, most likely they never went beyond a bachelors degree.

3. Entrepreneurs cannot tolerate mediocrity. Most have had some work experience (although little, if any, management experience) with a large organization, where they were frustrated by the slow pace, politics, and inefficiency. They are thrilled by the prospect of starting a new company free from those encumbrances (not realizing that if they become truly successful, these same inefficiencies could ultimately creep into their own organizations). They strive to maintain absolute control over their destinies.

4. Entrepreneurs are goal-oriented to a fault, and they cannot tolerate failure. Success is the only result acceptable to them, and they often become workaholics in their quest for success.

5. While entrepreneurs are willing to make great sacrifices in their quest for success, they are also impatient and tend to be bored with the planning and administrative aspects of their work, often letting them slide.

6. Entrepreneurs generally have large egos that need to be nurtured. They tend to believe they are always right, and it is difficult for them to heed the advice of others, no matter how good the advice, when it differs from their own beliefs.

7. Entrepreneurs are calculated risk takers. They tend to have a good feeling for what choices to make, and they are willing to "bet the store" on their choices.

8. Entrepreneurs are good communicators who can generate enthusiasm within others because they believe so deeply in their cause. However, they sometimes have trouble accepting the fact that other employees are not driven by the same inner motivation. Therefore, they often fail to motivate their own employees.

9. Most entrepreneurs are not strong in money matters. They see cash only as a means to an end, rather than as an essential commodity that needs to be constantly and carefully monitored. Either they are so positive they will succeed that financial planning seems irrelevant to them, or they are so uncomfortable in dealing with finances that they

avoid this aspect of their work as much as possible, hoping it will go away.

10. Entrepreneurs are so focused on their product that, left to their own devices, they will manufacture enough super widgets to fill an entire warehouse before they realize they should have worried about marketing long before they began the production process.

11. Because they are so self-confident, energetic, and driven to succeed, entrepreneurs may come to believe they are infallible. If they have read about something, they believe they can accomplish it. They fail to realize, often until it's too late, that no amount of drive or raw talent can substitute for experience.

12. Above all, entrepreneurs are visionaries. They see a vision of the future, and they strive against all odds to make their vision a reality.

As the above profile demonstrates, the entrepreneurial personality is a mixed bag of positive and negative attributes. The same all-consuming drive that provides the creative energy to launch a business can also lead to its downfall. In particular, the entrepreneur's sense of infallibility, failure to motivate employees, and single-minded focus on product development all weigh heavily in the business mortality statistics, as we shall see.

What Makes for Success?

Now you know what entrepreneurs are like, and some of the reasons why their businesses fail, but what makes a handful of them successful? That question will be addressed throughout the book, but it should be stated up front that the quality of management and the quality of marketing are the two most critical factors in the success of a business. Why isn't financing involved? Because management and marketing alone will determine if you secure the capital you need.

Management Experience: An Essential Ingredient

In order to determine the probable success of a business venture, investors typically use a weighting system that attaches more importance to certain facets of a potential business deal than to others. A typical weighting scheme, in the eyes of venture capitalists, is pictured below (and I recommend that you embed this chart indelibly in your subconscious, or at least write it in your notebook):

*Factors Contributing to Business Success**

The management team	54%
The industry	24%
The product	16%
The planning	6%

Note that the management team's contribution to the success formula is almost four times greater than the product's contribution. The truth is, an experienced team beats a dynamite product any day. Given the choice between backing a superior product produced/marketed by inexperienced managers, or a mediocre product produced/marketed by experienced managers, investors will inevitably choose the mediocre product marketed by experienced managers, because the odds for success are far greater.

We've all seen this happen. An executive with a solid track record leaves an established company to start a new business with a "ho-hum" product, and he quickly finds financing. At the same time, a young engineer with an exciting new product but very little in the way of a track record tries to find financing and is unsuccessful.

Because the management team is the most highly rated factor contributing to success, you had better assemble a strong team for your company before approaching potential investors.

And if you don't have the requisite management experience, have no fear, because I'll be showing you how to present at least the appearance of this experience to potential investors.

A Better Mousetrap Is Not Enough

In 1970 my first company created an industry: agricultural monitoring systems. Our first product (with the trade name Farm Alarm®) was

---

*The author's firm, The HTC Group, periodically polls a select group of national venture capital firms throughout the country on a number of issues relating to venture investment. This chart is extracted from those polls.

designed to monitor the hundreds of thousands of hog and poultry confinement buildings in rural America, because power or fan failure could wipe out the farmer's entire investment in less than an hour. Why? Because as soon as the forced air flow stops, the animals rapidly suffocate from the toxic gases.

Why had no one else come up with a system? Because the environment is so corrosive to electronics. With ammonia, methane, and hydrogen sulfide gases present in abundance, electronic gadgets were being destroyed. Stainless steel turned black in just a few months; if the farmer brought a small portable radio into the building to provide music, he had to throw it away after six months because the circuit board and components had become badly corroded.

Enter Farm Alarm. Using circuitry from the space program (because the confinement building environment is just as hostile as is deep space), we created a system that was rugged enough to withstand the environment and reliable enough to have a lifetime guarantee against failures!

Our unit was a smash hit with the media. As a result, I found myself in the situation that every entrepreneur dreams about: a new product with no competition and mountains of free publicity in major national publications.

Then the insurance companies got into the act. Because of our excellent reliability record, they offered farmers a rate reduction of up to 30% on their livestock insurance if they had one of our systems.

The farmer could pay for our system in one year with his insurance premium reductions; then the rest was "gravy." I found myself being asked to make major presentations to national meetings of insurance groups throughout the country, as well as to the American Society of Agricultural Engineers.

But I was also panicking. How would I be able to fill the orders that would be coming in? I was focused on expanding our facility and building up an inventory of systems. Then I waited for the orders to come flooding in. But do you know what? The telephone did not ring off the wall, and I was not inundated with orders.

In fact, I almost went bankrupt, because I had focused on *building* product rather than *marketing* it. I learned a hard lesson: No matter how good your product is, no matter how much of a monopoly you have, no matter how much free publicity you get, it won't sell itself!

I had lots of product, but my coffers were empty. Only because I was able to secure four new investors who believed in our dream was I able to get back on my feet. And every dollar that I raised this time went into marketing! As a result, we grew to become the largest company of our type in the country, and I subsequently sold the company to an Australian conglomerate at a handsome profit.

Although this story does have a happy ending, it almost did not. My company, with everything going for it, almost drowned under the weight of excess inventory because I had ignored marketing. But then, I was like most greenhorn entrepreneurs who want to believe that they know it all.

Most aspiring entrepreneurs believe that the key to success lies in developing an innovative and exciting product. After all, remember Emerson's adage "Build a better mousetrap, and the world will beat a path to your door." I'm here to tell you that if you believe in that adage, then you are doomed to failure. No matter how exciting the product, it won't sell itself. The truth is, it's far better to aggressively market a mediocre mousetrap than to build a superior trap and wait for the phones to ring.

This is perhaps one of the most common traps that ensnare the enthusiastic entrepreneur. Most entrepreneurs, myself included, are so in love with their products that they automatically assume everyone else will feel the same way. As a result, they tend to minimize their financing and marketing efforts and focus exclusively on perfecting their products. Unfortunately, what investors want to see is just the opposite: a focus on marketing the product.

This realization was a key to the success of my early business financing efforts. I learned other key points as well, and you will be encountering these axioms throughout the pages of this book. Because they ignited sparks of awareness within me, thereby keeping me on track with the growth of my businesses, I highlight them for you. You may want to list these points in your notebook to refer to as you develop and execute the strategies for your own business.

Key Point: *Profit is the only factor that motivates investors to finance a business.*

Investors are not putting money in your company because they love your company or your product. They are investing in you for one reason and one reason alone: They want to make money. Potential investors, whoever they may be, want to be shown that they can make significantly more money from their investment in you than with other, safer alternatives. And to ensure this, they want to know that you can sell your product, not just build it. Otherwise, they would be better off putting their funds into a bank certificate of deposit, where they would have none of the risk.

If you are to persuade investors to finance your company, you'd better show them that you're smart enough to concentrate on making the sale that generates the profit. This means you need to have a strong marketing person on your management team.

So how do you, having been focused on your company's product for so long, suddenly shift your focus to profit? The easiest way is to understand and put into practice this next Key Point:

Key Point: *The <u>sale</u> of your product (or service) is the only activity of your business that contributes to profits.*

All other activities within your company (manufacturing, engineering, proposals, advertising, etc.) contribute only to expenses.

Until I understood this axiom, I was totally embroiled in the creation of my first product. I suddenly realized that if I wanted this business to grow and provide a significant measure of compensation to my family in return for all of our sacrifices, I had to alter my thinking and concentrate on achieving sales and profits.

The Human Factor

Let's assume that you and I are conversing after one of my Company Doctor™ presentations in your city. As the lights are extinguished, we're standing in a dark and somber auditorium (which seems oddly appropriate to our conversation about the bleak odds against starting a successful business).

Our dialogue takes a personal turn as you discuss your own ailing business and ask me for a diagnosis. You explain that you've been trying to launch your company for the past two years, but it's contracted a bad case of stagnation. The reason it has failed to grow, in your opinion, is the indifference of area financial institutions. You believe that a big infusion of cash is all that it will take to restore a healthy glow to your anemic company.

I offer a preliminary diagnosis based on my experience with a number of other companies suffering from the same symptoms. Although I would need to examine your company in greater depth to make an absolute diagnosis, I suspect that more cash is not your answer. In fact, it may create deeper problems. What your business is probably lacking is something entirely different. Without it, your company is probably destined to become just another statistic in the annals of business failure.

What is the ingredient that, when absent, causes so many businesses to wilt before they have a chance to grow? It's something I call *the human factor,* and you can acquire it by expending quiet contemplation, not dollars. The human factor is a measure of your ability to put yourself in another person's shoes. Think of it as a sensitive microphone that picks up on the thoughts, feelings, needs, and desires of others. We begin life with our microphone at full volume, trying to pick up every clue we can about what motivates the people around us so that we can get them to feed us or comfort us. But by the time we get ready to start a business, we have been battered around just enough that we have usually turned the volume way down (or even off). We become defensive, focused on ourselves, forgetting that we need to please the other person in order to meet our own needs.

Furthermore, entrepreneurs are hampered by the belief that they are almost always right and assume others should realize this and adopt their perspective.

Those few entrepreneurs who are able to "turn up their microphone" are the ones who have the ability to constantly analyze what motivates the other person. The majority of entrepreneurs make no effort to regain this lost ability to relate to people as people, seeing them only as potential sources of capital or new business.

I am asking you, during the course of this book, to make the commitment to crank up your microphone, to pay close attention to what your customers, bankers, and suppliers are saying (by their actions and expressions, as well as their words) so that you can have a strong advantage in all of your business dealings. When people urge you to take a particular course of action you are opposed to, before you react against it spontaneously ask yourself, "Why are they insisting I do this?" Put yourself in their shoes, and see if their request makes sense. This newfound perspective (and the subsequent understanding you develop of other people's beliefs) will help you to close orders, solve problems, negotiate contracts, and cement lasting professional relationships. It isn't important that you always agree with others, but it is essential you understand where they are coming from.

Is that all there is to it? Will success then be inevitable? No. When you have successfully assimilated the human factor, you will have found the key to unlocking one of the rusted shackles that is tightly wrapped around your treasure chest labeled "Success." One of the goals of this book is to tackle the other relevant shackles as well, so that you can break free of all of them.

But to accomplish this, I must begin at the beginning.

Ten Levels to Small Business Success

Now that I've gone over the preliminaries, let me introduce you to my overview of the entire process of starting and managing a business. This is the system that I introduced in the Preface: Microgenesis.

This process involves the mastery of ten levels (see Figure 1-1). Each level by itself is merely a tool, but collectively they add up to a powerful program. No matter what your business, conquering these ten levels will increase your odds for success. They are straightforward but by no means easy. Each level involves a tremendous amount of effort and a lot of street smarts to work effectively. As in playing an arcade game, you should master each level before moving on to the next one.

Now let's look at each of these levels in detail:

LEVEL I: *Develop your personal and company goals.*

Your written goals (and the operative word here is *written*) serve as your road map. They give you a sense of direction and help you get to your destination, a successful business of your own, with a minimum of time, effort, and expense.

LEVEL II: *Define a viable market segment for your product or service.*

It is critical to define an unmet consumer need first, before you develop a product to satisfy that need. Logical as that might seem, the

Figure 1-1.   The ten levels of Microgenesis.

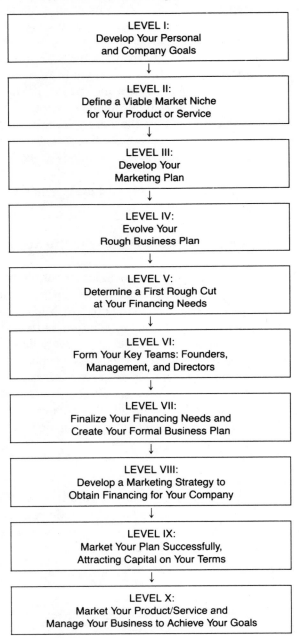

LEVEL I:
Develop Your Personal
and Company Goals

↓

LEVEL II:
Define a Viable Market Niche
for Your Product or Service

↓

LEVEL III:
Develop Your
Marketing Plan

↓

LEVEL IV:
Evolve Your
Rough Business Plan

↓

LEVEL V:
Determine a First Rough Cut
at Your Financing Needs

↓

LEVEL VI:
Form Your Key Teams: Founders,
Management, and Directors

↓

LEVEL VII:
Finalize Your Financing Needs and
Create Your Formal Business Plan

↓

LEVEL VIII:
Develop a Marketing Strategy to
Obtain Financing for Your Company

↓

LEVEL IX:
Market Your Plan Successfully,
Attracting Capital on Your Terms

↓

LEVEL X:
Market Your Product/Service and
Manage Your Business to Achieve Your Goals

majority of entrepreneurs instead come up with what in their view is a "hot" product before verifying that a sufficient demand for the product exists. You may have the most exciting product in the world, and people might think that it's the most interesting thing they've seen in a decade, but if you can sell only a handful (to your immediate family and in-laws), you are probably doomed to failure. In order to verify that there is a need for your product, you must test the market by conducting a variety of market research.

LEVEL III: *Develop your marketing plan.*

The purpose of the marketing plan is to articulate whom you are going to sell to, how you are going to penetrate the market, why you will be successful with your sales campaigns, and finally, how much you will sell annually over the next five years. The marketing plan will ultimately become an integral part of your overall business plan, but it must be completed first.

LEVEL IV: *Evolve your rough business plan.*

The rough business plan is an outline of the direction in which you plan to take your company, an analysis of your business strengths and weaknesses, and a skeleton from which your formal business plan will later be developed. It will assist you in securing the key people you need, and it will also help you to begin developing your financial projections.

LEVEL V: *Determine a first rough cut at your financing needs.*

Once you have developed a rough business plan, you can begin to determine your financing needs, which will be incorporated into your formal business plan. Your marketing analysis leads to sales forecasts, which determine your staffing level, which defines your operating budget, from which you can generate pro formas (financial projections) and determine your projected cash flow.

LEVEL VI: *Form your key teams: founders, management, and directors.*

Before developing your formal business plan, you must make sure you have put together a solid management team. If there are any holes in your team at this point, they should be filled. The rough business plan you developed in Level IV should help you to attract top talent to your company. In addition, it will help you to build a strong board of directors or board of advisors.

LEVEL VII: *Finalize your financing needs and create your formal business plan.*

Starting with the rough business plan developed in Level IV, put together a full-fledged formal business plan. This is the document you will use to secure the financing you need to get your business off the ground. It will also serve as an operating manual for your business once it's been funded.

LEVEL VIII: *Develop a marketing strategy to obtain financing for your company.*

I'm not talking here about the marketing strategy to sell your product or service, but a strategy to sell yourself and your company to financiers in order to raise the capital that your business needs.

LEVEL IX: *Market your plan successfully, attracting capital on your terms.*

Once you've developed a strategy for approaching financing sources, you must make use of the negotiating tools that will give you an inside edge on the competition and enable you to attract capital on your terms rather than just on your investors'.

LEVEL X: *Market your product/service and manage your business to achieve your goals.*

The last step in the process involves the ongoing management and marketing of your business. Getting a company started is only half the battle. Once you're in business, you will need strong management tools and marketing skills in order to make sure you stay in business.

Each step, executed in order, builds a solid foundation for the steps that follow. By progressing in this manner, rather than using the typical haphazard approach, you begin to gain the needed experience.

What's It All About?

Just in case you haven't picked up my not-so-subtle hints by now, let me state this bluntly: You will not be successful in raising the money you need to open your business if you do not have some level of business experience (and lemonade stands and Girl Scout cookies don't count). If you are not an experienced businessperson, you must at least present the *appearance* of one. (Twenty years ago I tried to acquire this experience by attending seminars and reading books, but the answers weren't there. So I decided to write this book, to provide you with the guide I never had. During your journey through these pages, you are going to gain a great deal of wisdom, from the agony and the ecstasy of my successes and failures, to the experiences of other businesspeople with their own companies. Then it's up to you to put this new-found knowledge to work!)

The Goal-Setting Road Map

Suppose I told you that, as a final exam for this chapter, I wanted you to travel from New York to Los Angeles by car, using as little fuel as possible. And, by the way, you would assume that road maps did not exist.

Sure, you would eventually get there, after many stops to ask directions and after wasting a lot of time and gas. Then you could look back on your zigzag route and reflect how much faster you could have gotten there with a good road map.

A set of written, clearly defined goals is your company's road map for success. It serves to minimize both time and fuel (people and dollars) required to get the job done. This brings us to our next Key Point:

Key Point: *You cannot decide what you truly want from your business until you know what you personally want from life.*

Most entrepreneurs ignore the need for a road map. Even worse, they believe they already have a mental map, with their key goals existing in their head. This brings us to the corollary of the above Key Point: *You haven't done it until you've written it down.*

It is amazing how goals kept in our heads somehow change radically with time. If you don't believe this, then I challenge you to write down a set of goals, commit them to your perfect memory, and lock them in a safe deposit box. Six months later (because you have retained them perfectly), write them down on a blank piece of paper. Then retrieve your copy from the safe deposit box and compare the results.

Now that you have an overview of the entire Microgenesis process of achieving business success, let's begin by entering the first level:

LEVEL I: Develop Your Personal and Company Goals

The ideal time to analyze what you want out of your life is before you launch your business. The overall goals that will emerge from such an analysis will serve as your pair of personal and professional road maps.

If you can honestly say that you have already compiled a detailed, written list of your personal and business goals, you have my congratulations. However, even then you should take out your lists and compare them with the exercises that follow, completing those exercises that will enhance the goals lists you've already developed.

As you set down your goals, don't worry about whether or not you'll be good enough to achieve a particular goal. If it motivates you, you will be good enough; if it doesn't, you won't, and you can hire someone who will be.

SMART Goals

When developing your list of goals, keep in mind that each goal should be SMART:*

Specific:	"Earning an annual income of $100,000 within three years" is specific; "having a good time" is not.
Measurable:	What is your definition of success, and how will you measure it?
Attainable:	Don't set your goal so high that you can never achieve it (but do set it high enough that it requires you to stretch yourself and realize your full potential).

---

*The SMART concept was originally presented in Ken Blanchard, Patricia Zigarmi, and Drea Zigarmi, *Leadership and the One Minute Manager* (New York: William Morrow & Company, 1985).

You Are Here
→

LEVEL I:
Develop Your Personal
and Company Goals

↓

LEVEL II:
Define a Viable Market Niche
for Your Product or Service

↓

LEVEL III:
Develop Your
Marketing Plan

↓

LEVEL IV:
Evolve Your
Rough Business Plan

↓

LEVEL V:
Determine a First Rough Cut
at Your Financing Needs

↓

LEVEL VI:
Form Your Key Teams: Founders,
Management, and Directors

↓

LEVEL VII:
Finalize Your Financing Needs and
Create Your Formal Business Plan

↓

LEVEL VIII:
Develop a Marketing Strategy to
Obtain Financing for Your Company

↓

LEVEL IX:
Market Your Plan Successfully,
Attracting Capital on Your Terms

↓

LEVEL X:
Market Your Product/Service and
Manage Your Business to Achieve Your Goals

Relevant: Make sure that a particular goal is meaningful for
                   your life-style. Don't declare that you want a yacht if
                   you tend to get seasick.
Trackable: Ensure that you can assess your periodic progress.

EXERCISE: Your Personal Goals

Now you are ready to develop some SMART goals of your own.
The following exercise is designed to help you identify your personal goals.* Get your notebook out again and do each of the five
steps in order:

1. Perform a simple inventory of the skills you presently have:
   those things you do well and enjoy. Aim for a list of about six
   to ten skills, as follows:

   My favorite and strongest skill:_____
   My second-favorite and strongest skill:_____
   My third-favorite and strongest skill:_____
   . . .

2. Write an answer to this simple question:

   "If I could have any kind of a job, what would it be?" Be specific; even invent a job if need be, but let your imagination
   really take over here.

3. Write down your vision of your future, taking only four or five
   sentences. Again, let your imagination wander!

4. Write a short essay entitled "On the Last Day of My Life, What
   Must I Have Accomplished So That I Can Look Back on My
   Life as Having Been Truly Satisfactory?"

5. Draw three columns on another piece of paper, labeled as follows:

---

*Portions of this exercise have been adapted from concepts presented in Richard N.
Bolles, *What Color Is Your Parachute?* (Berkeley, Calif.: Ten Speed Press, 1985).
Updated annually, this is an excellent skill and goal assessment resource.

Column 1: *Things I Have Accomplished*
Column 2: *Things I Want to Accomplish*
Column 3: *Steps Needed to Complete Column 2*

Now, looking back at the accomplishments you detailed in your short essay, place each individual point in either column 1 or column 2, as appropriate. Finally, for those points listed in column 2, complete the third column with the remaining steps required. Note that the items in column 3, although probably not goals themselves, will help you focus on your actual goals.

The next step is to develop a list of your personal goals based upon the data you just gathered. Your goals should be derived from those specific actions needed to satisfy the requirements of your short essay and from columns 2 and 3 above. Remember each personal goal must meet all of the SMART criteria.

Record these goals in your notebook under the heading Personal Goals. State these personal goals clearly, and include a specific time frame for the accomplishment of each one.

EXERCISE: Your Business Goals

Now that you have developed a realistic set of SMART personal goals, it's time to repeat the procedure for your business, as shown below. Record your responses under the headings indicated:

1. *Company skills.* Perform a simple inventory of the skills that your company employees have (or will have). Again, aim for a list of about 6–10.
2. *My ideal company.* Write an answer to this simple question: If my company could be anything, what would it be?
3. *Vision of my company's future.* Express your vision of your company's future, taking only four or five sentences.
4. *Desired company accomplishments.* Write a short essay entitled "Before I Finally Leave or Sell the Company, What Do I Want to Have Accomplished With It?"
5. *Accomplishment status.* Draw three columns on a new page in your notebook, labeled as follows:

Column 1: *Things My Business Has Accomplished*
Column 2: *Things I Want My Business to Accomplish*
Column 3: *Steps Needed to Complete Column 2*

Now place each individual point from your company essay in either column 1 or column 2, as appropriate. Then, for those points listed in column 2, complete the third column with the remaining steps required.

Finally, develop a set of SMART goals from the data you have gathered for your business.*

The Persistence of Your Goals

Anytime that you make decisions for your business, you will want this list of personal and business goals available so that you can easily refer to it. As you examine various alternative courses of action, you must ask yourself, "How does this particular option contribute to the accomplishment of each of the goals that I have established?" It is not necessary for any particular alternative to strengthen all of your goals, but it should certainly contribute to several of them.

Only when you have accomplished the above exercises will you (1) have some initial tools with which to assess progress and (2) be able to state clearly to potential investors exactly what your company goals are.

And you may rest assured that potential investors are going to ask what your goals are (because they are looking for evidence of experience, remember?). Experienced businesspeople know their specific goals and can communicate these goals with great fervor, because they embrace them with a passion. Furthermore, the experienced businessperson has imbued all members of the management team with these goals. Investors therefore know that the goals are not merely empty

---

Caution: As you develop each company goal, you must clearly ascertain whether that goal also helps contribute to one or more of your personal goals. If it does not, then you should seriously question that particular company goal. Once you have developed these goals (along with a time frame for each one), record them in your notebook under the heading Company Goals.

words but represent a real commitment. A process this simple demonstrates the experience that investors are looking for.

By the way, your goals are not meant to be cast in concrete. In fact, they should be reviewed every 6 to 12 months and revised if conditions warrant. But you must write them down and save them so that you can refer to them periodically to assess how far you have progressed.

A Final Note About First Things

Now it's time to make the transition from goals to growth. If you're like most entrepreneurs, the first thing you do is come up with a product, then launch your company, and finally realize you need to convince people to buy your product. A far better way to create a business is to first recognize an unmet need in the marketplace and then develop a product to satisfy that need. I cover this tactic in Chapter 2.

However, I am assuming you have followed the typical path and have already developed your widget (but if you haven't, then Level II in Chapter 2 can still help you find it).

*   *   *

Thus far you've been introduced to the process, you've christened your notebook, and you have some tangible results. With a strong set of personal and business goals in hand, you are now ready to determine how much demand exists for that widget you're building.

CHAPTER
2

Will It Play in Peoria?

*Finding and Verifying
Your Niche*

Most new companies start with only a single product. Several years ago, I knew a company that I'll call Short-Sighted, Inc. It manufactured a fantastic full-color dynamic light display that hooked up to home stereo systems. This was a quality product at an attractive price with a good profit margin, and the company had excellent sales outlets. During the first two years, the company made sizable profits, and the business expanded. Suddenly, offshore competition arrived with a lower-quality unit at half the price. As a result, Short-Sighted, Inc.'s market dried up overnight, and six months later the company died a quiet death.

This was an obituary that should never have been written. If only the company had plowed its profits into more cost-effective models, versions for other market niches, or other related products, it might still be here today. But because it had only one "seed" (or product), when that product failed, so did the company.

Whether you are a new or an existing business, you should have several different "seeds" for your field. Even if you concentrate on only one of them, have the others ready to grow and harvest.

Key Point: *A company cannot survive with only a single product aimed at a single market niche.*

Look at how fast-food chains are constantly expanding their menus, automotive manufacturers their car lines. The same holds true for nonprofit corporations. For example, a few years ago, our city's symphony orchestra was in serious trouble. Even with only eight concerts a year, future survival was in doubt. Enter new management and a new conductor who understood the above Key Point; today our symphony orchestra has a classical concert series, a pops concert series, a chamber concert series, a young people's concert series, and even a music school. Revenues and interest in the symphony have increased dramatically because there are a number of different products to meet the needs of different people.

Sounds good in theory, right? But in practice it took you three long years to come up with your flagship product. Just how are you supposed to come up with a warehouse full of other products when you're spending every waking hour struggling to get your company on solid footing?

Well, the good news is that when you arrived at your first product, you probably defined the industry that you are specializing in, along with a particular market segment. All you need now is a little bit of refinement to discover other products with sufficient demand. The trick is to realize the next Key Point:

Key Point: *Customers do not buy products; they purchase solutions to their problems.*

Give that Key Point some thought for a moment, from your own perspective as a customer: Virtually everything you have purchased was not acquired because you wanted to buy a "thing" but rather because you wanted to solve a problem. These problems might have been anything from "How am I going to get to work?" to "How am I going to spend my leisure time?" but in every case you were responding to filling a perceived need that you had. The majority of would-be entrepreneurs never understand that perspective, but most experienced businesspeople do, and remember, you want to present the image of experience.

I've already made the point that, regardless of your market segment, in order to survive a company cannot be devoted to a single product. Taking the foundation of the business goals you have developed and adding in the wisdom of the above Key Point, you are now ready to identify ancillary products for your company, ensure that there is enough demand to support your products, and develop a solid plan for bringing those products to the marketplace.

LEVEL II: Define a Viable Market Niche for Your Product or Service

The Magic of Market Niche Analysis

So you have a product idea. How do you know if it's a good one? One effective way of determining if there is sufficient demand in the market-place for your product is by conducting a Market Niche Analysis (MNA).* How do you determine other ideas for your company's stable of products? Again, MNA is the answer.

Market Niche Analysis is a powerful tool for uncovering those niches in the market where demand for a product far exceeds supply. A well-run MNA will help you to identify potentially lucrative market niches not currently being addressed by other companies and products.

If you are just starting a business, MNA can be used to verify that there is sufficient demand in the marketplace for your proposed new product or service. If you have an established company, it will help you to develop a host of ideas for new products. In fact, it's a good idea for established businesses to conduct a Market Niche Analysis periodically as a regular part of their strategic planning process.

MNA is a two-tier process: First, you verify that there is an apparent need (that activity will occupy the rest of this chapter), and second, you quantify the strength of your selected product to meet that need, determining how many you can expect to sell (we will accomplish that activity in Chapter 3).

If you already have an initial product, this probably defines the market you are focused on. However, MNA can also uncover ancillary and second-generation products and markets for your business, so don't overlook its power.

A well-run MNA can convert readily available raw data into lucrative product niches never before uncovered. However, don't lose sight of the fact that I am initially focusing upon the needs of the consumer, and this will ultimately lead to *products* (although the typical entrepreneur invents a "product" first and then tries to figure out how to sell it).

---

*The Market Niche Analysis presented here is modeled after the concept of market gap analysis originally presented in Richard M. White, *The Entrepreneur's Manual* (Radnor, Penn.: Chilton Books, 1977).

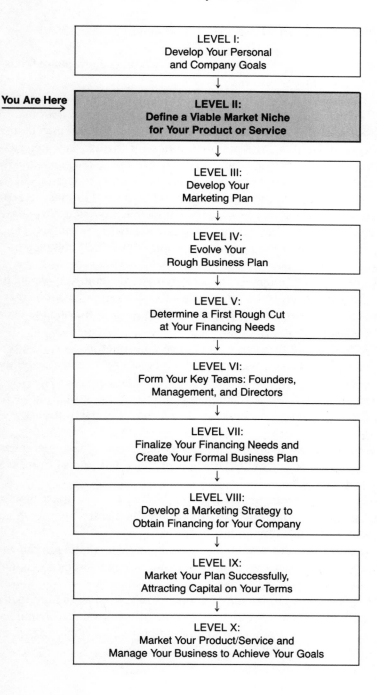

You Are Here →

LEVEL I:
Develop Your Personal
and Company Goals

↓

LEVEL II:
Define a Viable Market Niche
for Your Product or Service

↓

LEVEL III:
Develop Your
Marketing Plan

↓

LEVEL IV:
Evolve Your
Rough Business Plan

↓

LEVEL V:
Determine a First Rough Cut
at Your Financing Needs

↓

LEVEL VI:
Form Your Key Teams: Founders,
Management, and Directors

↓

LEVEL VII:
Finalize Your Financing Needs and
Create Your Formal Business Plan

↓

LEVEL VIII:
Develop a Marketing Strategy to
Obtain Financing for Your Company

↓

LEVEL IX:
Market Your Plan Successfully,
Attracting Capital on Your Terms

↓

LEVEL X:
Market Your Product/Service and
Manage Your Business to Achieve Your Goals

How Market Niche Analysis Works

The first tier of Market Niche Analysis consists of an eight-phase focus-narrowing process, as follows:

PHASE 1: *Define your company's objectives for this analysis.*
To initiate this phase, you must identify a market and then define initial broad objectives for a product/service for that market. Let's assume that you have defined your initial focus to be the *telecommunications market.* You know you want to develop some product to sell to that market, but you're not sure what would be a good product. Keeping in mind your company goals from Chapter 1, complete this phase by developing a list of broad objectives as you tackle this market. Here is a partial list of objectives from an example MNA that I completed:

> "Because of our engineering backgrounds, the company wants to develop an electronic product for the telecommunications market [if you already have a product, this product may define your market]."
>
> "We would like to concentrate on the consumer in a leisure environment, because we know this to be a sizable and expanding group."
>
> "We want a reliable yet simple design, to ensure attractiveness to the consumer, low start-up costs, and minimal warranty expenses."
>
> "We can't afford to spend time and money creating customer interest, so the product must be a new one that will create immediate customer acceptance."
>
> "We want to generate rapid profits, so the product must have a market potential of at least 100,000 units the first year, with no serious initial competition."
>
> "We don't have the resources to create a new marketing organization, so we must be able to sell the product through existing sales networks."
>
> "We want to minimize initial capital investment, so the product's design must be such that we can initially subcontract manufacturing, with the potential for later in-house manufacturing when justified by cash flow."

PHASE 2:   *Break down the market.*

This phase consists of a multilayered technique in which you look at your defined market and then (A) divide, (B) subdivide, and (C) subdivide again, reducing the market into increasingly smaller increments for analysis. A visual representation of this example is shown in Figure 2-1 with each phase clearly marked. Note that for purposes of illustrating this process, we will only consider one category in each phase. However, during your MNA, you should investigate all criteria at each phase (as indicated by the dashed lines). Armed with a large sheet of paper, begin this activity with a focus on your target market: the *telecommunications market*. Your analysis should proceed from left to right, similar to the flow in Figure 2-1.

2A. Investigate the different ways in which you can segment the market. This segmentation might focus on the demographics of potential users, such as their age, where they live, or their income levels. It could look at the market in terms of time, dividing it into months of the year or seasons. It might focus on different levels of experience of potential users. The key here is to use your imagination. The more ways you can think of to break down your target market, the more potentially lucrative market niches you are likely to uncover. Here are some examples of segmenting the target market:

Segment approach 1	By family structure: children, adults, family
Segment approach 2	By marital status: married, single
Segment approach 3	By sex: male, female, both
Segment approach 4	By season: spring, summer, fall, winter
Segment approach 5	By employment: working persons, retirees (etc.)

Record these level (2A) categories in the far left column of your spreadsheet. Note that each different market segmentation looks at the same overall group in a different way, thus allowing you to scrutinize your market from several different perspectives.

2B. The next step is to focus on each of these segment perspectives and determine how they could be subdivided into smaller elements. These might be broken down by time, age, or other criteria. For example, if we consider the *telecommunications-adult* segment from (2A), we could focus on the different times when adults might use tele-

Figure 2-1. A one-segment example of the market breakdown process by phases.

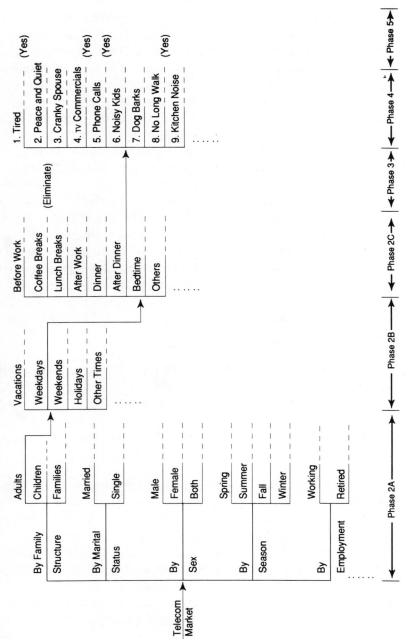

communications products, such as weekdays, weekends, vacation days, holidays, and other times. Record each of these level (2B) criteria to the right of their appropriate level (2A) categories.

2C. The third step is another subdivision. Your goal is to break the level (2B) criteria into even smaller market segments. As an example, the level (2B) sub-sub-subdivision *telecommunications-adult-week-days* might be further subdivided according to time of day, as follows: Before Work, Coffee Breaks, Lunch Breaks, After Work, Dinner, After Dinner, Bedtime, Others. Again, each of these should be recorded to the right of the appropriate level (2B) criteria.

Note that what I have done thus far is start with the target market and continually subdivide it into smaller segments, to at least three sublevels below the initial market. The initial goal is to generate sufficiently small market segments that you can easily analyze and work with. The ultimate goal is to arrive not only at a product, but a product with sufficient demand to meet your goals. If the market you identified is highly complex, you may have to subdivide to an additional level, until at last you begin to see individual segments you can easily work with.

PHASE 3: *Evaluate and eliminate inappropriate market segments.*

In Phase 1, we developed a number of objectives for entering the telecommunications marketplace. Now that you have divided your selected market into sufficiently small segments, it's time to examine them in detail and eliminate those that clearly do not meet your broad objectives. For example, assume the only segment that could be eliminated was *telecommunications-adult-weekdays-coffee breaks*. Don't be too eager to eliminate any segments at this point until you have examined them in greater detail. As a result of this phase, you now have a list of potentially viable market segments for further analysis.

PHASE 4: *Create a chart of problems that exist in each market segment.*

At this point, you will probably have to start a new sheet, because this phase will generate an immense list, probably 100 or more problems for each market segment on your list. Here is the start of a problem list for the *telecommunications-adult-weekdays-after dinner* segment:

"I am tired and want to relax."
"I want peace and quiet without interruptions."

"My spouse is worn out and cranky."
"I hate TV commercials."
"I can't stand solicitation phone calls."
"The kids are too noisy."
"The dog barks too much."
"I can't take a long walk because I've got chores and calls."
"There is too much noise in the kitchen."

Each problem requires serious brainstorming. Never stop too soon. The more problems you list, the more possible solutions—and potential new products for your company.

PHASE 5: *Evaluate and eliminate inappropriate problems.*

Don't be too quick to eliminate problems before thinking them through. "Inappropriate" means problems whose solution clearly would not meet your Phase 1 objectives, problems that are so insignificant the market would not pay for a solution, or problems whose solution would be too costly (if I invented a device to automatically screen out TV commercials but it sold for $5,000, I probably wouldn't sell too many of them).

For our illustration, let's assume only four problems survived the cut:

1. "I am tired and want to relax."
2. "I hate TV commercials."
3. "I can't stand solicitation phone calls."
4. "I can't take a long walk."

PHASE 6: *Tabulate the surviving problems with your original objectives.*

At this point, it's time to prepare your third large worksheet, which will be divided into three columns. In the left-hand column, list each of the surviving problems. Put the heading Solutions over the right-hand column. In the middle column, across the top, place the numbers of the objectives you developed in Phase 1. Your worksheet should look something like the abbreviated version in Figure 2-2 with the Objectives and Solutions columns blank.

Now review each problem against your original objectives. If a solution to a particular problem would appear to satisfy one of your objectives, place a check mark under that objective.

Figure 2-2. Example worksheet for phases 6 and 7.

Problems	Objectives							Solutions
	1	2	3	4	5	6	7	
Need to relax	—	—	—	—	—	—	—	
Hate commercials	—	—	—	—	—	—	—	
Phone solicitations	—	—	—	—	—	—	—	
Can't take long walk	—	—	—	—	—	—	—	

The Solution column should be blank at this point. Your intention at this stage is not to come up with a solution (a product), but simply to determine if a solution to a particular problem would satisfy a number of your objectives. However, if having a particular solution would assist your process of completing the matrix, then feel free to "cheat" and add a preliminary product as a solution. But if you modify the product later, you must redo the matrix.

When you have completed this analysis, select only those problems that appear to be the most promising in terms of developing a solution. To do this, look at your Objectives column. Select those problems that have the most check marks (i.e., those problems that, if solved, would meet the greatest number of your objectives) or those that have check marks under your most important objectives.

PHASE 7: *For the remaining problems, make a list of probable solutions.*

Assume that three of the four problems outlined above made the final cut. You should come up with as many solutions as you can for each problem, even though I've only indicated one for each in our example:

Problem	*Solutions*
Need to relax:	Vibrating recliner chair automatically turns off phone ringer.
Phone solicitations:	Automatic phone device silently screens incoming calls, letting only friends through.
Can't take long walk:	Long-range portable headset link to home phone.

When doing this exercise, be creative; use your imagination. List any solution, and strive for spurts of inspiration that may yield several innovative products.

PHASE 8: *Clean up.*

At this point, take out your red pencil, study your proposed product solutions in detail, and eliminate those that are not feasible. Prioritize the remaining ones on the basis of your Phase 1 objectives, narrowing them down to a list of a dozen or less.

Finally, you must pick one of the finalists for your pursuit. This selection might be made on the basis of your earlier check marks (again, not just the greatest number but the most important). Assume for the continuing examples you have selected the automatic phone screening device.

This selection must be considered tentative at this time, until sufficient demand is verified through market testing.

Doing It Right

So important is the MNA process that a poorly run analysis can result in the failure of your business even before it gets off the ground. This brings us to the subject of Fatal Errors. Entrepreneurs make a variety of mistakes as they develop their businesses; mistakes are inevitably part of the learning process. However, there are certain errors that can be fatal to a business, even after many years of successful operation.

Fatal Error: *Poor market niche analysis.*

Because you are likely to uncover a large number of market niches when you run your MNA (10–100 is typical), the process can be a euphoric experience. Suddenly you find yourself faced with dozens of product possibilities. The challenge is to run the MNA as objectively and dispassionately as possible, not to get stuck on a particular "pet" product idea just because it intrigues you. MNA is just a tool; it will only work properly when it's used properly. That means you must be honest about your objectives and willing to accept the fact that there might not be sufficient demand for your most cherished ideas. In order to avoid the above Fatal Error and to come up with a more balanced perspective, it's best to have more than one person develop the MNA. Two or more people can play creative ideas off of each other.

In identifying market niches, three things should be kept in mind. Ideally, the niche you select should be relatively free of competition, giving you a head start in the marketplace. At a minimum, it should not be occupied by an industry giant. Even if your product is superior to the giant's, you can be sure your marketing dollars won't be any match. Many small companies have regretted taking on IBM's computer business.

On the other hand, don't be afraid to go against a major company if your niche is so narrowly defined, so specialized, that it's not worthwhile for the giant to pursue. If you develop a specialized computer system, with hardware and software, for veterinarians who monitor drug levels in prize-winning race horses, you just might succeed. IBM probably won't bother competing for such a specialized niche of the market.

However, while you may have solved the problem of competition, in this case you may be facing a worse problem. You may have defined your market niche so narrowly that it is not big enough to support an ongoing business. The key is to define a niche that is large enough to make a profit, but not so large that it attracts major competitors who can "outmuscle" you in the long run.

EXERCISE: Developing Your Own Market Niche Analysis (MNA)

At this point, you are ready to perform an abbreviated first-tier MNA, similar to the one just described. For this abbreviated MNA, select just one or two segments at each stage (similar to what we did in the example). In this manner, you will uncover only a few potential niches by the time you reach stage 9. When you run a full-blown MNA later, considering all of the alternatives available to you at each stage, you might end up with several hundred potential market niches; there's no need to run such an involved analysis at this point. However, you should include every one of your stage 1 objectives in the abbreviated MNA.

Once you have completed your MNA and have selected the most promising market niches, as defined by your Problems list, you must begin verifying through market testing that each niche (i.e., the market for a problem solution) is large enough to make the development of a solution profitable. You must also ensure that the niche is not already occupied, or at least that it is not occupied by an industry giant. This will be covered later in this chapter under "The Mystique of Market Testing."

The Water Witch: Testing for Viable Niches

Now that you have a sheaf full of niches, how can you determine whether the niches you uncovered in the process are large enough to support your product or service? This is where the second tier of the MNA comes in, because it is critical that you answer this question *before* proceeding to develop any new products. Nothing is more dispiriting than coming up with a surefire, innovative solution to a real problem only to find that the problem affects just a handful of potential customers! It's easy enough to rule out the niches that are obviously large and already occupied; the difficult task is to uncover the potentially lucrative areas of the market that have been overlooked by others and are just waiting to be filled by your company.

But it doesn't take a water witch to give you the answer. You can determine if a market niche is big enough to justify development of a solution by running some inexpensive market tests. The key word here is *inexpensive.* In a good MNA, your problem is that you will uncover not too few potential niches for your product, but far too many. You'll be faced with so many options to pursue that you'll feel like the proverbial kid in the candy store. Unless you are independently wealthy (a characteristic few would-be entrepreneurs share), you must find a way to check out each of the options within the limits of your budget.

My experience has been that a typical in-depth MNA may uncover between 10 and 100 potential opportunities for new products or services. Of these, typically:

- *60% will be mirages,* which have no real potential for new product development, usually because of some barrier to entering the market (e.g., price, size). There is no true niche for a useful new widget that engineers love if it can only be manufactured and marketed for twice the price they are willing to pay.
- *10% will be short-term targets of opportunity* that will lead to lucrative but short-lived markets. The hula hoop and Cabbage

Patch dolls are two classic examples. Don't throw these ideas out; just realize that they will only last for a few years.

- *30% will be viable long-range market niches* that will lead to long-term products. These are the niches that you want to focus on, the ones that will support an ongoing business.

To check the viability of a market niche, to find out whether it's a bona fide niche or just a mirage, it is necessary to run several independent market tests and see how they correlate. In the next section, I'll discuss how you accomplish this.

The Mystique of Market Testing

If you don't perform sound market testing, you're playing Russian roulette with the life of your business. You are also showing the world of financiers that you lack experience, something you definitely want to avoid. You're going to need the financiers' dollars, and you can be sure that when you approach them, they are going to ask about your market testing. You had better have some good answers.

Disguising Your Market Testing

When you perform your initial market tests, you must do so in a disguised manner, in order to protect your company. In other words, you should not reveal the exact product that you propose to introduce until you are almost ready to introduce it. Otherwise, you run the risk of losing the niche you're pursuing to another company that is better positioned (by sales force, manufacturing ability, more cash, reputation) to act more rapidly than you. Alas, the real world is filled with pirates.

These tests require some time, and I won't ask you to stop reading and perform them now. However, as you read the examples below, you may want to make notes about how you would use these tests with the niches you just uncovered in your MNA. Place these entries in your notebook after the MNA results, and indicate the specifics of your tests (either what action you would accomplish or what people or what companies you would contact).

I recommend your market testing be conducted in a two-stage approach. The first stage is the "qualifying" stage. At this point you are going to contact a variety of people (wholesalers, dealers, users) to see if sufficient demand really exists. You will conduct this research in a highly disguised manner.

If the demand does appear to be sufficiently intense, you proceed to the second stage, where you identify your key customers and conduct marketing tests on them. During this stage you may be slightly more candid regarding the real nature of your product, because these are the people who will be placing orders with you.

STAGE 1: *Two Potential Qualifying Techniques*

Let's assume that you are concentrating on the automatic phone screening device as the potential product uncovered in our earlier example MNA. Here are examples of two disguised qualifying techniques to find out whether or not the product idea is a sound one:

Technique A

Devise several cover stories to make your subjects want to give you accurate information:

- To telecommunications retail stores, you could pose as a potential customer with obscene phone call problems.
- To telecommunications wholesalers, you could indicate that you were considering opening several stores that would purchase their products.
- To the public, you could pose as an author researching the problem of unwanted phone solicitation for articles and books.

Technique B

Announce you may release a similar product in the near future; then openly test the potential of that product.

- For example, you might pose as the potential founder of an answering service to screen all calls to customer homes.

STAGE 2: *Cheap But Effective Marketing Tests*

Once you verify that a significant market exists, then you need to identify who your key customers will be, and remember this:

Key Point: *80% of your sales will come from 20% of your customer base (this is known as the 80-20 rule).*

It is critical that you identify those 20% of your customers who will represent the bulk of your business. How do you do this? By going directly to the marketplace and using one or more of several relatively inexpensive testing techniques that can give you the confidence that your potential product will be based on a foundation of strong demand. An added bonus is that, if your testing is solid, potential financiers may just verify a few points and accept the balance. On the other hand, if your testing is not complete, you'll have to wait for the financiers to do it anyway, because no one is going to invest major dollars in you without being certain that there is a significant market demand for your product.

Here are several inexpensive market tests that you can conduct to complete your market analysis:

TEST 1: *Data Base Research*

There are a tremendous number of data bases available on virtually any topic. All you need to do is tap into them. Here are some ways to begin: Get information on your industry from the Department of Commerce, the Small Business Administration, larger stock brokers, investment bankers, commercial banks, and public and university libraries (you don't have to be a student to use many college libraries; you may not be able to check books out, but you can usually do your research there).

In a major city, use your library's professional researchers. They will usually help you free of charge; however, you will have to come to them with specific, tightly defined questions. For example, you might ask, "How many telephone answering machines were sold to residences last year?" or "Who are the primary manufacturers of telephone answering machines?"

Many universities and some libraries have computerized data base searches, but you must carefully select the "key words" for the search, or you will get 2,000 pages instead of the 20 you really wanted. It's best to make judicious use of these services because they can often become expensive to use, depending on how broad your search is.

If you have a computer and a modem, you can plug in directly to many of the larger data bases on the market through services like Compuserve, Easylink, and The Source.

TEST 2: *In-Person Interviews With Potential Key Customers*

This is the best method for testing your product ideas, because you can see facial expressions of the people you are interviewing in addition to noting their voice inflections. At the same time, this is the toughest marketing test to set up. To be effective, you must select the largest and most knowledgeable users, and you must target their key management staff. Their time is valuable, and you probably won't get more than 10–15 minutes with each person.

In pursuing these interviews, you should aim for someone at the executive level (ideally a vice-president or above). Interviewing someone at a lower level will not generally yield much information, because the person will probably be afraid of disclosing any proprietary information. Company executives, on the other hand, like to demonstrate their knowledge and expertise. They will typically share with you the results of market studies that their companies probably spent thousands of dollars to complete.

Right now you are likely muttering, "This may be a great test, but just how am I supposed to get an interview with one of these people?" Let me share with you one of my favorite tactics:

Suppose I wanted to reach Bob Martin, vice-president of marketing for Northwestern Telcom Distributors, a major wholesaler in Los Angeles. True, he probably won't take a direct call from someone he doesn't even know. So, I call the company and ask for the name of Bob Martin's secretary. I learn her name is Betty Smith, and then I thank the switchboard operator and hang up. I wait at least an hour, then I place another call to the company and ask for Betty Smith.

When Betty comes to the phone, I introduce myself and my company, explaining we are developing a new product line that Northwestern will probably carry, and I indicate that I would like to set up a 15-minute appointment with Bob to get his input on several key features in the design. I indicate when I plan to be in Los Angeles, and I give her two options for meetings during that period.

I try not to be aggressive but rather, pleasantly persistent. Executive secretaries are powerful people, and I want Bob's secretary to be my ally rather than my adversary. Most executive secretaries have the authority to schedule such short meetings. If Betty does not, then she may insist that Bob will have to get back to me.

If I accept this answer, I will never hear from Bob. Therefore I indicate I may be in and out of the office today. Rather than have Bob play telephone tag, I should probably call back, and I ask Betty for the best time to call again.

I try to establish a first-name basis for our conversation as soon as possible. If my subject answers the phone with "This is Betty Smith," or "This is Bob Martin," I am home free. I respond with "Hello, Betty, I'm Scott Clark and I'm calling . . ." Then you retain a first name conversation. If the subject answers the phone with "This is Mrs. Smith," or "This is Mr. Martin," immediately respond with, "Is this *Bob* Martin?" When the subject answers yes, you can again transition into the previous response, placing the conversation on an informal basis.

The less formal the situation appears, the more willing the secretary will be to schedule the meeting. When I've successfully scheduled the appointment, I thank Betty for her help and tell her I look forward to seeing her on the day of the meeting. This reinforces the positive tone of our conversation and ensures that I have an ally in the distributor's camp.

When you do finally have your face-to-face meeting, after a few short pleasantries, try to get right to the point, stating why you are there, what your product is, and then ask the few specific questions you had prepared. Then allow the interview to expand into a brainstorming session in which the distributors will share their expertise with you about where they see the industry (and the market you are targeting) going in the next five years.

Finally, make an attempt to end the meeting on time. Even if your executive wants to keep on talking, remind him that the 15 minutes you asked for are up, and you wouldn't want to keep him from his next appointment. If he wants to continue, then at least you are now operating on his nickel. After the meeting, be sure to follow up with a letter of thanks. This keeps your name in front of the executive, reinforces your professionalism, and probably ensures that you will be able to see him again, if need be.

TEST 2-A: *Two-Tier Method for In-Person Interviews.*

If you aren't comfortable with the above "cold-call" approach, this is a modified version. First, write to Bob Martin. Explain who you are, what you are trying to accomplish, and why you need his input. Then indicate you will call him on a specific date to set up a meeting, and suggest two possible days and times for the meetings.

In this manner, when you make the initial call to Bob Martin's office, both he and his secretary have seen your letter and know who you are. If you still can't succeed in arranging a meeting during that call, follow up with another letter and another call at a future date. Remember, pleasant persistence pays off.

TEST 3: *Telephone Interviews With Potential Key Customers*
What if you can't afford to pay a visit to these people? The telephone interview is faster and less expensive than Test 2. However, it is also less versatile and less flexible (you can't see the facial expressions or gestures of your interviewee).

If you choose this method, you should still use the same technique above to get through to Betty, but now you are asking for five minutes on the phone. If she replies that Bob is busy now, simply ask for the best time to call him back. Betty will remember you when you call again.

When you do get through, you should expect no more than 5–10 minutes of discussion. Therefore, your best tactic is to let your subjects lead you so that you can see where they are headed during this shorter interview time. It would help if you have a written script, so that you can get through the preliminary introduction and explanation for your call in a timely manner. One caution here: You cannot make it sound as if you are reading your script, and the script itself must sound exciting so that your interviewee wants to talk to you.

I want to emphasize that when you are conducting either Test 2 or Test 3, the secret is to let your subject to do most of the talking. Don't try to get your interviewees to validate your ideas; instead, ask for their valued judgment as experts on your particular market. Keep your spoken portion short and be prepared with a series of questions to ask your subjects. Also, be prepared to take copious notes as they respond. If your questions are well thought out, not only will you get more meaningful answers, but you will also gain the respect of your interviewees for knowing how to conduct research effectively.

TEST 3-A: *Two-Tier Method for Combination Mail-Phone Survey*
Once again, if you are uncomfortable with making a "cold" telephone call, this method uses a one-two punch: It ensures you are known when you call and that the executive knows exactly why you are calling. Therefore the executive should be more willing to take your call.

Just as in Test 2-A, first write to Bob Martin, explaining who you are, what you're trying to accomplish, and why you need his input. Also, include in this letter the specific questions you would like to have him answer. Then indicate that you plan to call him on a specific date at a specific time to conduct a brief interview.

By prebriefing the executive in a letter, you can make more efficient use of the telephone interview. Furthermore, you will most likely impress the executive with the professionalism of your approach. By the time you call, he will have had time to think about your questions, so the odds are that you'll get much more accurate, in-depth responses from him. In addition, because he has already received your letter, you will find it easier to get through to him. Now, both he and his secretary will remember you and will be expecting your call.

TEST 4: *Direct Mail Survey*

This test method is the next best if you can't reach key people by phone. However, it is limited, for a number of reasons. First, you must ask simple, short answer questions; you will rarely get people to spend more than five minutes on five questions in a mail survey. Also, if you send out 100 questionnaires, consider yourself lucky if you get five of them back. Finally, you will likely have to wait a month to receive all your responses.

It's true that a 3%–4% response to a questionnaire is considered good. But I will let you in on a secret, one that can increase your response rate to as much as 50%. It's this simple: Tape a dollar bill to your questionnaire. I get so many questionnaires with a dime taped to them "for a cup of coffee" that I collect the dimes and throw out the questionnaires. After all, my time is worth more than 10 cents. But when I receive a questionnaire with a dollar taped to it, I feel sufficiently guilty to keep the dollar *and* fill out the questionnaire.

TEST 5: *Mail Order Survey*

This will cost you the price of an ad in several publications, but it will also provide invaluable information about consumer interest and will help you to identify the correct publications for later advertising. The first step is to determine the appropriate trade publications for your market, then you place a small display advertisement like the one shown in Figure 2-3.

Rather than go to the expense of getting your own 800 number, look in the Yellow Pages under Telephone Answering Services. You

Figure 2-3. Example of a display advertisement in a trade publication.

SCREEN INCOMING PHONE CALLS!

Our company is about to introduce a new product
that will automatically screen phone calls
to your home, letting only your friends get through.
If you are interested in this product, and
if you would be willing to participate in a short
survey, we will send you a coupon providing a
50% discount off the purchase price
for one of these innovative systems.
To participate in this survey,
please call 1-800-123-4567 today.
This offer is strictly limited to the first 100 respondents.

should find a number of 800-number shared services listed. Contract with one of them, and it will usually provide the names and addresses of the respondents for a small per-person fee. After you have the names, send out your survey form to these people, with a letter stating that when you receive the completed survey form, they will be notified when the first units are ready for delivery (specify an approximate date) and will receive a coupon for a 50% discount well in advance of that date. This method will ensure a high percentage of returns, and respondents will tend to make a number of suggestions for the product, because they believe they are part of the development process (which they are) and because they anticipate owning one of your products.

TEST 6: *Trade Show Presells*

A final useful method of market testing, if you have a working prototype, is to rent a booth at a trade show appropriate to your market and attempt to presell your product from prototype samples and preliminary literature. Frequently, the information you can gain at a good trade show (one that is attended by your primary customers) can be far more useful than years of personal interviews.

Trade show attendees in some markets expect to be quoted long lead times. Therefore, if you are lucky enough to actually land a big order at a show, you could consider quoting a long lead time for first delivery. If the customer accepts this quote and gives you a purchase order, you may actually be able to take the order to financiers and get funding to fill it.

Even if you do not have a prototype, you could still attend key trade shows for your niche market without renting an exhibit booth. In a few days, you will be able to rub shoulders with major customers and glean critical information for your market testing far more easily than calling and/or writing all over the country.

Key Point: *A good trade show in your specific target market is one of the least expensive ways to get good sales leads.*

Trade shows afford you an excellent opportunity to "rap" with recognized experts in your target market. If you have an exhibit booth, you should have another team member who can periodically man your booth while you are tracking down these key people at the ancillary workshops.

Verifying Your Test Results

Let's assume that you have conducted several of the above tests and analyses on your intended product. As you review your results, are the data from different tests in agreement? If not, one of four factors is responsible:

1. You may have contacted some of the wrong people (those who are not part of the critical 20% of your market or who do not understand the dynamics of this market).
2. You may have used poor procedures (vaguely or improperly wording questions, or even infusing your opinions into others by not keeping quiet).
3. The dynamics of your chosen market are changing so rapidly that a portion of your data is already obsolete.

or (and this next one is most likely)

    4. You are chasing a mirage rather than a valid market niche.

You must decide which of the above statements is true. If it is item 1 on the above list, you had better throw out the data from the inappropriate people and replace them with valid data. If it is item 2, you had better revise your test procedures, because something is wrong. If it is item 3, you may have a chance for significant near-term profits, but only if you can get to market in a timely manner. If it is item 4, then you had better discard your product and consider another one, because you simply won't sell enough to make a profit.

The Significance of Market Testing

The process of testing for the viability of niches uncovered by the MNA is every bit as critical to the success of your business as the MNA process itself. You may be tempted to rush through the testing process or skip it altogether. I strongly urge you to resist this temptation, which leads to the second Fatal Error that puts entrepreneurs out of business.

<u>Fatal Error</u>: *Improper market testing.*

If you are like the typical entrepreneur, you believe so strongly in your product idea that you may be tempted to minimize the importance of properly testing the validity of the concept in the marketplace. But as I've emphasized, many entrepreneurs have been put out of business by their blind adherence to a product idea for which there simply wasn't sufficient market demand. The only way to determine whether or not there is enough demand for your product to support a business is to go through the time and effort necessary to conduct thorough market testing.

Besides, because we can assume that you want to be successful in your quest for capital, you must realize that financiers are not going to put funds in your business if they don't believe that you have verified the strength of the market. Improper market research brands you as inexperienced.

Should you wish to explore the topic of market research in greater detail, there are several excellent market research books in the recommended reading list at the end of the book. They will cover the advantages and disadvantages of the different types of market testing.

The Niche Shift—A Reverse MNA

So you've completed your MNA and your market testing, and it all checks out. That's great, but before you go charging ahead I want you to consider another wrinkle.

You have used MNA to identify a niche that, in turn, led to a primary product or a secondary product, and your market testing verified that the apparent demand for the product is real. What if you have a product in a market where there is potentially serious competition? You may want to consider a niche shift into better turf. In other words, you may want to take your product into a less competitive marketplace, in order to gain a strategic advantage.

When Dial soap arrived on the American scene in 1951, its maker did just that. When Armour Meatpacking decided to get into the soap manufacturing business, the company developed Dial as a unique round-corner bar with a pleasant scent. Because of the formidable competition in traditional soap markets, Armour did a niche shift, evolving a unique strategy. Dial soap was introduced in a distinctive 12-pack available exclusively through men's clothing stores. Here was a soap product being introduced into a smaller-niche market where no competition existed. Armour structured the price to give the retailer a high profit. Only after significant exposure in this market (where Dial gained a reputation as a "designer" soap) did Armour shift distribution into the conventional soap marketplace—and Dial immediately realized a 7% market penetration.

In my first small manufacturing business, I executed a similar play. Previously, I discussed the agricultural monitoring system at the heart of my first company. However, the company did not start out in that market. Through MNA I created a unique, rugged reliable alarm system. My initial niche was the business alarm market, and I had formidable competition. Subsequently, I saw a need for rugged alarm monitoring systems in the agribusiness community, where there was virtually no competition. I did a niche shift with this product and went on to build an entire industry. A decade later, when I sold the business, my company had more market share in the agribusiness niche than did all the competition combined.

As the quarterback of your team, you need to review this option as well. Given all the niches your MNA uncovered to develop your new product, could you shift this product into another market initially, thereby gaining a significant advantage?

If you do elect to make a niche shift, you should repeat the market testing in this new niche, to verify sufficient demand (note that the ideal price may vary considerably in the new marketplace).

The Advantages of Certain Industries

If you plan to raise your required capital through bank loans and private equity placements, you probably needn't concern yourself with this topic. However, if you plan to approach professional venture capital sources for funding, the industry you are in may be a very real concern.

At any point in time, certain industries are "hot" in the eyes of venture capitalists, and they won't touch other industries with a ten-foot pole. For example, after a love affair with computer companies in the early 1980s, venture capitalists regarded them as poison in the mid-1980s. The same held true for semiconductor companies.

So how do you know which industries are blacklisted and which are "goldlisted"? The best way to determine this is to query several venture capital firms, not about your specific product but, rather, about your specific industry. Furthermore, keep in mind that the "in" industries are constantly changing, so make sure that your analysis is concurrent with your MNA. If you last visited with the venture capital world a year ago, you had better repeat your venture capital analysis before approaching venture investors for financing.

* * *

By the time you have completed your testing, you should know if the market for your product is real (and if it isn't real, you will have elected to concentrate on one of the other products resulting from your MNA). You should also have a basic overview of the characteristics of the segments of the market you are targeting. And you have further verified you have the right market for your product.

However, having a product with apparent demand is not enough. In order to convince consumers to buy your product (and financiers to invest in your business), you must also understand your customer base. Otherwise, you cannot hope to penetrate the market (or raise the money you need). And understanding the market is what the next chapter is all about.

CHAPTER
3

Putting the Pieces Together—The First Course

The Marketing Plan

In the last chapter, you found your niche and utilized market research to verify sufficient demand for your product. Most highly charged entrepreneurs believe the next step is to develop a business plan. But how can you raise the money you need if you can't convince potential investors that you understand your market and its dynamics so well that you will be able to achieve your sales projections? For that matter, how will you formulate your sales projections—the one set of numbers that all your other financial summaries depend upon?

I suggest you put aside premature thoughts of a business plan and concentrate instead on your specific market and its unique facets. The next Key Point says it best:

Key Point: *In order to penetrate your market, you must understand your market.*

The sins of failing to make the effort to understand the market are not limited to small companies. Here are some classic examples where large companies committed major market blunders: A young San Jose computer software company called VisiCorp created the first computer spreadsheet program, called Visicalc, in the late 1970s. It could have had the tiger by the tail, but the company really never understood the needs of its users and never built in the features that their customers wanted. As a result, several years later a young Boston upstart, Lotus Development Company, studied the needs of the market, incorporated features the potential users wanted, developed a strong marketing plan, and launched Lotus 1-2-3, which buried Visicalc. Was 1-2-3 that much better? Not really. But because of a strong marketing plan, potential customers perceived that it was better, and as a result Lotus soared to dizzying heights while Visicalc floundered.

Another truly visionary company created the first personal computer for office use: In 1979 Tandy-Radio Shack introduced the TRS-80 Model II microcomputer. The machine was a winner for its time, and Tandy had the opportunity to control the entire market. But as effective as its market niche analysis had been in verifying the strength of the market, Tandy never really understood the market. Tandy developed a proprietary operating system, kept the "innards" of its product confidential, and insisted only Tandy peripherals and software be utilized with the product. To ensure this, the company mandated that its Radio Shack stores sell only Tandy products. Even with these impediments, Tandy systems sold well (I bought three of them myself), and a small number of other companies began offering Model II add-on products, but Tandy's efforts did not lead to the Model II (or its successors) capturing a significant share of the potential market. Several years later, IBM entered the market with its first PC (personal computer). The IBM PC was more expensive than the Tandy Model II, but IBM did a far better job of ensuring a product legacy in the marketplace. Big Blue made schematic diagrams of its system available to other peripheral hardware and software companies that wanted to develop products compatible with the IBM PC. As a result, within a few years there were thousands of companies manufacturing ancillary products for the IBM PC, and Tandy, which should have been king of the hill, was buried in IBM's dust.

In the early 1980s, as computers became more widely accepted in the office place, another computer giant, Wang, entered the picture with its own office computer system. However, it committed sins akin to Tandy's, developing a unique system with unique connectors that could only be utilized with Wang peripherals. The companies that committed to Wang systems were unable to expand into other technologies (for example, the Wang system would only work with the company's own expensive laser printer). As a result, another computer giant failed, and when An Wang, the company's brilliant founder, died in 1990, the company had still not recovered.

So much for big failures. Now let's look at some small companies that did the job right: They utilized effective strategies gleaned from market analysis to achieve success. John, a midwestern entrepreneur, opened a meat market in a major metropolitan area. How could he hope to compete with the big supermarket chains in his area? John analyzed his market and knew that his potential customers had limited budgets for their meat products, as well as limited time to devote to meat purchasing. So in addition to high-quality meat, he offered a unique service. His customers filled out a form indicating the size of their family and the types of meat their family liked and disliked. The family then specified a weekly meat budget. Each week he would put together a package of meat for each family, varying according to meat prices, specials, and the family preferences, and he would then deliver the package to the customer's home, for the specific price each customer had quoted in his or her survey form. The result? John had all the business he wanted.

Meredith, a southeastern entrepreneur, launched a new office supply/computer products company in a large city, amid fierce competition. Through Market Niche Analysis, her company targeted a large niche market of area companies that had PCs in their offices. But in doing an additional survey of the market, she discovered that potential customers didn't like to spend time dealing with office supply salespeople. So her company devised a system offering customers a free software communications package and modem. This allowed the customers to communicate over local phone lines directly to the company's order entry computer. Customers could check availability and pricing whenever they wanted. Then all they needed to do was enter their customer number, operator name, purchase order number, and quantities to place the order. The system provided instant hard copies at both ends, virtually eliminating errors and reducing labor costs. Many times the orders were delivered the same day. And Meredith smiled all the way to the bank.

Entrepreneurs are impatient by nature. Because they want things done yesterday, they launch sales programs into markets that they don't really understand. As a result, they close only a mere fraction of sales possible if they really knew what they were doing. This chapter is going to help you gain that understanding and thereby ensure that you have the potential to maximize your sales.

To understand your market, you must first complete a survey of that market. To do this, it's time to play "20 Questions." Review the checklist below. I have included comments with each of the questions. I would strongly recommend that you have a complete understanding of the items in this checklist, as they relate to your specific market.

If you want another secret weapon in your arsenal, then please don't take this checklist lightly. If you understand the answers to every question on the list and can execute your plan based upon these answers, you will have a decided advantage over 90% of your competitors, even if you are new to the market. Why is this such an advantage? Because entrepreneurs typically believe the public will readily switch to their product or service; therefore, they don't take the time to analyze their markets and competition.

Market Survey Checklist*

1. *What different customer segments are involved in your market?* A customer segment is a specific subset of your market with unique needs that require a specific channel for sales. As an example, with my telephone call screening machine from the previous chapter, there are a number of market segments: the home market segment and the business market segment. (In fact, each of these segments could be broken down further. The home market segment could be broken down into home market retail segment—sales through stores—and home market direct mail segment—sales through magazines to areas that lack a sufficient number of stores.)

2. *What is the size (in potential customers) and the geographic distribution of each segment?* Through the same data base that you utilized in your disguised market testing, you should be able to obtain a realistic number. However, most entrepreneurs grossly overestimate the size of their market. Be conservative in your estimates; otherwise potential investors will not accept your projections.

---

*Several of these categories were adapted from checklists presented in Richard M. White, *The Entrepreneur's Manual* (Radnor, Penn.: Chilton Books, 1977), pp. 72–73.

3. *Who are the* major *end users in each market segment (remember the 80-20 rule), and what are these customers' profiles?* It is not enough to merely identify who the buyers will be. It is critical that you also understand their life-styles: typical income, age, marital status, number of children, typical annual dollars spent in your product's category, etc.

4. *What are the top prices you can command in each segment?* Price should be a function of the buyer's perceived value of your product. For example, even though I could sell my telephone screening system for $150 and still make a profit, this screening service may be worth $500 to the buyers. You must determine this by conducting several different surveys (phone, mail, interviews) in which you "try out" various prices and test the customer's reaction. *This step is absolutely crucial for success.*

5. *What are the unique product (or service) requirements for each segment?* Here you are looking at the specific needs (related to your product) of each segment. In other words, why will they buy? The needs of the home market segment will be different from those of the business segment. This may even lead you to further break down your segments (the home market, for example, might be further broken down into the urban home segment and the rural home segment).

6. *Who are the existing major competitors in the market?* You should determine not only their names, but how they market their products, where they advertise, and their annual sales figures. To identify the competitors, talk to salespeople, consumers, and distributors. Try to get copies of their annual reports.

7. *What are the existing competitive products (or services) in each segment?* From the same sources, determine the complete product line of each competitor, and then determine which of these products are being marketed within each of your segments. This will help you formulate the most effective competition within segments.

8. *What are the competitors' strengths? weaknesses?* From your data gathering to answer the last two questions, along with casual conversations with salespeople, consumers, and distributors, you should be able to formulate a pretty good idea of your competitors' strengths and weaknesses. Note that "weaknesses" refers not only to design flaws but also (because you know the needs of each segment) to missing features.

9. *What are the areas that competitors are serving well? serving poorly?* Again, from your data gathered thus far, you should be able to assess that your competitors are serving certain market segments better than others. One competitive strategy might be to concentrate in those areas where the competition is doing poorly.

10. *What would be probable new competitive products (or services) after entry into the market?* For this one you need to put yourself in the shoes of your competitors. Ask yourself how they are likely to respond when you introduce your product line.

11. *What companies would be probable future significant competitors within the next five years?* If the market is really as large as you believe it is, there will be additional competition. Determine companies in ancillary markets that might be motivated to enter this market.

12. *What products or services will each segment want next year? in five years?* If you have the understanding of the end user's needs, you should be able to project a reasonable scenario of the potential growth of your product line over the next five years.

13. *What will overall product sales be in each segment for each of the next five years? and what will your share be?* Because you have determined the number of potential buyers or size of the market (SIZE), and you know what unit price these buyers are willing to pay for the products (PRICE), you only need to determine what percentage of the market will purchase products each year (%). Then the yearly sales are calculated as $(SIZE) \times (PRICE) \times (\%)$. Finally, you should determine what reasonable portion of that market you could capture during each of the next five years. These figures become your yearly sales projections. Remember, be conservative in your estimates so that your figures will be believable to the financiers.

14. *What is the appropriate sales network to penetrate each segment?* There are many options: retail sales, catalog sales, telephone marketing, direct mail, sales reps. And only one method is best for each segment. If the best option is not obvious to you, then you may want to visit with other marketing people or representatives of each of these channels to determine which is most appropriate for each market segment.

15. *What* image *do you need to effectively penetrate each specific market segment?* Again, look at the consumer's needs. They need

something that they are not getting from the competition (many times it's better customer service). Determine what it is and then portray that image to the buyers.

16. *How do you educate the customer for best market penetration?* Remember that customers are not looking for features; they are looking for the solution to a problem. When you are intimately aware of their needs, then you only have to inform consumers that your product satisfies those needs.

17. *How do you educate our sales distribution network for the greatest possible market penetration?* The sales network must also focus on meeting the consumer's needs. They must not focus on your product's features. Provide them with training and sales tools emphasizing the fact that your product solves the customers' needs.

18. *What is the best probable advertising media in each segment for your products?* There are a number of options: newspapers, magazines, direct mail, radio, television, billboards, etc. Your challenge is not only to determine which type (for example, magazines), but further to determine which title is best in that type (for example, which specific magazine) by determining which magazine is read by the largest group of your target consumers.

19. *What are some effective ways to bypass the competition?* Most of your competition have not done the in-depth study of the market that you have. If you truly understand the buyers' needs, then you know which of these needs are not being met, and thereby you focus your strategy on meeting those needs, which leaves your competitors out in the cold.

20. *What is the probable number of sales calls required for a sales close?* A sales call could be defined as your representative contacting the consumer (for example, telemarketing) or the consumer contacting your representative (for example, walking into a retail store). If your product is low-cost, it will probably sell on the first sales call. However, if it is a "high-ticket" item (such as a computer or a car), several sales calls may be required. You need to determine how many sales calls are required so that you can factor this into your projections (for example, if three sales calls are required and the sales force will be making 900 effective sales calls per month, then you could expect to close 300 sales during the month).

The Critical Situational Analysis

So far I have been concentrating on gathering market data. If you've begun the process of switching gears from the typical "product-oriented" entrepreneur to the rarely seen "marketing-oriented" entrepreneur, you have already learned a great deal about your market, your potential buyers, and your competition. In this section, I'll begin to condense the information you have assembled.

The next step is to construct a situational analysis of the market, which is the creation of a one-page narrative summary of your compilation of data.

This one-page summary must address the following critical areas:

- The total size of the market, as well as your share of it, for the next five years
- A statement of your strengths and weaknesses
- Who your competition is and their strengths and weaknesses
- A description of your customer base (how many there are and where they are located)
- How you will identify, contact, and sell to customers
- How you will price your products
- What type of sales force you will utilize
- Why you will succeed

It is not a trivial task to condense all of your relevant data into a single page that addresses all of these points. However, it is necessary in order to (I) provide you with a major section for your marketing plan and (II) allow you to succinctly brief a potential investor with the highlights of your market and your marketing strategy, thus giving the *appearance* of experience.

EXERCISE: Your Own Market Analysis

It's time to take out your notebook again. For the first part of this exercise, I want you to complete a survey of your intended market. Write all of the Market Survey Checklist questions in your notebook, even if you do not yet have all the answers. This will help you to see which areas of the market survey you still need to concentrate on in order to complete the task.

When you have answered all of these questions to the best of your ability, then I want you to turn to a new page in your notebook and label it Critical Situational Analysis. Proceed to write a one-page summary, based on the data gathered from your Market Survey Checklist, that answers all eight "bullets"(•) from the previous section. When you have completed this exercise, you are ready to proceed to the next Microgenesis level.

However, lest you think that most of the market data gathering is over at this point, let me assure you that it is never over. Your data are only current as of today; some data will become obsolete tomorrow. Therefore, you should ensure that whoever heads up marketing within your company periodically updates this marketing analysis (probably every six months), because you will need the most current information when you have to make future strategic product decisions.

LEVEL III: Develop Your Marketing Plan

Once you are satisfied with your product or service and you understand your market, you need to start the transition process from an idea into a business (if you already have an established business, this is a transition process integrating your idea into your existing product line).

When I launched my first company, I had never seen a marketing plan. However, I still had one, so to speak. We had a single product, Farm Alarm. My first marketing plan consisted of a single objective. It was written in large letters on a sheet of typewriter paper and taped to the wall over my desk. It said, "We will do whatever it takes to sell 500 Farm Alarm systems this year!"

Happily, we achieved that goal. However, because we did not have a marketing plan to guide us, we made some bad decisions. What we had was one good objective. What we needed were additional objectives, clear-cut strategies to meet those objectives, and detailed tactics for implementing the strategies. Armed with these, we would have avoided some trouble spots and realized our objective more quickly and inexpensively.

For example, one of our strategies to achieve sales of 500 Farm

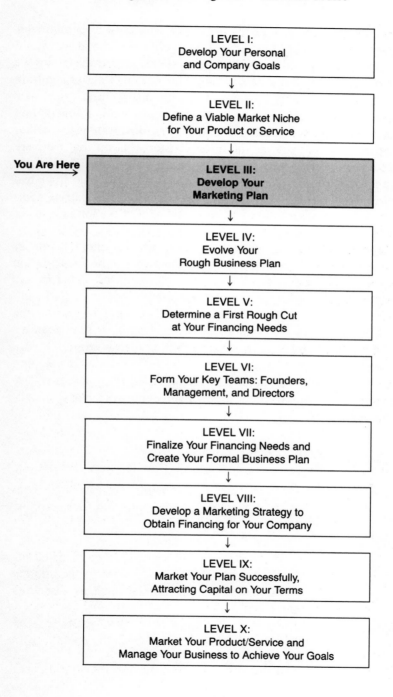

LEVEL I:
Develop Your Personal
and Company Goals

↓

LEVEL II:
Define a Viable Market Niche
for Your Product or Service

↓

You Are Here →

**LEVEL III:
Develop Your
Marketing Plan**

↓

LEVEL IV:
Evolve Your
Rough Business Plan

↓

LEVEL V:
Determine a First Rough Cut
at Your Financing Needs

↓

LEVEL VI:
Form Your Key Teams: Founders,
Management, and Directors

↓

LEVEL VII:
Finalize Your Financing Needs and
Create Your Formal Business Plan

↓

LEVEL VIII:
Develop a Marketing Strategy to
Obtain Financing for Your Company

↓

LEVEL IX:
Market Your Plan Successfully,
Attracting Capital on Your Terms

↓

LEVEL X:
Market Your Product/Service and
Manage Your Business to Achieve Your Goals

Alarm systems might have been "Develop a base of at least ten major distributors." This would have increased the likelihood that we would find enough customers to buy 500 of our systems. One of the tactics we could have used to accomplish this might have been "Recruit and train four manufacturers rep organizations to secure distributors."

Instead, we concentrated on a few major distributors directly and fortunately landed one of them, who took our entire 500-system order. We were ecstatic that year as the roller coaster went up, but we were dismayed the following year when it came crashing down: The distributor ran into financial problems and decided to drop our line. If we had had a well thought out plan, we would have focused on acquiring additional distributors during that first year and spared ourselves a lot of grief down the line.

Despite this setback, we managed to develop another smaller alarm system called MinAlert™. By our third year in business, it had gone on to be an even bigger success than Farm Alarm. This time we got smart and put together a detailed marketing plan that forced us to concentrate on multiple distribution channels, vastly increasing the range of our customer base and guaranteeing far higher sales than we would have realized by focusing on a handful of distributors.

With this lesson in mind, let's turn to the subject of developing your marketing plan. The major purpose of a marketing plan is to outline the specific market for your product and detail your plans for selling to the market.

Your Marketing Plan's Format

Now that your situational analysis is complete, you can begin constructing the marketing plan. A good marketing plan has four sections:

1. Introduction: *An overview of the market.*

     This is basically your previously completed situational analysis. You may want to incorporate additional marketing points, such as discounts and profit margins.

2. Objectives: *The specific broad MARKETING goals you are striving to achieve (these should be tied to a specific time frame).*

Your marketing plan's objectives should be based (at least in part) on the objectives that you created as part of your Market Niche Analysis and may also include some of the marketing-oriented goals that you set for your business in Chapter 1.

For example, XYZ Corporation's first-year objectives might include generating sales of $2 million, closing ten major key accounts in a five-state area, and closing four major catalog accounts.

3. Strategies: *The individual programs utilized to achieve the objectives.*

Strategies are your detailed plans for realizing your individual objectives within a specific time frame.

For example, XYZ's strategies might include the introduction of a strong co-op advertising program (whereby you offer to share in the cost of your dealers' local advertising) and the appointment of at least five experienced sales reps to reach its objectives of $2 million in sales and closing of key accounts.

4. Tactics: *The detailed actions required to implement a given strategy.*

For example, XYZ Corporation's tactics for implementing its strategy of recruiting sales reps might include creating an effective sales rep interview procedure and implementing a creative rep training/incentive program.

A typical marketing plan is five to ten pages in length. After the introduction, each subsequent section is progressively longer than the previous one. The objectives section should consist of four to eight primary marketing goals. The strategies should be at least twice that many, since a single objective will require multiple strategies. Finally, the tactics should be even more numerous, because each strategy will generally demand several tactics. Each of the objectives, strategies, and tactics should be stated and then explained in several sentences. You may choose to break down activities by year or by quarter; in any event, each action should be tied to a specific time frame.

Prototype Marketing Plan

Figure 3-1 illustrates an abbreviated sample marketing plan for XYZ Corporation, which shows how the objectives, strategies, and tactics are incorporated into a plan. This is not presented as the "ideal" marketing plan but simply as an example of a workable plan. It contains a shortened introduction section, followed by an objective section with only a single objective (instead of your multiple objectives). The strategies and tactics relate back to that single objective, making it easy for you to see how the three categories intermesh.

EXERCISE: Creating Your Company's Marketing Plan

Armed with the marketing data that you've accumulated and the situational analysis that you just completed, it is now time for you to pause from your reading and create your own marketing plan based on the marketing plan format and sample outline presented above.

Leave a blank page after completing each of the four major sections (Introduction, Objectives, Strategies, and Tactics) because you will be making additions to your plan during the remainder of this book. As a rough guideline, you should probably have one page for objectives, two pages for strategies, and three pages for tactics. In each section, you should state the item and then follow with a several-sentence description (this was omitted from our example plan).

Tactical Consistency

Your marketing plan objectives were probably established with an obvious link to your marketing analysis. However, by the time you pro-

Figure 3-1. XYZ Corporation marketing plan (an abbreviated example).

Introduction

The purpose of this document is to outline a marketing plan which gives XYZ Corporation consistent direction and firmly positions the company as a viable leader in the _____ industry.

XYZ Corporation plans to market a new product, _____ . Potential customers for this product are home-owner consumers with an income of at least $30,000/year, that are plagued by [*define the problem you are solving*]. Having completed an extensive analysis of the marketplace, we believe that a conservative estimate of the total size of the market within our five-state area is _____ units/year for the next 10 years. Nationally, the market is estimated to be _____ units/year. [*If the market is growing each year, you may want to use a graph or a chart to depict this*].

The product will be sold through retail outlets in our five-state area and through major electronics catalogs [list the target catalogs] elsewhere. The product will retail for $199. We will use a network of sales reps to market the product to distributors throughout our five-state area. The typical distributor discount will be 50% off list, at which level we will realize a 55% gross profit margin.

We will generate sales leads for the five-state area through newspaper advertising, utilizing a computerized lead-tracking system. We will also place articles in several electronics magazines about this exciting new product.

Our competition consists of _____ . Although they have manufactured a similar product for several years, they require large stocking orders from their dealers, have alienated their distributors with a lack of field support, and are not willing to adapt their units to meet the specific needs of our target niche market.

XYZ Corporation's business philosophy focuses on a strong orientation toward customer service. We plan to appoint a national spokesperson who will stress our commitment to quality, meeting the consumers' needs, and customer service. With the implementation of our marketing plan, we will realize the objectives detailed in the following section:

I. Objectives [*the specific marketing goals*]

The primary objective for XYZ Corporation's first year of operation is as follows:

- Generate first-year sales of $800,000.

(*continues*)

Figure 3-1.   (continued)

[*Continue with subsequent years and additional objectives.*]

II. Strategies [specific action programs to achieve objectives]

The first year's strategies are as follows:

- Introduction of national advertising campaign, coupled with regional co-op program
- Appointment of at least eight experienced sales reps, covering major urban areas
- Appointment of major catalog sales rep
- Secure stocking contracts with 50 major distributors

[*Continue with subsequent years and additional strategies.*]

III. Tactics [detailed actions required to implement strategies]

The first year's tactics are as follows:

- Signing of contract with national spokesperson
- Introduction of new brochure, display ads, and "point-of-purchase" poster
- Placement of advertising in major print media
- Personal appearance tour of spokesperson in major cities
- Implementation of creative sales-rep training program
- Initiation of national sales rep kickoff meeting with spokesperson
- Unveiling of new rep sales incentive program
- Creation of color catalog slicks
- Initiation of catalog stocking bonus program
- Launching of sales incentive program for distributors
- Scheduling of training carnivals with each distributor and its dealers

[*Continue with subsequent years and additional tactics.*]

gress to the level of developing specific tactics for your plan, you are three generations away from your original marketing analysis.

Therefore, as a final check, review each of your tactics carefully against the details of your original market analysis. Are each of these tactics consistent with your marketplace (and with your pocketbook)?

Fatal Error: *Inappropriate market tactics.*

The wrong tactics can cause even the most sound strategy to back-fire and jeopardize your business. For example, a small business cannot afford to use the same tactics for recruiting and rewarding sales reps as a large organization can. To try to do so would result in financial dis-aster (in trying to match the perks of a big company) or a sales force greatly disillusioned when employees realize they have been lured by promises that can't possibly be kept.

To avoid this error, keep in mind that bigger is not always better. For example, many a sales rep leaves a large company to join a smaller one where the commissions may not be as high but the rewards in the form of recognition, increased responsibility, and sense of accomplish-ment are far greater.

Marketing vs. Sales

Before we conclude this chapter, it's worth noting that there is a key difference between marketing and sales. A description of the difference is hard to come by; yet if you know and can articulate this difference, you will impress your potential financiers.

When I was researching this topic several years ago, I searched all the literature I could lay my hands on. Because I couldn't find a clear distinction, I called up the president of one of the national advertising agencies that I use, and I asked him, "Jerry, can you give me a good definition that will clarify the distinction between marketing and sales?"

Jerry thought a moment and then replied, "That's really a good question. I'll have to think about it for a while and get back to you." I hung up the phone, realizing he didn't have the answer either.

Then I proceeded to develop my own definition, and when I was done, I called Jerry back and told him what I had come up with. He replied, "Scott, you have hit the nail on the head!"

So, it is with his endorsement that I present you with the next key point:

Key Point: *MARKETING consists of those actions by which you make potential customers aware of your product or service.*

Examples might include:

- *Handing out a business card at a party*
- *Giving a speech about your company*
- *Giving out literature at a trade show*

while SALES consists of those actions specifically tailored to close an order.

(Examples of these actions are the typical activities of, e.g., the retail clerk, the telephone salesperson, the car salesperson.)

If you intend to be a major contributor to your company's business strategy, you must know (and understand) this distinction, so record it in your notebook and remember it well.

In most start-ups, the sales and marketing functions are in the same department (for the sake of economy), but as you grow, you may need to split them, because their basic missions are different.

*   *   *

With this knowledge and a firm marketing plan in hand, you are one step farther in the process of turning your product idea into a business (and you are miles ahead of most of your competition). In the next chapter, you will learn how to draft a rough business plan to attract key players to your management team and prepare for a visit to the financiers.

4

Putting the Pieces Together—The Next Course

Rough Plans and Initial Projections

The time has now arrived to consider developing a business plan. For now you will need only a rough, preliminary plan. The rough business plan covers the same major areas as the formal business plan does, but it is less detailed and contains far fewer pages.

You can rest assured you won't be duplicating your efforts by preparing a rough business plan; most of the information in it will be absorbed in the full-fledged plan we'll be discussing in Chapter 6. Your work in developing a rough business plan will help you to clarify all of the issues surrounding the development of your business and ensure that when the time comes to write your formal business plan, it will be well thought out, professional, and polished.

CAUTION: If you are not planning to raise vast amounts of capital, you may be tempted to skip this chapter. Please don't. The rough business plan serves several purposes, *none of which is to raise capital.*

Bringing in the Barrister and the Bean Counter

The first considerations in developing the rough business plan are the legal questions surrounding your business. It's time to go shopping for a lawyer.

You might be considering using your family attorney to help launch your business. A word of caution: Don't!—unless, of course, he or she happens to specialize in business law. Attorneys are like doctors: Some are generalists, and some are specialists. If you needed heart surgery, you would definitely seek out a specialist, because your very life is at stake, and you want a physician intimately familiar with that organ. When selecting an attorney, keep in mind that the very life of your business is at stake; you will want to secure an experienced specialist for this activity as well.

Just like heart specialists, attorneys who specialize in small business are going to charge more than generalists do. However, they can usually do the job far better and in less time, so you are likely to come out ahead financially anyway.

How do you find one of these experts? If you have a family attorney, ask him or her for a referral. Otherwise, ask your banker or business associates or look in the Yellow Pages under "Lawyers" for a lawyer referral service. Explain that you are looking for a lawyer who is an experienced business law specialist.

You will want someone who can deal effectively with the nitty-gritty of labor law, among other things. For example, make sure the attorney is intimately familiar with the Fair Labor Standards Act, to determine which employees can be on salary and which ones must remain on hourly status, thereby avoiding this young CEO's situation:

The CEO of a new manufacturing company asked his family attorney for business advice. He had an employee responsible for the stockroom and custodial duties. The employee was working 50–60 hours each week for $5.00 per hour. The CEO promoted the employee to material manager, with the same duties, at a salary of $300 per week. The employee was pleased to be promoted to the ranks of management, and the CEO was happy to save the costs of overtime pay. Everything seemed to be working out fine.

One year later, though, the company was audited by the Labor Department. The audit determined that the material manager was not a qualified salaried worker, as determined under Part 541 of Title 29 of the Code of Federal Regulations. The reason? He wasn't supervising any people, and his job required no formal training. As a result, the CEO was required to give the employee back pay for overtime and to pay back withholding plus penalties and interest to the government. The total tab amounted to more than $4,000. This CEO was lucky; imagine what he would have owed if he had not been audited for several more years.

The moral of this story is to make sure the attorney to whom you are entrusting your business has the background to merit that trust. Interview candidates to clarify two factors: First of all, make sure they have experience not just in business law, but in your type of business. For example, if you are starting a manufacturing business and a candidate's experience is strictly with retail businesses, you should probably continue looking.

Second, make sure the chemistry between the two of you is good, because your relationship with your attorney will probably be lengthy. If it is to work well, there must be a good "fit."

Once you find the right attorney, use this person wisely and prudently. This is something I had to learn the hard way. When I secured my first business attorney, I expected him to do everything for me, and I paid through the nose as a result. For example, one of the first tasks I gave him was to create an agreement for my sales representatives in the field. I provided him with samples of similar agreements and told him I wanted a contract that was legally sound, and that ensured I was well protected in the event that relations soured between me and my field reps.

Two weeks later, the attorney handed me a 16-page document that covered every possible contingency you could think of, and then some—along with a bill for $1,500. The agreement was so lengthy and intimidating that my field sales force refused to sign it. So I was out $1,500 and still had no agreement.

Subsequently I reviewed the document, condensed it into a few short paragraphs, written in my own words, reducing it from 16 pages to 2. Then I took it back to my attorney and asked him to review it, keeping in mind two questions: (1) Had I done a good job in protecting the company and myself? and (2) Was there anything that I had failed to do? This time he took 45 minutes to review the document, told me I had done an excellent job, and handed me a bill for only $100.

My advice to you is to use your business attorney judiciously, mainly to "polish up" work you have already done. I guarantee it will be a lot easier on your pocketbook. By using your attorney primarily for making corrections, you gain a working understanding of the legal issues surrounding your business, avoid getting drowned in unnecessary "legalese" (and having to redo documents nobody but the lawyer can understand), and save yourself a bundle of money in the process.

When you've chosen the right attorney, one of your first discussions should cover the current status of your business development efforts and legal structures for the company. Don't be surprised if your attorney advises you not to form any specific legal entity yet; the legal structure of the business can be determined further down the line (I'll be discussing this issue in the next chapter). Probably all you need to do at this point is file for a trade name and, if several of you are involved in the planning of the business, execute a mutual letter of agreement that defines in detail each person's level of participation in the business.

There is another professional you should be seeking at this point in time—a professional independent accountant. If you are planning a company that you expect to grow, I strongly recommend that you locate an experienced certified public accountant (CPA) at this stage. If you ultimately plan on raising venture capital or going public, I would recommend that you immediately contact one of the"Big Six" accounting firms (Ernst & Young, Peat Marwick & Main, Deloitte-Touche, Coopers & Lybrand, Arthur Anderson, and Price-Waterhouse), because you are going to need a nationally recognized independent auditor as soon as possible.

Before you pass off this suggestion as unrealistic because of the size of your company and your pocketbook, let me assure you that regional Big Six affiliates are constantly looking for new clients that they believe will be the superstars of tomorrow. If they think you have potential, they may be willing to assist you by critiquing your initial financial projections for a low fee. Once your business is launched, they will serve you initially at a cost that is far below their usual fee. Then, as you become profitable (and they will know it because they are auditing your books), their charges will rise accordingly.

It's worth the cost to have a Big Six firm on your side at this early stage. If for no other reason, it will lend credibility to your financials, your business will gain considerable respectability, and you will enhance your chances of getting the funding you need later on.

How do you find the right CPA firm for your business? Ask your banker and your lawyer for recommendations, then interview potential

CPAs just as you did your attorney. Make sure the chemistry is right, and find out what they can provide to help you at this stage. The major CPA firms offer a number of manuals, books, and other programs to assist new businesses. These may be available to you at little or no charge, because the firms want your business as you grow.

Once you have your lawyer and accountant, don't hesitate to refer questions to them as you proceed with the document you will develop in the next level.

LEVEL IV: Evolve Your Rough Business Plan

A well-prepared rough business plan accomplishes the following:

1. It will begin to give your business a sense of direction. Up to this point you have given a lot of lip service to your plan for launching the business. Now you will see the blueprint start to emerge on paper.
2. It will help you pinpoint your strengths and weaknesses by answering a number of questions and addressing a number of concerns, such as, How far along should my product design be before I seek capital? What other critical staff positions do I have to fill? Should we start manufacturing in-house or "farm it out"? What kind of company structure should we have?
3. It will assist your recruiting of key managers as well as your board of directors or advisors.
4. It will help you begin your financial projection process. Your marketing plan includes yearly sales projections. These sales projections dictate your staffing level (how many people you need). And the staffing level determines your operating budget, which in turn determines your net profit.

In developing your rough business plan, keep in mind that you want to reveal enough information about your business to whet the appetite of potential investors and recruit the key people you need, without giving away so much that a potential competitor could rip off your business idea before you have a chance to launch it. There's always the possibility that a potential competitor (or a potential competitor's investor) may see a copy of your plan, so never reveal too much in writing.

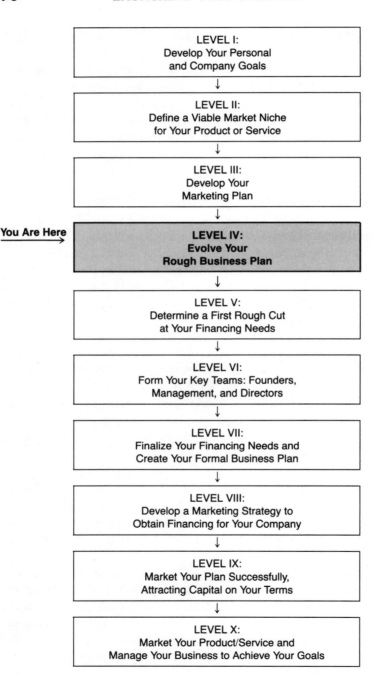

You Are Here →

LEVEL I:
Develop Your Personal
and Company Goals

↓

LEVEL II:
Define a Viable Market Niche
for Your Product or Service

↓

LEVEL III:
Develop Your
Marketing Plan

↓

**LEVEL IV:
Evolve Your
Rough Business Plan**

↓

LEVEL V:
Determine a First Rough Cut
at Your Financing Needs

↓

LEVEL VI:
Form Your Key Teams: Founders,
Management, and Directors

↓

LEVEL VII:
Finalize Your Financing Needs and
Create Your Formal Business Plan

↓

LEVEL VIII:
Develop a Marketing Strategy to
Obtain Financing for Your Company

↓

LEVEL IX:
Market Your Plan Successfully,
Attracting Capital on Your Terms

↓

LEVEL X:
Market Your Product/Service and
Manage Your Business to Achieve Your Goals

The goal of the rough business plan is to get the attention of would-be investors or managers. Save the details for face-to-face meetings.

The Lay of the Land: The Format and Contents of the Rough Business Plan

There are certain key elements that your rough business plan should include:

SECTION A: *Executive Summary* (1 page)

Think of this section as a *Reader's Digest* condensation of the entire plan, captured in a single page. At a minimum, this page should cover the purpose of your company, discuss your market potential (with some data to back it up), mention significant product features, and include a statement as to why your company will succeed as well as a summary of anticipated financial results.

If you have trouble accomplishing this with one page, then just jot down a few key points and go on to the next section. Some people find this section easier to finalize after they have completed the remaining sections of the plan.

SECTION B: *The Company* (2–3 pages)

In this section, describe your business. Discuss your products or services, markets, applications, and any other factors that will contribute to your success. Think of this section as a short newspaper article on your company. (Example questions to help you begin this section are included in the next exercise.)

SECTION C: *The Market* (3–5 pages)

This is the longest section of the business plan, and probably the most critical. It incorporates parts of the marketing plan you have already developed. The purpose of the market section is to present detailed marketing data that show you have done your homework thoroughly. Explain existing and future markets and how you will capture them. Summarize the objectives, strategies, and tactics you discussed in your marketing plan. List specific marketing milestones for a five-year period and detail how they will be reached.

SECTION D: *Product Development* (optional—1 page)

If you are developing a product, discuss in this section the technology utilized by the company. Indicate the current stage of development of the product, and provide details about how and when the development process will be completed.

SECTION E: *Manufacturing* (optional—1 page)

If you are in a manufacturing business, discuss whether your product is assembled in your plant or is subcontracted out. If you have, or plan to have, in-house manufacturing operations, the equipment used should be described in detail. What kind of equipment is it? How old is it? Is it state-of-the-art?

SECTION F: *Management and Ownership* (1–2 pages)

In this section, list your company's present management team (even if it consists of only you). Discuss the skills and experience of your management team and how they will relate to the success of your venture. You don't need to include résumés here, just a paragraph or two for each executive.

If you need to recruit some members of the management team, list the positions you have yet to fill as well as the requirements for each position. If you have stockholders, list them. If you have a board of directors, list them and indicate what relevant background they bring to your board.

SECTION G: *Organization and Personnel* (1–2 pages)

List your key staff people, those who are critical to the company. If you are still recruiting key people, list those positions you have yet to fill, the requirements for each position, and how you intend to fill them. Include an overall organizational chart for your company.

SECTION H: *Funds Required and Their Uses* (1 page)

As we discussed at the beginning of this chapter, the purpose of this rough business plan is not to raise capital, so there's no need to include detailed financials. However, you should include two financial tables in this section: "Sources of Capital" and "Uses of Capital."

Even though these tables will include only estimates of your capital needs, the information will be invaluable to you. Sources of Capital will show where your funding will be coming from (how much from the founders, how much from loans, and how much from sale of stock, etc.). Uses of Capital will show how these proceeds are to be allocated. A typical example of these two tables follows:

Sources of Capital		*Uses of Capital*	
$120K	Private investors	$110K	Purchase inventory
$100K	SBA bank loan	$130K	Purchase equipment
$ 80K	Founders team capital	$ 60K	Working capital
$300K		$300K	

This completes the format of the rough business plan and results in a concise document that is probably 10–12 pages in length.

EXERCISE: Create an Outline for Your Own Rough Business Plan

Now that you understand the basics of developing a rough business plan, develop a brief outline for your own plan. Tackle one section at a time, using no more than one page for each. Leave some space in your workbook at the end of each section for additional ideas you may have later on.

To get you started in the right direction, here are some sample questions and answers to help you assemble your outline for Section B:

SECTION B: THE COMPANY

WHAT: Our business will be to sell computer products to businesses.

WHO?   Our target market is the small businessperson, retail and wholesale.

WHY?   We will offer products, software, and service at a discount.

HOW?   We will utilize a direct sales force to call on businesses.

OTHER?   We will offer free system setup and training, as well as on-site service.

As you develop your outline, make sure that it is clear, precise, and realistic. Avoid any vague statements that will peg you as an amateur. For example, in Section C (The Market), do not make vague statements such as "The market is huge, and we will need to capture only 2% of it." Instead, specify how large is "huge" and how you arrived at this figure, and indicate in detail how you plan to capture the 2%, for example, "According to U.S. Commerce Department figures for 1989, the domestic market for widgets is currently $800 million. We project that within four years our company will be able to capture 2%, or $16 million, of the current market, utilizing a direct sales force in five states, supplemented by print ads and direct mail marketing."

Completing this exercise for every section of your rough business plan will start you in the direction of building a formal, professional business plan down the road. It will help you to articulate—for yourself as well as for others—the current status of your business and what you will need in order to accomplish your ultimate objectives for the business.

LEVEL V: Determine a First Rough Cut at Your Financing Needs

Some Financial Perspectives

Visiting an investor makes most entrepreneurs about as happy as going to the dentist. Many of us don't really understand the moneylending process. We only know that our company needs cash, and we have been trained to believe that, no matter how solid our idea, the moneylenders are going to give us a rough time.

Banks are not the only sources of funding for your business. I'll be discussing many financing sources in Chapter 6. However, they are the most common source for entrepreneurs, so you will do well to understand how they think and what they will require from you in exchange for a loan.

Some people say that bankers are a mysterious lot, that when business is going well, they are all too happy to help. However, when we

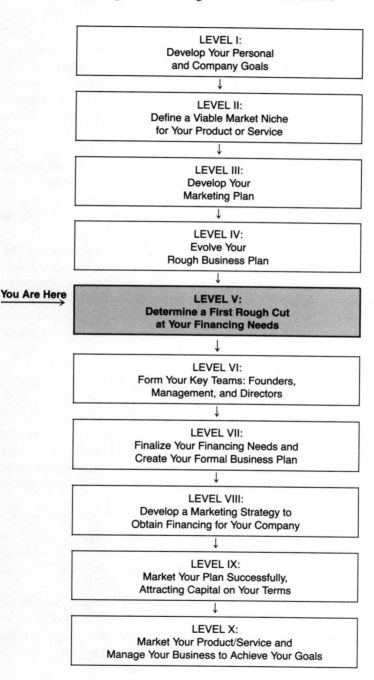

LEVEL I:
Develop Your Personal
and Company Goals

↓

LEVEL II:
Define a Viable Market Niche
for Your Product or Service

↓

LEVEL III:
Develop Your
Marketing Plan

↓

LEVEL IV:
Evolve Your
Rough Business Plan

↓

You Are Here →

**LEVEL V:
Determine a First Rough Cut
at Your Financing Needs**

↓

LEVEL VI:
Form Your Key Teams: Founders,
Management, and Directors

↓

LEVEL VII:
Finalize Your Financing Needs and
Create Your Formal Business Plan

↓

LEVEL VIII:
Develop a Marketing Strategy to
Obtain Financing for Your Company

↓

LEVEL IX:
Market Your Plan Successfully,
Attracting Capital on Your Terms

↓

LEVEL X:
Market Your Product/Service and
Manage Your Business to Achieve Your Goals

entrepreneurs need them most, when our business is struggling and we need another capital infusion to get it back on course, they are nowhere in sight. But fortunately, this is just a myth. The people who created it do not understand how to deal with bankers. The reality is this: Bankers are there to help you. If you show them respect, are honest with them, keep them informed about the progress of your business, and, in short, show integrity in all your dealings with them, you can expect to be treated fairly by them.

But remember at the same time that bankers are businesspeople, and they are in business to make a profit. If they don't believe your company will be a success and return them a reasonable profit (the interest on their loan), they won't lend you money. It's as simple as that.

Because banks operate on low profit margins, they are unwilling to accept high risk. Therefore, if they do give you a loan, they will require you to provide collateral for it. This means you will have to pledge some of your property (with a value greater than the loan) as a guarantee for the loan. Bankers require this additional collateral because if you defaulted on the loan the bank would sell the remaining inventory at auction and would be lucky to recover 20 cents on the dollar.

One way to look more attractive to a banker (that is, less risky) is to have a good track record of borrowing money and paying it back. If you don't already have a good financial history with your banker, I suggest you obtain one by beginning to borrow money long before you need it. Approach the loan officer at your bank and borrow $500 on a 90-day note, making sure to borrow in the name of your business. (You should be able to borrow this amount with your personal guarantee.)

Next, go to one of the bank's investment officers and put the money you just borrowed into a 90-day certificate of deposit. The loan officer will probably never know what you did. (If the bank is so small that the loan officer and the investment officer are one and the same, you may want to make the investment at another bank.)

Then pay the note off on time. A month later, borrow $1,000 for 90 days, and repeat the procedure, each time increasing the dollar amount of your loan request. This process of borrowing ever-increasing amounts of money when you don't really need it, and paying it back on time, will cost you the "spread" (the difference between the interest rate on your loan and the yield on your certificate of deposit), but it is very worthwhile because you will build a favorable credit history with the bank. Then, when you really need short-term capital for your business, the bank may overlook a weak balance sheet, thanks to your solid credit history and demonstrated reliability.

Bankers are not the only ones who may be nervous about providing you with financing. As a start-up business, you will find out quickly that if you don't have money in the bank, your suppliers won't let you buy on credit (and, believe me, they will check with your bank, which will, at a minimum, convey your "average" account balance). If you just placed an order for $10,000 worth of merchandise and the vendor learns your average account balance is only $5,000, you can bet your bank balance you will receive a call from the vendor informing you the order must be either prepaid or COD.

At first it was hard for me to understand this concept of suppliers needing to see "backup" money in the bank. I reasoned that if I failed to pay, the suppliers would get their material back (after all, this is what happens if I personally buy something on time and then don't make the payments).

However, business law is different from personal law. As a business, if you default on payments to your supplier, the supplier might not be able to get its merchandise back. That's why suppliers want cash up front or a company with a solid financial track record.

Suppliers may accept other financing arrangements. For example, they might accept a "letter of credit" (which is nothing more than a guarantee of payment from your bank) in lieu of advance payment. There are times when this may be appropriate, but you will have to pay your bank a fee (and probably provide your personal guarantee as well) in order to get the letter of credit issued.

The Evolution of Your Financial Projections

Even if you hate numbers, you must grit your teeth and pay attention to this part of the book, in order to present the best possible image of financial competence to potential investors. Financial novices make some classic mistakes when it comes to developing the financial projections bankers and others use in determining whether or not they will fund a business. Two of the most common mistakes are overestimating sales and underestimating the risks of the business.

A banker who picks up a business plan and thumbs through the financials can spot an amateur a mile away. In this section we'll take you step-by-step through the process of developing credible, realistic estimates of your company's financial needs and developing financial statements that will increase your likelihood of securing the funding you need to launch your business.

Some of you know nothing about financial statements, so I'm going to start with the basics. For those of you who have a more solid background in finance, please bear with me. You might well review the points I make in the next few pages as a brief refresher course; there are some "need to know" points hidden in these next few pages that you would do well to read.

Projections of future financial statements are often referred to as pro formas. These pro formas represent your current best estimates of your company's future financial performance. If you are starting a new company, all of your financials will be pro formas; if you have an existing company, you will use actual financial statements for past performance and pro formas for your future financial estimates.

In simplest form, a pro forma income statement is little more than a summary of your projected "cash in" (sales revenue forecast) minus your projected "cash out" (operating expenses). Any money left over is profit; any negative sums are losses. In developing pro formas, many would-be entrepreneurs fail to come up with realistic projections. Part of the reason is that their numbers are biased according to their areas of expertise. Here are two examples:

1. Entrepreneurs coming from the ranks of manufacturing or engineering tend to make maximum production the cornerstone of their business plan. They make the invalid assumption that the sales department can sell everything manufacturing can produce. Thereby, these maximum production quantities become their sales forecasts.

2. Entrepreneurs coming through the administrative ranks usually evolve sales forecasts based on the profits that the founders wanted to realize. Therefore desired profits become the cor-

nerstone of the business plan, and the founders work backward to arrive at sales essential to produce these profits.

In either case, investors will see right through these biases. Therefore, when you prepare your financial projections, I urge you to widen your perspective and base your projections on realistic expectations from a broad range of experts. If you're not sure your numbers are realistic, run them by several people you respect in different areas of expertise.

At this point you have already begun the process of preparing your financial projections. From your marketing plan you have developed yearly sales forecasts for the next five years. The next step is to break these numbers down into monthly sales projections for at least the first two years, then quarterly thereafter. If your business is seasonal, factor this into the projections.

Next, determine what personnel (sales, manufacturing, and administration) you will need to achieve the level of sales shown in your forecasts. This will help you develop an operating budget for each department and ultimately for the entire company. The operating budget projections should also be broken down monthly for the first two years, and quarterly thereafter.

With the exception of pro formas, financial statements typically show the present fiscal state of the company. If you are preparing a business plan for a company already in existence, you should include "actual" financial statements that show the past and current status of the company, along with the pro formas.

Keep in mind that you can set up your company to operate on a fiscal year (FY) that might be different from the calender year (CY). There are a number of reasons why you might wish to choose a fiscal year that doesn't conform to the calendar year. For example, if your primary customer is the U.S. Government, you may choose a fiscal year that begins on October 1 and ends on September 30, just as the government's does. Or you may choose to start your fiscal year on July 1 and end it on June 30, so that your accounting bills will be lower, because you will be using your accountant during the "off season" rather than during prime time.

Let's discuss some of the basic financial documents you will need for your business. The example documents we present here are not offered as "ideal" illustrations (for one thing, some of them show lousy results!) They are presented here because they are all extracted from real companies, permitting you to analyze real results. We will review the statements and then show you how you can develop pro forma equivalents.

The Income Statement

The income statement is also referred to as the P&L, or Profit and Loss Statement. It is a summary of income and expenses for the company, totaled over a period of time. The typical income statement shows the totals for "this period" (the current month) in the left-hand column and cumulative totals for the year to date (YTD) in the right-hand column. Most businesses prepare an income statement each month, in a form similar to the one shown in Figure 4-1.

XYZ is an established company with more than $1.1 million in annual sales. Let's review the YTD column, from top to bottom:

Total sales for the year through November amount to $1,104,330. Subtract from this the *cost of sales (COS)*, also known as *cost of goods sold (COGS)*—which consists of the direct expenses to make and sell the product—and you have *gross profit* ($496,030).

When gross profit is expressed as a ratio to sales, the result is known as the *gross profit margin (GPM)*. The GPM for XYZ Company is $496,030 ÷ $1,104,330, or 45%. This is slightly low; ideally, you would like to see a GPM higher than 50%.

Next, total all of the operating expenses (note that manufacturing wages are not listed here, because they have already been included in the cost of sales) and deduct that sum from gross profit to determine *operating profit*.

Then, add any additional income not previously accounted for (for example, dividends and interest), and subtract any interest paid (for example, interest on loans). The result is *profit before taxes* (PBT).

Finally, deduct a provision for income taxes (note that when you are starting your company and have losses initially, you won't need a provision here; you'll only need it when you start turning a profit). The final result is the *net profit* (or *net loss* if the amount is negative). This net profit is the number investors are referring to when they ask about your bottom-line performance.

Figure 4-1. XYZ Company Income Statement (P&L), November 19XX.

	This Period	Year to Date
TOTAL SALES	$91,250	$1,104,330
Cost of Sales (material and labor)	54,820	608,300
GROSS PROFIT	$36,430	$ 496,030
Operating Expenses (typical)		
Management salaries	$ 4,410	$ 48,210
Admin salaries and wages	3,550	39,870
Payroll taxes and fringes	5,310	58,420
Travel	2,220	23,470
Marketing/Advertising	6,450	67,870
Shipping	1,870	22,010
Office supplies	1,680	19,200
Insurance	700	13,880
Utilities	650	7,100
Legal and accounting	2,120	23,030
Dues and subscriptions	110	4,110
Miscellaneous	290	7,080
TOTAL OPERATING EXPENSE	$29,360	$ 334,250
OPERATING PROFIT	$ 7,070	$ 161,780
Other Income (dividends, interest)	180	5,070
Less Interest Paid	− 1,070	− 13,510
PROFIT BEFORE TAXES	$ 6,180	$ 153,340
Less Provision for Taxes	− 1,850	− 45,920
NET PROFIT (or loss)	$ 4,330	$ 107,420

The Balance Sheet

Where the income statement expressed the financial condition of the business over a period of time, the balance sheet provides an instantaneous "snapshot" of the company at a specific point in time (usually the end of the month, the quarter, or the fiscal year). The balance sheet (see Figure 4-2) lists all *assets* (what you own) and all *liabilities* (what you owe) as they exist at this moment in time. If assets minus liabilities equals a positive number, you have a positive net worth. If it is negative (meaning that you owe more than you own), then you are technically bankrupt. However, keep in mind that most start-ups have a negative net worth early in their history.

The balance sheet derives it name from the simple fact that the top half of the sheet (*total assets*) must "balance" with the bottom half of the sheet (*total liabilities* + *total equity*). Let's review each major area of the balance sheet in Figure 4-2.

Current assets usually consists of cash and accounts receivable (less an allowance for any bad debts that may not be paid to you); *fixed assets* are the land, buildings, equipment, and machinery that you own (not lease), less any depreciation based on how long you have owned each item; *current liabilities* include what you owe to others within the current year (including the current year's portion of any long-term loans); *long-term liabilities* include debt that extends beyond the current fiscal year.

Note that *stockholders' equity* is also the company's net worth (defined as assets minus liabilities). Knowing this definition, you should realize that raising money with loans (debt capital) increases your liabilities and decreases your net worth as you spend the proceeds. However, if you sell stock, you add to your equity, thus increasing your net worth. (The advantage of debt capital, though, is that you don't have to sacrifice any ownership of the company).

In summary, an income statement (or P&L) presents a record of your financial performance over a period of time, while a balance sheet is an instantaneous snapshot of your company's financial condition at the end of the month, quarter, or year.

As we turn our attention to the pro forma financial projections required for your business, in addition to the above two financials, the *cash flow statement* is another essential document. Most entrepreneurs fail to understand the importance of cash flow, believing that their in-

Figure 4-2.   XYZ Company Balance Sheet, November 19XX.

Year to Date

ASSETS

Current Assets:

Cash		$ 45,210
Accounts receivable	$302,180	
Less reserve for bad debts	− 3,010	
		299,170
Inventory		209,870
TOTAL CURRENT ASSETS		$554,250

Fixed Assets:

Land	$ 45,800	
Buildings	370,250	
Machinery	96,110	
Office equipment	15,260	
	527,420	
Less accumulated depreciation	179,120	
NET FIXED ASSETS		$348,300
Payments and deferred charges		8,500
Intangibles (patents, trademarks, etc.)		50,000
TOTAL ASSETS		$961,050

LIABILITIES

Current Liabilities:

Accounts payable	$ 98,720	
Notes payable	84,900	
Accrued expenses payable	32,860	
Taxes payable	45,920	
TOTAL CURRENT LIABILITIES		$262,400

(continues)

Figure 4-2. (continued)

TOTAL LONG-TERM LIABILITIES (mortgage, bonds, debentures, etc.)		225,800
TOTAL LIABILITIES		$488,200
STOCKHOLDERS' EQUITY		
Preferred Stock	$ 60,000	
Common Stock	220,000	
Accumulated Retained Earnings	192,850	
TOTAL EQUITY		$472,850
TOTAL LIABILITIES + TOTAL EQUITY		$961,050

come statement's bottom line shows their cash status. But this is equivalent to believing that your monthly checking account statement from the bank shows your true account balance, even though you have another 15 outstanding checks that haven't been cashed.

A cash flow statement is essential to your business because it reflects your ability to pay off immediate debts. No matter how solid sales are, they won't pay your bills until you actually receive the money from those sales. The monthly sales figure at the top of your income statement does not translate into ready cash. Some of it will show up within 30 days, and the balance (hopefully) within 60 days. In the meantime, you can hardly pay your staff with IOUs.

Even for an established business, cash flow can be a problem if the business grows too slowly, or expands too rapidly, or has seasonal sales fluctuations. Even a well-established company must prepare cash flow statements regularly, so it can anticipate its cash needs and secure short-term financing to cover them.

Basically, you compute cash flow by calculating the cash sources and the cash uses for each month.

Pro Forma Income Statement With Summary Cash Flow

The pro forma income statement shown in Figure 4-3 indicates monthly results for the entire year. In this manner, cash flow shortfalls can be easily spotted. The cash flow summary at the bottom of the statement merely shows cash sources and cash uses; I'll discuss methods of calculating these later.

Now note that net profit is positive for this company during each month of the year. Sales are generally increasing during the period; however, there is a slight seasonal downturn during January.

But even though the profit picture looks good, note the negative glitch in the cash flow. The company will have to find some source of money during March and April. Hopefully, the company made these projections during the previous year and approached its banker at that time to arrange a credit line to see it through. If company executives waited until March to approach their banker, they would probably be turned down, because they would be perceived as a bad risk (and this is most likely true—after all, if company executives haven't foreseen this negative cash flow, what else have they overlooked that may be fatal to the company?).

Now let's consider one way you can calculate your cash flow (your accountant may recommend alternative methods, but this technique helps you clearly to understand the process). Study the pro forma income statement for ABC Corporation, shown in Figure 4-4. This young company shows a growing net profit for each month of its fiscal year.

The company's monthly cash flow can be computed by reviewing its January figures. Begin with the company's checking account balance at the end of the previous month ($1,200). Let's assume that 50% of the company's invoices will be paid within 30 days and the remaining 50% within 60 days. Thus, you would add 50% of the previous December's sales ($11,300, the amount paid within 30 days) and 50% of the previous November sales ($9,100, the amount paid within 60 days). The sum of these figures ($21,600) equals all of the sources of cash that should be available to the company during January.

Next, compute the cash uses for the month. First, consider the cost of goods sold (or COGS). This is the material and labor utilized to make the product. Let's assume the material was purchased for inventory during the previous month, and that the company paid the material invoices this month. The hourly workers must be paid each week, because the products are manufactured. Therefore the entire COGS ($20,862) will probably be paid out during January. Similarly, all of the company's operating expenses will probably be paid during the current month ($12,475) and are recognized here. Although it could be argued

(*text continues on page 90*)

Figure 4-3. DEF Manufacturing Company Pro Forma Income Statement and Projected Cash Flow, FY 19XX.

	OCT	NOV	DEC	JAN	FEB	MAR	APR	MAY	JUN	JUL	AUG	SEP
Pro Forma Income Statement												
SALES	$283,702	$300,747	$300,919	$285,459	$291,404	$399,132	$447,858	$431,585	$434,948	$438,312	$443,675	$449,038
COST OF SALES	133,340	141,351	141,432	134,166	136,960	187,592	210,493	202,845	204,426	206,007	208,527	211,048
GROSS PROFIT	150,362	159,396	159,487	151,293	154,444	211,540	237,365	228,740	230,522	232,305	235,148	237,990
Operating Expenses												
Administrative	$ 18,592	$ 18,592	$ 18,592	$ 18,592	$ 18,592	$ 18,592	$ 18,592	$ 18,592	$ 18,592	$ 18,592	$ 18,592	$ 18,592
Marketing	4,838	4,838	4,838	4,838	4,838	4,838	4,838	4,838	4,838	4,838	4,838	4,838
Engineering	23,288	23,288	23,288	25,875	25,875	25,875	28,463	28,463	28,463	29,000	29,000	29,000
Clerical	9,085	9,085	9,085	9,085	9,085	9,085	9,085	9,085	9,085	9,085	9,085	9,085
Total Salaries and Wages	$ 55,803	$ 55,803	$ 55,803	$ 58,390	$ 58,390	$ 58,390	$ 60,978	$ 60,978	$ 60,978	$ 61,515	$ 61,515	$ 61,515
Employee Benefits and Taxes	15,625	15,625	15,625	16,349	16,349	16,349	17,074	17,074	17,074	17,224	17,224	17,224
Facility Rental	6,000	6,000	6,000	6,000	6,000	6,000	6,000	6,000	6,000	6,000	6,000	6,000
Equipment Rental	20,250	20,250	20,250	20,250	20,250	20,970	22,648	24,459	26,416	28,529	30,812	33,277
Legal and Accounting	1,918	1,918	1,918	1,918	1,918	1,918	1,918	1,918	1,918	1,918	1,918	1,918
Marketing	20,000	20,000	20,000	20,000	20,000	20,000	20,000	20,000	20,000	20,000	20,000	20,000
Conventions	2,000	2,000	1,000	0	2,000	1,000	2,000	2,000	1,000	2,000	2,000	2,000
Training	0	0	2,500	0	0	1,500	0	0	2,500	0	0	1,500
Travel	3,450	3,450	3,450	3,450	3,450	3,450	3,450	3,450	3,450	3,450	3,450	3,450

	OCT	NOV	DEC	JAN	FEB	MAR	APR	MAY	JUN	JUL	AUG	SEP
Office Supplies	500	500	600	500	500	600	500	500	600	500	500	600
Maintenance	800	800	800	800	800	800	800	800	800	800	800	800
Telephone	4,000	4,000	4,000	4,000	4,500	4,500	5,000	5,000	5,000	5,500	5,500	5,500
Utilities	2,400	2,400	2,400	2,400	2,400	2,400	2,400	2,400	2,400	2,400	2,400	2,400
Dues and Sub- scriptions	250	250	250	250	250	250	250	250	250	250	250	250
Insurance	1,950	1,950	1,950	1,950	1,950	1,950	1,950	1,950	1,950	1,950	1,950	1,950
Freight	450	450	450	450	450	450	550	550	550	550	550	550
Entertainment	250	250	250	250	250	250	250	250	250	250	250	250
Depreciation	4,435	4,435	4,454	4,454	4,454	4,473	4,532	4,532	4,551	4,551	4,551	4,570
Miscellaneous	1,500	1,500	1,500	1,500	1,500	1,500	1,500	1,500	1,500	1,500	1,500	1,500
TOTAL EX- PENSES	$141,581	$141,581	$143,200	$142,911	$145,411	$146,750	$151,799	$153,611	$157,187	$158,888	$161,170	$165,254
OPERATING PROFIT	8,781	17,815	16,287	8,382	9,033	64,790	85,565	75,129	73,335	73,418	73,978	72,736
Interest	2,142	4,616	5,096	5,418	5,948	6,478	6,850	7,429	8,009	8,306	8,687	9,069
PROFIT BE- FORE TAX	6,639	13,199	11,191	2,964	3,085	58,312	78,715	67,700	65,326	65,112	65,291	63,667
Taxes	1,328	2,640	2,238	593	617	11,662	15,743	13,540	13,065	13,022	13,058	12,733
NET PROFIT	$ 5,311	$ 10,559	$ 8,953	$ 2,371	$ 2,468	$ 46,649	$ 62,972	$ 54,160	$ 52,261	$ 52,089	$ 52,233	$ 50,934

Projected Cash Flow

	OCT	NOV	DEC	JAN	FEB	MAR	APR	MAY	JUN	JUL	AUG	SEP
CASH SOURCES	$297,500	$295,723	$303,835	$318,394	$332,542	$336,109	$344,029	$401,914	$481,282	$548,478	$615,459	$681,619
CASH USES	273,628	284,113	286,274	279,041	284,865	337,347	365,611	360,353	366,071	369,649	374,833	381,801
CASH FLOW— →	$ 23,872	$ 11,610	$ 17,561	$ 39,353	$ 47,677	$ −1,239	$ −21,581	$ 41,560	$ 115,211	$178,829	$240,625	$299,818

Figure 4-4. ABC Corporation Pro Forma Income Statement and Incomplete Cash Flow Forecast.

Pro Forma Income Statement

	JAN	FEB	MAR	APR	MAY	JUN	JUL	AUG	SEP	OCT	NOV	DEC
SALES	$ 34,200	$ 41,040	$49,248	$59,098	$70,917	$85,101	$102,121	$122,545	$147,054	$176,464	$211,757	$254,109
COGS	20,862	25,034	30,041	36,050	43,259	51,911	62,294	74,752	89,703	107,643	129,172	155,006
GROSS PROFIT	$ 13,338	$ 16,006	$19,207	$23,048	$27,658	$33,189	$ 39,827	$ 47,792	$ 57,351	$ 68,821	$ 82,585	$ 99,102
Operating Expenses												
Payroll/Taxes	$ 4,500	$ 4,950	$ 5,445	$ 5,990	$ 6,588	$ 7,247	$ 7,972	$ 8,769	$ 9,646	$ 10,611	$ 11,672	$ 12,839
Insurance	200	200	200	200	200	200	200	200	200	200	200	200
Rent	900	900	900	900	900	900	900	900	900	900	900	900
Equipment/Rent	243	243	243	243	243	243	243	243	243	243	243	243
Legal/Accounting	200	200	200	200	200	200	200	200	200	200	200	200
Marketing	900	1,500	1,500	1,500	1,500	1,500	1,500	1,500	1,500	1,500	1,500	1,500
Trade shows	500	500	500	500	500	500	500	500	500	500	500	500
Training	600	600	600	600	600	600	600	600	600	600	600	600
Travel	850	893	937	984	1,033	1,085	1,139	1,196	1,256	1,319	1,385	1,454
Office supplies	175	184	193	203	213	223	235	246	259	271	285	299
Cleaning supplies	35	35	35	35	35	35	35	35	35	35	35	35
Maintenance	200	200	200	200	200	200	200	200	200	200	200	200
Telephone	620	651	684	718	754	791	831	872	916	962	1,010	1,060
Utilities	810	810	810	810	810	810	810	810	810	810	810	810
Shipping	342	410	492	591	709	851	1,021	1,225	1,471	1,765	2,118	2,541

Depreciation	400	400	400	400	400	400	400	400	400	400	400	400
Miscellaneous	1,000	1,000	1,000	1,000	1,000	1,000	1,000	1,000	1,000	1,000	1,000	1,000
TOTAL EXPENSES	$ 12,475	$ 13,676	$14,339	$15,073	$15,885	$16,786	$ 17,786	$ 18,897	$ 20,135	$ 21,515	$ 23,057	$ 24,782
OPERATING PROFIT	863	2,330	4,868	7,975	11,773	16,403	22,041	28,895	37,216	47,306	59,528	74,321
INTEREST	0	0	780	0	0	780	0	0	780	0	0	780
NET PROFIT	$ 863	$ 2,330	$ 4,088	$ 7,975	$11,773	$15,623	$ 22,041	$ 28,895	$ 36,436	$ 47,306	$ 59,528	$ 73,541

Cash Flow Forecast (Incomplete)

Last Month End	$ 1,200	$ −11,537										
50% M-1 SALES	11,300	17,100	20,520	24,624	29,549	35,459	42,550	51,060	61,272	73,527	88,232	105,879
50% M-2 SALES	9,100	11,300	17,100	20,520	24,624	29,549	35,459	42,550	51,060	61,272	73,527	88,232
CASH SOURCES	$ 21,600	$ 16,863										
COGS	$ 20,862	$ 25,034	$30,041	$36,050	$43,259	$51,911	$ 62,294	$ 74,752	$ 89,703	$ 107,643	$129,172	$155,006
TOTAL EXPENSES	12,475	13,676	14,339	15,073	15,885	16,786	17,786	18,897	20,135	21,515	23,057	24,782
− Depreciation	−400	−400	−400	−400	−400	−400	−400	−400	−400	−400	−400	−400
+ Capital equipment and interest	200	200	980	200	200	980	200	200	980	200	200	980
CASH USES	$ 33,137	$ 38,510	$44,960	$50,922	$58,945	$69,277	$ 93,450	$110,418	$128,959	$152,029	$180,368	
SOURCES-USES	$ −11,537											

For clarification, the label M-1 means one month prior, while M-2 means two months prior.

that some individual invoices could be deferred until next month (telephone, etc.), the effect of this is probably minimal and there is no need to consider it here.

Next, add depreciation back in, because this is not a true cash expense but rather an accounting entry that recognizes the aging of the company's assets. Note that to add depreciation back in, subtract it from the other cash uses.

Finally, include any capital equipment that the company is planning to purchase (this company has a budget of $200 per month) along with any interest being paid. Note that interest is paid quarterly, so it appears every third month ($200 + $780 = $980). This yields the total cash uses for the month.

As a result of all these computations, ABC Corporation showed a negative cash flow for January ($-11,537). This monthly result becomes the starting point for the next month. Note that we have not completed the figures beyond January.

This company appears sound, and its sales and net profit are projected to grow steadily each month. Assuming that the income statement figures are accurate, when would you expect this company's cash flow to "turn the corner" into positive numbers? Month 3? Month 6? Month 9? Write your answer down and then read on.

Now look at Figure 4-5, which is the completed Cash Flow Forecast for ABC Corporation. Note that cash flow continues to be negative each month, reaching a maximum of $-45,678 in July. What happened?

This is a perfect example of a company that is growing too fast. Sales are increasing so rapidly that every available dollar must be utilized to purchase more material to fill the increasing orders. At the same time, cash coming in from customers is lagging behind.

The only way this company could survive at these projected levels is if it had approached its bank the previous year and arranged for a line of credit of at least $46,000 that the company could draw on as a loan during the current year. Otherwise, the company would have to decrease expenses and delay product deliveries in order to survive.

Now you should have a better idea of the difference between the income statement and the cash flow statement. As you can see, it is possible for an income statement to paint a very rosy picture of the company's situation at the same time that the more critical cash flow statement indicates the company is in danger of going out of business.

Figure 4-5. ABC Corporation Complete Cash Flow Forecast.

	Cash Flow Forecast, ABC Corporation (complete)											
Last Month End	$ 1,200	$ -11,537	$ -21,647	$ -28,987	$ -34,766	$ -39,537	$ -43,807	$ -45,678	$ -45,517	$ -43,602	$ -37,761	$ -28,031
50% M-1 SALES	11,300	17,100	20,520	24,624	29,549	35,459	42,550	51,060	61,272	73,527	88,232	105,879
50% M-2 SALES	9,100	11,300	17,100	20,520	24,624	29,549	35,459	42,550	51,060	61,272	73,527	88,232
CASH SOURCES	$ 21,600	$ 16,863	$ 15,973	$ 16,157	$ 19,407	$ 25,470	$ 34,202	$ 47,933	$ 66,816	$ 91,197	$ 123,998	$ 166,080
COGS	$ 20,862	$ 25,034	$ 30,041	$ 36,050	$ 43,259	$ 51,911	$ 62,294	$ 74,752	$ 89,703	$ 107,643	$ 129,172	$ 155,006
TOTAL EXPENSES	12,475	13,676	14,339	15,073	15,885	16,786	17,786	18,897	20,135	21,515	23,057	24,782
− Depreciation	-400	-400	-400	-400	-400	-400	-400	-400	-400	-400	-400	-400
+ Capital Equipment and interest	200	980	980	200	980	200	200	980	980	200	200	980
CASH USES	$ 33,137	$ 38,510	$ 44,960	$ 50,922	$ 58,945	$ 69,277	$ 79,879	$ 93,450	$ 110,418	$ 128,959	$ 152,029	$ 180,368
SOURCES-USES	$ -11,537	$ -21,647	$ -28,987	$ -34,766	$ -39,537	$ -45,678	$ -45,517	$ -43,602	$ -37,761	$ -28,031	$ -14,288	

For clarification, the label M-1 means one month prior, while M-2 means two months prior.

Now that you have been introduced to the three basic financial documents you will need to develop for your plan, let me also mention there are probably a number of organizations in your area, some providing free assistance, to help you put these projections together. You may want to refer to the "Free Sources of Help" section in the Appendix for further details.

A Few Words About Profits

Entrepreneurs tend to focus more on the fun of growing the business then they do on profits. Unfortunately, lenders don't really care whether or not you are having fun. Never lose sight of the fact that there is one and only one reason investors will give money to you: THEY EXPECT TO MAKE A PROFIT. Furthermore, if they don't believe you are focused upon this same objective, you won't get their money. You must show them that you are doing all you can to maximize the potential profit of your business.

<u>Key Point:</u> *In order to maximize profits, you must set your price as high as the market will bear.*

One way to ensure maximum profits is to set a price for your product that is as high as the market will bear. At this point, you should have an idea, from your market survey, of just what is the maximum price consumers are willing to pay for your product. If you are still unsure, even after surveying the market, then you should gather more data; you cannot afford to leave any money lying on the table. Try contacting potential customers or dealers, describe the product to them, and ask them what they would expect to pay for this product or service. You must know the perceived value of your product in the minds of potential customers.

There's an additional reason for striving to maximize profits. This will not only please investors but it will help you to recoup start-up and development costs, and enable you to build a source of funding for future development efforts.

<u>Fatal Error:</u> *Most start-up companies set their selling price too low.*

Many entrepreneurs make the mistake of setting the price of their product too low, in an attempt to capture market share more easily. But if your product is priced lower than its perceived value in the marketplace, you are sending potential customers the message that it is worth less than they think (remember the old adage that you get what you pay for). As a result, they may be reluctant to buy it, even though they would have been happy to buy it at a higher price!

Suppose I am starting a new company that manufactures TV sets under the HTC brand, and my strategy for capturing market share is to sell my sets at a lower cost. You walk into an area electronics store, in search of a small portable color TV set for your mother, and you spy two almost identical sets on the shelf. One is a 15″ RCA for $279 and the other is a 15″ HTC for $199. They look identical, but when you look at the HTC set, you start thinking to yourself: "What's wrong with this set? What did they leave out to get the lower price? Since $279 is an acceptable market price, the HTC set must be lower quality, and I want the best for Mom, so RCA, here I come!"

I would have been better off using a reverse strategy, setting a slightly higher price and backing my TV set up with a stronger warranty than RCA's. Now you might walk into the store and see that my HTC set is built as well as the other brands are, and it also carries a five-year warranty, whereas the others carry only a one-year warranty. My price is slightly higher: $299 versus $279 for the other major brands—but you figure it must be a higher-quality set, and it's worth the extra $20 because of the superior warranty. "Nothing but the best for Mom!" you think, and purchase the HTC set.

When I detailed this strategy in one of my national workshops, a young electronic parts distributor in the front row jumped up and shouted, "That's it!" When I asked him to share his inspiration, he explained he had been trying to sell a new Toshiba electric motor as a replacement for the current industry-standard GE motor. His Toshiba was a better-quality product, was lower in price, and was guaranteed for five years, while the GE was only guaranteed for one year. Yet this poor man had trouble selling his Toshiba motors because GE had kept spreading the word to customers that the Toshiba model couldn't be superior to theirs because it cost less.

So the entrepreneur decided to start marketing his Toshiba at a price greater than the GE motor, emphasizing its stronger warranty as a selling point. Six months later I heard his sales were booming.

Key Point: *Your optimum sales price is primarily a function of your product's value as perceived by your customers—not your cost to produce the product.*

In only a minor way is your optimum sales price a function of your product costs. More than a decade ago, I heard a story about two California chemists who developed a new product as a joke. The product was supposedly an "anti-aging" cream. Their total cost for the product was 28 cents per jar. They began to test market it in several stores at a price equivalent to 5,000% of their cost. It may have been a joke, but the result was two new California millionaires.

EXERCISE: Your Initial Financial Calculations

Armed with your understanding of the financial statements you will need, take a break from reading and write down some initial numbers for your financial projections.

Start with a breakdown of projected sales—by month for the first two years, then quarterly for the next three. Ultimately your sales projections should be broken down into both (A) number of units sold and (B) dollars. If you expect to sell nationally, your projections should be broken down by state or region. If your product has seasonal fluctuations, they should be clearly shown (see Figure 4-6, Section I).

From these data, determine the staffing your company will need during the same period. Break your projections down by category: management, marketing, administrative, supervisors, manufacturing, other (purchasing, shipping, etc.).

Next, derive a company budget based on this level of staffing. For the overhead employees (anybody not involved in manufacturing the product), assign a total salary figure to each category, and show it increasing by a reasonable rate at the start of each year (see Figure 4-6, Section II). To determine direct labor costs for manufacturing, determine the average hourly wage of manufacturing workers (WAGE), and the number of hours required to manufacture one unit of your product (HOURS). Then (WAGE) × (HOURS) = the labor portion of cost of goods sold (COGS) for a single unit. Multiply this figure times the number of

Figure 4-6. Example financial calculations worksheet.

SECTION I—SALES PROJECTIONS

	JAN	FEB	MAR	APR	
Units sold	30	36	45	56	. . .
Unit price	$198	$198	$198	$198	. . .
Total sales	$5,940	$7,128	$8,910	$11,088	. . .

SECTION II—STAFFING PROJECTIONS

NUMBER OF PEOPLE

	JAN	FEB	MAR	APR	
Management	1	1	1	1	. . .
Marketing	0	0	0	1	. . .
Administrative	1	2	2	2	. . .
Manufacturing	2	2	3	3	. . .

SALARY BUDGET

	JAN	FEB	MAR	APR	
Management	$3,500	$3,500	$4,000	$4,000	. . .
Marketing	$ 0	$ 0	$ 0	$3,000	. . .
Administrative	$1,500	$3,000	$3,000	$3,000	. . .
Manufacturing	$2,600	$2,600	$3,900	$3,900	. . .

SECTION III—AVERAGE HOURLY WAGE EXAMPLE

$$\text{Wage} = \$7.50 \qquad \text{Hours} = 6.5 \text{ hours/unit}$$
$$\text{Labor/Unit} = (\$7.50) \times (6.5) = \$48.75/\text{unit}$$
$$\text{Material/Unit} = \$47.80/\text{unit}$$
$$\overline{\text{Total COGS/Unit} = \$96.55/\text{unit}}$$

SECTION IV—ASSIGNING REALISTIC COST PROJECTIONS

CATEGORY	JAN	FEB. . .	NOTES
Total wages	$5,000	$6,500	← These do not include COGS wages.
Benefits and taxes	1,672	2,002	← 22% of total wages plus COGS wages.
Facility rental	600	600	← Show an increase each year.
Legal and accounting	400	400	← Show an increase each year.

(*continues*)

Figure 4-6.   (continued)

Facility rental	600	600	← Show an increase each year.
Legal and accounting	400	400	← Show an increase each year.
Advertising	800	900	← Show an increase as business grows.
Travel	600	600	← Show an increase as staff grows.
Office supplies	80	80	← Show an increase as staff grows.
Telephone	400	500	← Show an increase as staff grows.
Utilities	280	300	← Show an increase as staff grows.
(etc.)			

units manufactured each month to determine the total labor portion of COGS. Finally, add in the cost of raw materials to produce those units, to arrive at the total COGS (see Figure 4-6, Section III).

Compute your employee benefits (health insurance, sick leave, vacations, etc.) and taxes as a percentage of wages and salaries. Be sure to include *both* "direct labor" workers already included in COGS as well as overhead staff not included under COGS.

Next, assign realistic cost projections to each of the other budget categories (facility rent, utilities, legal and accounting, travel, office supplies, marketing supplies, maintenance, etc.). Apply an inflation factor to these categories at the start of each year and also at other times when the company is expected to add staff (to account for things such as increased telephone usage). See Figure 4-6, Section IV.

Now total the numbers, again computing totals by month for the first two years, then quarterly thereafter. You now have a pro forma income statement (Figure 4-3).

To generate your cash flow forecast (Figure 4-5), prepare a detailed list of cash sources minus cash uses (remember to include interest paid and capital equipment less depreciation). This will show how much money you will need over the same time period as the income statement. That's all there is to it.

Creating your initial balance sheet (Figure 4-2) may require the assistance of your accountant. If you already know the value of your current assets, inventory, fixed assets, current liabilities, long-term liabilities, and equity, you can complete the balance sheet on your own. Most novice entrepreneurs utilize their accountant to help assemble these numbers for the first time.

If your pro forma income statement indicates you can't make a reasonable profit, then you had better take one or more of the following steps:

- Reduce the direct costs to build your product.
- Reduce the operating expenses.
- Increase the price of the product.

If none of these options works, it's time to find a different line of business.

How to Live While You Start Your Business

It should be obvious that your business is not going to make a profit for the first year or two. Since the salary you receive during this preprofit period may be minimal, how are you going to supplement your income and survive during this period?

The best way to accomplish this is to put money in a savings account before you launch your business, so that you have a small nest egg to live on. Keeping your new business going will be difficult enough without the added worry of how you will support yourself or your family during this time.

* * *

I have thrown a lot of facts at you in this chapter, but as a result you have advanced two more levels and are this much closer to launching your company. You now have developed your rough business plan and a preliminary set of financial projections. At this point you may still be missing key elements of the business: most likely certain key members of the company, possibly a sales manager, an operations manager, or a finance manager. And what about a board of directors? Or a group of outside advisors? In the next chapter, I'll talk about putting together the teams you will need to operate your business effectively, as well as appropriate structures for the company.

CHAPTER
5

Make-or-Break Teamwork

Structuring and Staffing Your Business

You and your attorney should probably consider giving some serious thought to the structure of your company about now, particularly if you plan to bring other executives onto your management team. Although nothing needs to be cast in concrete at this point, you should discuss with your attorney the pros and cons of various legal structures for the company.

Planning Your Company's Structure

Should you form a proprietorship, a partnership, a full corporation, or a Subchapter "S" corporation? Following is a brief summary of each option, along with a few comments about the relevance of each.

Proprietorship

The proprietorship is the simplest legal form of doing business. Under this structure, an individual is the sole owner of the business. Most small businesses start out as proprietorships.

A proprietorship is simple and inexpensive to set up (in some states you don't even have to register the company if the proprietorship uses your own name). Furthermore, it is not considered a separate entity for tax purposes; you simply add the income or losses from the proprietorship to your personal tax return.

The main disadvantage is that, under the proprietorship structure, the individual who owns the business also has personal liability for the obligations of the business. That means that if the company goes bankrupt, creditors can legally go after the personal assets of the proprietor in order to secure payment.

Partnership

In a partnership, ownership of the business is divided among two or more people. There are two types of partnership structure. In a general partnership, all of the co-owners (partners) are active in the business. In a limited partnership, in addition to the general partners who are active in the business, there are limited partners who invest in the business but do not take an active part in running it. The limited partners' liability is generally limited to the amount of their investment, whereas the general partners are exposed to the same liability as in a proprietorship. That is, their personal assets as well as the company's assets are at risk.

A partnership is also not considered a taxable entity subject to the payment of income taxes. However, after the annual proceeds of the business are divided among the partners, the partnership must file a tax return (under its own federal I.D. number) specifying what the partners must report on their personal tax returns.

It is common for a general partnership to consist of several friends with a mutual interest. Unfortunately, a large number of two-party partnerships erupt into battlegrounds over disagreements about the direction of the business. The end result is usually the dissolution of the partnership and the loss of a friend. (Curiously, partnerships between married couples seem better able to withstand these battles.)

Corporation

Many entrepreneurs want to incorporate because of the status they attach to it; somehow it sounds more important to have an Inc. after the company name. But incorporation should never be undertaken for such a superficial reason. It involves a great deal of time and expense, along with the creation of a new legal entity that entails a lifetime of reporting documents. Furthermore, undoing the corporation takes an enormous amount of additional paperwork.

If you and your attorney jointly agree that the corporate form is the way to go for your company, proceed slowly and with caution. Setting up a corporation is a lot like building a mansion; a corporation that is initially constructed poorly will prove both difficult and costly to maintain and to modify later. In a corporation, the business is owned by stockholders, each of whom owns a number of shares in the company. Because a corporation is considered a separate legal entity, a separate tax return is filed for the corporation, even if it consists of a sole owner.

The subchapter S corporation (or just plain S corporation) is a special version of this structure. The S corporation has several additional restrictions: It can issue only one class of stock and can have no more than 35 stockholders, to name two restrictions. Beyond the restrictions, the S corporation functions basically like a full corporation (except that certain medical, charitable, and other deductions must be declared by the individuals rather than by the corporation).

One major difference between the S corporation and the standard variety (or C corporation) is that the S corporation does not pay any income taxes. However, like the partnership, the S corporation must still file a tax return under its own federal I.D. number. Then the corporation's profits (or losses) are added to the shareholders' individual tax returns. Typically, people consider forming S corporations if they anticipate losses for the next several years, because these losses can offset personal income taxes (with some limitation), which may be higher than business taxes. (The Subchapter S structure was more favorable prior to the 1986 income tax reform act, which lowered individual tax rates).

Once you decide to choose the subchapter S structure, you cannot restructure later as a standard corporation, except during a narrow time window in subsequent fiscal years. Therefore, you must choose wisely, selecting the S corporation structure only if you anticipate losses for the first few years of operation. I started my first company, a manufacturing firm, as a proprietorship. I ran the company under this structure until I developed our first product. When we were ready to introduce the product, I knew I would ultimately want to raise money, so I decided to incorporate. Because I did not have an experienced corporate lawyer to counsel me, I elected to form an S corporation (believing that I would lose money for the next few years). I did not plan to sell any stock until the second year, so I was the sole owner for the first year.

During the year I formed the S corporation, however, I closed a very large order. I suddenly found myself swimming in profits. Unfortunately, all of these profits were applied to my personal tax return that year, and it cost me dearly. Had I foreseen the near-term potential for this large order, I would have chosen differently.

Let me offer you a few final guidelines regarding incorporation. There are two basic reasons to form a corporation: (1) for increased protection from liability and (2) to raise money. The C corporation can also provide pension, insurance, and other benefits.

If you are going to incorporate to raise money, I recommend you incorporate with a large number of authorized shares, say 10 million, at no par value (the face value of the stock), and plan on offering the stock initially to investors at a price in the vicinity of $1.00 per share. There's a psychological reason for this. If you offer someone 10,000 shares in your business at $1 a share, he or she is likely to feel "wealthier" than if you had offered that person 1,000 shares of stock at $10 a share.*

LEVEL VI: Form Your Key Teams: Founders, Management, and Directors

Now that you have moved through the first five levels of Microgenesis, you may find that you still have "holes" in the fabric of your management team. By now you understand that the most important facet of your company to potential investors is the strength of your management team. Therefore, you should be prepared at this point to attract the highest caliber of people for your management team, in order to attract investment dollars and, more importantly, in order to ensure the success of your company.

---

*Please note that my comments regarding any legal matter in this book represent the opinion of an experienced business executive and not an attorney. They may not be appropriate for your particular situation. In all cases involving your company's legal matters, please consult with your attorney to determine the most appropriate course of action for your type of business in your specific location.

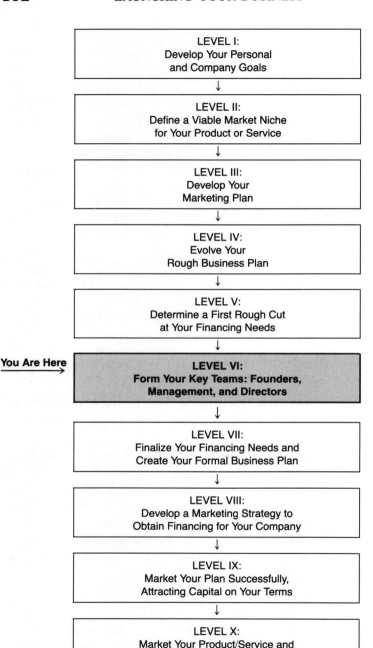

LEVEL I:
Develop Your Personal
and Company Goals

↓

LEVEL II:
Define a Viable Market Niche
for Your Product or Service

↓

LEVEL III:
Develop Your
Marketing Plan

↓

LEVEL IV:
Evolve Your
Rough Business Plan

↓

LEVEL V:
Determine a First Rough Cut
at Your Financing Needs

↓

You Are Here
→

LEVEL VI:
Form Your Key Teams: Founders,
Management, and Directors

↓

LEVEL VII:
Finalize Your Financing Needs and
Create Your Formal Business Plan

↓

LEVEL VIII:
Develop a Marketing Strategy to
Obtain Financing for Your Company

↓

LEVEL IX:
Market Your Plan Successfully,
Attracting Capital on Your Terms

↓

LEVEL X:
Market Your Product/Service and
Manage Your Business to Achieve Your Goals

Depending on the requirements of your business, you may need to recruit for three kinds of teams at this stage. If you plan to secure equity capital initially or if you require a critical executive from the outset of your business, you may need additional members for your founder's team—those people so essential to the business that they will receive a chunk of stock up front and will be intimately involved with the planning process. Even if you will be the sole founder, you will need a strong management team to run the company. The members of this team may or may not receive an ownership stake in the business, but they may be part of the business planning process, at least as it affects the departments they'll be managing. If you plan to incorporate, you will need a strong board of directors comprised of experienced businesspeople who will lend credibility to your company.

If you do not plan to incorporate, you should strongly consider recruiting a board of advisors made up of experienced businesspeople who can assist you in important business decisions as the company develops.

I'll discuss the creation of your founders team and management team together, because the recruiting process is the same for both.

If you're like 98% of the typical entrepreneurs who find themselves at this stage in their business development, you will be tempted to recruit for your management team friends, acquaintances, fellow workers, and other people whom you believe will work well with you. In doing so, you raise the potential for immediate problems. Here's why:

Key Point: *First-rate people will recruit other first-rate people. Second-rate people will recruit third-rate people. These third-rate people will then hire most of your company's employees, and they will tend to select fourth-rate people.**

Let me explain this key point. First-rate people are those who will give everything for the success of your company. As a result, they will only want to work with the strongest possible team—i.e., with other

---

*This Key Point is adapted from an axiom originally presented in Richard M. White, *The Entrepreneur's Manual* (Radnor, Penn.: Chilton Books, 1977).

first-rate people. If you empower them to recruit for the company, you will have the makings of a championship team.

But here is what usually happens. You recruit a friend to join your team. You've known this person a long time, and both of you are excited at the prospect of working together. However, this first-rate friend may in fact be a second-rate person when it comes to your business, and here is where you run into trouble.

Second-rate people are worriers. If they hire another person who is *too* good, they worry this person might ultimately take their job. So a second-rate person can't afford the risk of hiring someone as good as he or she is. Therefore, when your friend recommends other team members, the candidates will probably be less capable than your friend is.

These third-rate people recommended by your friend will then hire the bulk of your company's employees. Because these third-rate people are equally threatened by competition from other third-rate people, they will probably fill your company with fourth-rate staff.

As a result, you will end up trying to win the World Series with only a minor league team and wondering why you keep striking out.

How do you avoid this dilemma? By hiring the best people available—no matter where you are located, no matter how small your budget. I'll discuss how to go about this in a moment, but first I'll discuss an additional Key Point:

Key Point: *You must attract personalities, talents, and disciplines to your business which complement rather than duplicate each other.**

Here's what typically happens when a fledgling entrepreneur starts to put a business team together: Most entrepreneurs try to recruit previous co-workers with similar education and work experience. It's understandable. Amid the trauma of starting a new company, it's comforting to be surrounded by friends. The problem is that the management teams created in this way tend to be comprised of clones and lack the broad perspective needed to expand the business into new areas.

I was one of those typical entrepreneurs. When I started planning my first company, I wanted to be surrounded by other engineers, so my

*White, op. cit.

pre-start-up group consisted of technically oriented managers. Eventually it became clear that the team lacked vision and was too narrow in scope; as a result, we missed out on some golden opportunities. We ultimately recognized the stifling nature of our team, and we infused the group with some first-rate visionaries from outside the ranks of engineering.

Although it's natural to want to be surrounded by friends, it's also human nature to want to be surrounded by people in your own age group. Again, it's the comfort factor at work.

The problem again is that in selecting for your team only those people who fall into your general age range, you miss out on a broad range of experience, attitudes, and creativity that varies with age. One of the best strategic moves I made in my first company was to hire a sales manager who was 61 years old. He had been in agribusiness marketing for three decades and had lost his last sales manager's position when his company merged with a large conglomerate. He told me he planned to retire at 65, but hiring him was the right choice. During the four years this man worked for my company, I benefited greatly from his depth of experience and his agribusiness contacts. He was a critical factor in getting our fledging company off to a good start.

Another thing to be aware of in selecting your team members: Perpetual optimists tend to pick other optimists. The result is much like a balloon soaring with no one holding the string. Overly optimistic staffs seem to lack the ability to make accurate assessments or to realistically measure the impact of risks. All too often they view the world of their company through rose-colored glasses and have a hard time accepting and addressing the less positive aspects of the business.

At the other extreme, realists tend to hire other realists, because they are not comfortable with optimists. Companies filled with realists are as unbalanced as those filled with nothing but optimists. An overly realistic management team is always worried about what can go wrong and tends to be overly conservative in its decision making. As a result, growth can be severely limited.

I encourage you to realize your tendency toward these "filters" and not to let them affect your process. Look for people with different perspectives, regardless of their age or their overall orientation toward risk. Do not select a staff filled with people just like yourself. You do not want people who will always agree with you, but rather people who will challenge you to grow.

Show me a company where the management team is always in agreement, and you've probably shown me a company in deep trouble or at least not living up to its potential. The CEO is surrounded by "yes" managers, and the company probably lacks creativity. On the other hand, show me a business where there are frequent clashes and sparring sessions within the management team, and chances are you've found a vibrantly alive company, healthy and growing. To me, the ideal management team is one that encourages all members to plead their case, that debates issues vigorously and ultimately reaches a consensus decision that all members can sincerely support.

One more word of caution: Do not seek a prima donna superstar for each executive position. It's important to find first-rate executives who fit well with all the other members of the management team. Note that the term "fit well" does not mean "always agree with," it means sharing mutual respect, welcoming challenges, and working together for the good of the business.

In order to assemble the right team, you will need to interview several top-notch candidates for each position. Remember, you're betting the success of your company on these people, so you had better take the interviewing process quite seriously.

Where to Find Team Members

There is probably an excess of qualified candidates available in your area, no matter where your business is based. Here is how you can proceed to locate them:

First of all, prepare a short marketing document designed to interest potential candidates in the positions you are trying to fill. The document should be informative but must not reveal too much information, because it will be widely disseminated. In case it should fall into the hands of potential competitors, you want to be protected.

Without disclosing any of the proprietary information essential to your company's success, prepare a *one-page* summary of your plans and your projected growth (do not include specific product/service information, but zero in on the general field of business, and make it sound exciting). Include a second page with brief one-paragraph job descriptions (including experience required) for each of the key positions you are attempting to fill.

Next, have someone not associated with the company critique the two pages you've just written, to ensure this summary will pique the interest of potential candidates. When you are satisfied with this document as a recruiting tool, make a large number of copies and contact the following groups:

- *Business associates.* Give them a copy of your document and ask for their recommendations.
- *Bankers.* Talk to several, not just your own, and leave them several copies of your document. They may know of experienced executives looking for a change.
- *Lawyers and CPAs.* They usually know some professionals who are dissatisfied with their present position.
- *Area salespeople and sales representatives.* If you are looking for sales executives, these people usually know of some prospects.
- *Management groups or associations.* These people meet regularly and probably know of some other managers looking for the right opportunity.
- *Companies in allied industries.* Don't expect competitors to help you, but the executives of other companies working in similar industries may be able to provide some excellent leads.
- *State job service agencies.* These people usually have some executives on their lists. In some cases, they may also have programs that will offset a portion of the salary during a training period.
- *College recruiting.* Don't be afraid to recruit at this level. You'll find some extremely bright graduates with the entrepreneurial spirit.
- *Venture capital groups.* They always know of experienced executives. An added benefit of contacting them is that, if they like your management team, they may be interested in later investment.
- *A large area newspaper.* Run a medium-size display ad in the Sunday business section (this will be a greatly condensed version of your earlier summary). Note this should be run for several weeks to promote credibility with the most qualified candidates.
- *Executive recruiting firms.* These organizations charge a fee

payable by the employer (typically 20% of the first year's salary) for the executives they place. If you decide to use one of these firms, shop around. Some of them may be willing to place executives with your company while offering you an extended payment plan, provided you can convince them you will utilize their services for future executives. If you are seeking venture capital, they may be willing to waive their fee until you get funding. However, expect them to ask a slightly higher fee and possibly a small ½%–1% stock option for the risk they are taking.

You'll be surprised how, once the word gets out, a number of interested candidates will begin knocking on your door. If they don't, then you simply haven't done a good enough job with your marketing document. If this happens, scrap the old summary and draft a better one, remembering that it needs to communicate the potential, the excitement, and the challenge of your new company.

Screening Team Candidates

As a result of these efforts, you should now have several candidates for each position. What is the best way to proceed with the interview process? Whether you already have a place of business or not, I recommend your initial screening interview be conducted at a neutral location. Meet the candidate for breakfast or lunch. In this way, you can plan a meeting of fixed duration, and you can also observe how the candidate interacts with people.

After some small talk, thank the candidate for taking the time to meet with you, and then have him or her sign a nondisclosure agreement. This is necessary because you are now going to be revealing proprietary material about your business, and the candidate must agree not to disclose any of this information, whether or not he or she is hired. Your agreement should be short and simple, so the candidate will sign it willingly.

The simplest nondisclosure agreement contains only a few sentences, stating that candidates realize they have been invited to interview for a position on the company's management team, that they will receive certain proprietary and confidential information to allow them to evaluate this position, and that they agree to treat all this information in strictest confidence and will not disclose any of this information to any parties outside of the company. You and the interviewees sign two copies of the form; the interviewee keeps one copy, and you proceed with the interview.

Now you can brief the candidate on the company, your objectives, and your goals. Let the candidate know you will be selecting only the top people for this team. Explain to candidates that you have only an hour to get a feel for the kind of person they are. If candidates bring résumés to this meeting, scan them only briefly to ensure they include references (if they do not, ask for references). Then put these documents aside and read them in detail after the meeting.

I like to ask candidates to give me some idea of their strengths and weaknesses (and I am wary of people who can give me no weaknesses). I also want to know what their personal goals are. However, if I specifically ask for their goals, they probably will not be able to give me the answer I want, so I achieve the same end by asking them what they want to achieve with their life. And I listen very carefully to the answer, because I want to see how their goals mesh with the company's goals (for example, if their goal is to be earning $100,000 per year in five years, and I know the best this position could offer is $60,000 within five years, it's a pretty safe bet neither of us is going to be very happy).

I ask the candidates why we should hire them for this position, and I pay attention not only to the words but also to their ability to organize, to communicate, and to motivate. From this first interview and from the results of subsequent reference interviews, I know if a follow-up interview is appropriate. If it is not, I send them a letter thanking them for their interest in our company.

For those who survive the first cut, the next interview can be held in your place of business (if you have one) and with the rest of the management team (if you have one). During this interview, I like to ask candidates how they would solve some specific problems that may arise with the business, and I judge the appropriateness of their response, and observe their interaction with our team.

After this session, you will probably be left with only one or two suitable candidates. In any event, schedule a final interview to discuss the specifics of the position before extending an offer.

Now that you have become focused on securing first-rate people for your team, realize as you bring these people on board, they will probably know other potential candidates as well. Don't hesitate to ask them for their recommendations on any unfilled positions.

Creative Offers for the Right Person

What if you find the right people, but you can't afford them? With the resourcefulness you've shown in the creation of your business, you should be able to apply the same ingenuity here as well. Suppose you've located Jim McKenna, a marketing manager with 15 years of experience, who is perfect for your director of marketing position. But there's a slight hitch: He is presently earning $80,000 per year, and the best you could offer is $40,000. Should you throw in the towel? Not without a fight.

First, look at your sales figures. Try adding a commission based on sales for the director of marketing. A $40,000 base with a $20,000 commission considerably reduces the disparity between Jim's former salary and what you can offer him. Try changing the title to vice-president of marketing, so Jim perceives he'll be making a move from manager to executive. If necessary, throw in some stock options. You want Jim to believe your company will be a smashing success, so he will want to be part of the action.

What if you can't offer all this to lure him on a full-time basis? Then try to land him part-time, possibly offering no salary but a generous commission, as well as payment for attending strategy meetings. By doing so, you can at least include a person of Jim's stature in your business plan.

Finally, if you absolutely cannot land Jim yet, hire him as a consultant to help you develop your company strategy. You can even bait the hook by asking for his recommendation for marketing manager, but keeping the vice-president of marketing position open for him to consider when you are able to make him a better offer in a year or two. Chances are, if he has helped you to mold the marketing strategy and to hire the marketing manager, and has continued to consult with you, he'll be interested in joining you when the time is right. And by the way, you can still list him in your business plan as a consultant.

Your Board of Directors

If you are forming a corporation, you will need to put together a board of directors at the same time you are assembling your founders team and management team. Once again, you're looking for experience in the running of a successful business (not just friends or those who will always agree with you). The board should meet once a month, with the president and key managers reporting to it.

I believe five people is the ideal size for a board of directors. A group of this size is large enough to accommodate different viewpoints but small enough to gain consensus and conduct business efficiently. I strongly recommend that the president be the only employee on your board, because you are striving to bring outside business experience to it.

Also, you do not want management to appear split before the board on major issues. Having only one management representative on the board ensures only one voice will be heard. (The management team might hash out a potential board issue for the purpose of developing a consensus prior to a board meeting, but by the time the board meeting is held, management should be able to present a unified position to the board.)

Your goal should be to develop a strong, no-nonsense board comprised of executives who will challenge your decisions, to ensure that your planning is sound. If you are planning to seek venture capital, the funding companies will also require representation on your board. Having strong business leaders already committed to your board will make your business plan all the more attractive to them.

Again, turn to bankers, CPAs, and other businesspeople for recommendations for board members. You want strong directors on this board, ones who will not be afraid to make tough decisions and challenge your plans where appropriate.

In a corporation, the president answers to the board of directors, and the board answers to the stockholders. Often, fledgling entrepreneurs are paranoid about ensuring they control a majority of the board, fearing the board may overrule them. I believe this fear is groundless.

Let me share with you my experience in putting together my first board of directors. I needed to raise additional equity for my company. I found four experienced senior business executives, all willing to invest in my company at my asking price, provided they each had a seat on the board.

This meant they would outnumber me four to one, but this didn't worry me. I reasoned if I came up with a specific plan and could not convince at least two of them to vote with me on the plan, then something was probably wrong with my proposal. In the four years we were together as a board, we never had a violent disagreement. Yes, there were times when I put a proposal before the board, and they would ask if I had done this or verified that. If I hadn't, they would suggest I table the proposal for a month until I completed the additional tasks. The following month I would either present the additional material and the proposal would be adopted, or I would withdraw the proposal from consideration in light of the new information. I truly learned the business of business from these four mentors. I will always be grateful to them.

Once you find well-qualified potential board candidates, how do you entice them to serve on your board? If your company's rough business plan sounds exciting, these senior executives may want to be on your board on the basis of that alone, to be part of another winning company. Nevertheless, you need to make it easy for potential directors to say yes when you ask.

You should plan to pay all outside members of the board a fee for each meeting. While you are still struggling to get "in the black," this fee can be small, say $50 per meeting. However, when you begin to show a profit, the fee should begin to grow accordingly.

I also suggest you have your attorney arrange a stock option plan for outside board members—for example, a block of 4,000 shares, exercisable over a four-year period at 25% per year, provided they are still board members. In this way, there's no risk that a director will be given a block of shares tomorrow and then immediately leave the company with your stock.

Your board members are senior business leaders and their time is therefore quite valuable, so you must conduct your board meetings as efficiently as possible. Because their daytime schedules are quite busy, consider a 6 P.M. meeting with deli sandwiches. Always start and end your meetings on time, and always set up the date and time for the next board meeting before adjourning.

One week prior to the next board meeting, send each board member a copy of the agenda for the next board meeting. Develop a reputation for keeping your board meetings on schedule as well as adhering to the agenda. If a special topic is raised that merits lengthy discussion, either table the topic until the next board meeting or schedule a special meeting.

As you gain a reputation for a no-nonsense style in the conduct of your board meetings, you will gain the respect and the gratitude of your outside board members.

Your Board of Advisors

If you do not have a corporation, then you will not have a board of directors. In this event, you should strongly consider a board of advisors. These are outside executives whose experience is invaluable to the success of your company.

When my first company was still a proprietorship, I set up a board of advisors headed by a local business executive. He was able to bring in several other senior businesspeople, and this gave me strong management assistance during my formative years.

In forming your board of advisors, you should approach the same sources as you would for directors. Although you cannot offer stock options, you must offer meeting fees and discounts on your products or services, if appropriate. Also, you must schedule and run your meetings in the same concise, no-nonsense fashion as you would if you had a board of directors.

Once again, in selecting your board of advisors, the way you present your company is critical. If potential advisors believe your company will be a winner, they will want to be part of it.

Getting "Recharged" by Your Personal Network

During World War II, the military was training pilots at a greatly accelerated rate. A psychological study by the Navy discovered that when pilots who were training intensely 16 hours per day were able to break from their training rigors for several hours, their productivity increased dramatically. That break was sufficient to recharge their personal productivity "batteries."

If you don't already know it, creating and running a company is an emotionally draining experience. It is imperative you recharge your own battery, or you will start "flying off the handle" and making reckless, even potentially fatal, decisions for your company.

To avoid this, you need to do several things. First, you must mentally "turn off" the business at the end of the day, and second, you must spend quality time with family and friends, because this is when your emotional productivity batteries are able to recharge.

Even though you spend long hours at the company, when you finally leave at the end of the day and close the door on the business, you really must close your mental door on the business as well—shutting out all thoughts of the company and giving your mind a needed rest.

It is easy to continue working, worrying, and struggling with projects still in your head after you arrive home. You may have spent the last few years working two jobs—your regular day job, and the job of launching your new business after hours. You may be accustomed to working round-the-clock. But now that the business has been launched, things are different. What little time you have with your family and friends needs to be quality time. What little you might gain by mentally rehashing problems from work will take a significant toll on you, on your family, and on your friendships.

This is a lesson I learned the hard way. It cost me the death of my first marriage. Now, almost two decades later, I am married to a loving woman who understands the demands of my work. In return, I try to ensure we have meaningful time together. When I have a lapse, she lets me know—thank God, because my family is best at recharging my emotional battery.

Your family is, too. If you don't have a family, then you need sharing friends to let down your hair with—away from the cares of business. This is the most effective way you can ensure maximum productivity the next day.

Another part of your personal network should be a small number of trusted professional friends who are not connected to your business. Periodically, when you have to make a difficult decision—about laying someone off, reorganizing a department, raising more capital, or selling the business—it's good to be able to turn to a fellow business associate in confidence for a second opinion. When I received my masters degree in business management, my faculty advisor was chairman of the Department of Industrial and Management Engineering at a major university. Before joining the faculty, he had been in industry for more than 25 years. He became my mentor, and over the years, although there were times when I could assist him, there seemed to be far more times when he would listen to difficult decisions facing me and lend his wisdom and experience to my problems. In addition, I had two other business executives who were part of my mentoring network, so I always had a professional friend to lean on when I needed organizational solace. These contacts made a world of difference and helped me over the years to maintain my peace of mind.

EXERCISE: Your Dream Team

Utilizing the ideas presented in this chapter, start a new page in your notebook, entitled "Contacts." This will be a list of people you know, with whom you should start your search for candidates to fill key positions. Remember to prepare your summary sheet prior to contacting them. As you contact each of these people, in addition to soliciting recommendations for candidates, you should also ask about other professionals who may be able to recommend possible candidates.

The next page of your notebook should be reserved for management nominees. List the positions you want to fill, and add a short job description. Then include the names of any potential candidates for this position. Really brainstorm at this point, listing people you would love to have but probably could not secure. Then contact these people. If they are not interested, ask them to recommend other candidates as well. Never forget that first-rate people will usually know of other first-rate candidates. Continue to add to this list as you visit with your contacts.

Finally, you should have a section for board candidates (either directors or advisors, as appropriate). Continue adding names here as well, remembering that you are looking for experience. Some of your contacts may make ideal candidates. However, don't ask anyone to join your board too soon; just ask if they are interested in being considered. Once you are farther along with the company formulation and you have a longer list, then and only then should you finalize your hiring plans. Before you extend any formal invitations to join your board, you should have some idea of what perks you will offer.

Again, my recommendation is to arrive at an ideal-size board of five people (or certainly seven at the maximum), with the CEO as the only employee on the board.

*   *   *

Once you have filled the critical positions on your management team and your board of directors or advisors, you should now have a solid, rough business plan in place. Whether your company is only a dream or a full-fledged operating business, whether you seek a small bank loan or major equity capital dollars, you are now ready to proceed to the next level—developing a formal business plan for your company. The race for financing begins in the next chapter.

6

Winning the Finance Game—The Starting Line

Assembling Your Formal Plan

We have thus far traversed six of the ten Microgenesis levels on our journey together. The next level involves a number of critical financial and structural decisions on your part. In this chapter I am going to present a host of financing options for your business and show you how to develop a full-fledged business plan that will help you secure financing.

Entire books have been written on the subject of financing options. In this chapter, I have culled them down to a manageable number, and I will guide you, step-by-step, through the process of selecting the correct alternatives for your business.

LEVEL VII: Finalize Your Financing Needs and Create Your Formal Business Plan

The Many Financial Avenues Open to You

When I started my first company, I was a babe in the woods when it came to understanding financing options. Now, three companies later, it feels as if I have used them all: personal loans, banks loans, lines of credit, notes, private stock placements, SBA-guaranteed loans, and venture capital. But I haven't even scratched the surface.

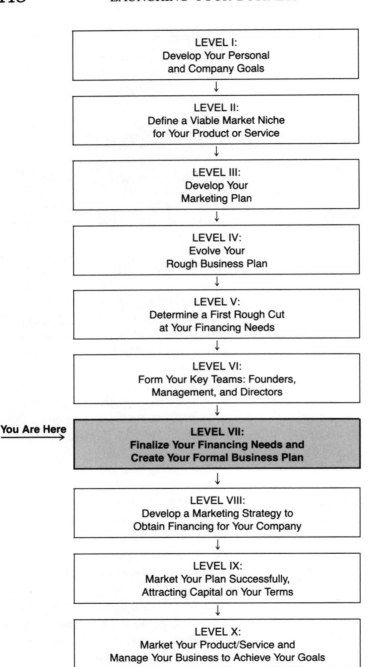

Before we consider some of the many financing options available to you, here's a pointer I learned the hard way: Whatever amount of capital you think you need, you will inevitably need a much greater amount. Here's why: When you put your financial projections together to determine how much money your company needs, you make certain assumptions—that your products will be manufactured on time, that the first version will work perfectly, that customer orders will arrive each month as stated, and that the economy will stay vibrant and healthy. If only half of your assumptions are realized, you will be lucky, because in the real world nothing ever goes exactly according to plan.

Furthermore, as hard as it is to raise money, it is usually easiest to raise it the first time around. Trying to go back to the well a second time when you haven't performed to promised projections (even if the reasons were totally beyond your control) is futile; it's almost impossible to get additional funding at this point. Therefore, whatever you project for your cash needs, double this amount to cover contingencies.

In addition to your own contribution, let's say your projections indicate you need $100,000. Does this mean that I'm telling you to raise $200,000 instead of $100,000? Absolutely, and I'm going to show you a technique to accomplish it.

You believe you have an exciting company, and people are going to want to invest in it, right? Then make them pay for the privilege. Tell potential investors that equity partnerships in your company are being offered in ten blocks of $10,000; however, as part of the price of admission, they will be expected to offer you in exchange a 36-month loan for $10,000 at prevailing interest rates. In this manner you raise $100,000 as equity and an additional $100,000 as debt capital, giving you the buffer you need to cover all those assumptions that don't quite work out right.

In all probability, the capital you raise will be a combination of both debt and equity, so let's look at the ramifications of each.

When you sell stock or a partnership, you are exchanging money for ownership. The cash you raise in this manner is known as *equity* capital. It will appear on the "plus" side of your balance sheet, which is good. On the other hand, by raising equity capital you have to give up some portion of ownership in your business, which is not so good.

When you borrow money for the company and promise to repay

these funds with interest, the cash you raise is known as *debt* capital. It will be recorded as a debt on the liability side of your balance sheet, which is not so good. On the other hand, you did not have to give up stock ownership in exchange for the money, which is not so bad.

Raising all of your funds as equity capital might result in your losing control of the company (owning less than 50% of the business), while raising all your capital as debt makes the company's balance sheet look shaky and ensures you will not be able to raise any additional debt funds. Clearly, the best option is a combination of both equity and debt financing. The exact structure of this combination should be determined initially by you and your attorney (using this chapter as a guide). However, you should expect the structure to be modified down the line as investors and their attorneys have their say.

Debt Capital

The primary source of debt capital is a bank loan. The interest rates charged and the collateral required can vary considerably from bank to bank, so don't be afraid to shop around. However, the bank you finally settle on will expect to handle your other financial business as well, so choose carefully.

When I started my first company, I went to my hometown bank, even though my business was located 45 miles away. Because my hometown bankers knew me to be creditworthy, they gave me a $50,000 line of credit, requiring my personal guarantee and my home pledged as collateral. Several years later, our business had grown, and I decided to transfer my accounts to a local bank that was closer to my business. The interest rate was slightly lower; however, my entire board of directors were required to sign personal guarantees. Three years later, after continued growth, I moved our accounts to a larger bank in the same city. Their interest rate was even lower, and this bank only required my guarantee along with the assets of the business as collateral. As you search for financing, don't be afraid to "shop around" for the best deal. But keep in mind the best deal does not just mean lower interest. It means the best all-around bank for your business. The other services the bank is willing to provide are an important consideration in which lender you choose.

More Than a Banker's Dozen

Most entrepreneurs think that a bank loan is a bank loan. In fact, there are a number of bank financing options available to you, provided you know what to ask for. Here are fourteen different types of loan mechanisms through which businesses can borrow funds from a bank, arranged in three broad categories: short-term, medium-term, and long-term:*

Short-Term Loans. These are the most popular business loans. Short-term loans are usually made for a maximum of one year, but may extend for several years. The bank will require collateral, but only as a secondary source of repayment. In granting a short-term loan, the lender expects to be shown that the growth of the business will generate funds for repayment.

- *Short-term operating loan or commercial loan.* This is a 3- to 6-month general business loan with a lump sum repayment at the end of the term. In approving this loan, the bank looks at how your company will generate sufficient cash to ensure repayment. However, if the due date approaches and conditions make it difficult to repay at that time, don't be afraid to ask for an extension. If your financial condition and projections look good, the bank will probably grant the extension by writing a new note, but you'll still be required to pay off the interest due.

- *Line of credit.* This is a kind of open-ended loan. The bank sets a maximum credit limit (or credit line) and gives the company a period of time to draw against this credit line, up to the limit. The period may be from 30 days to two years. This is essentially a "preapproved" loan, so you don't have to submit a new application each time you require additional funds up to the limit of your credit line. The bank may require an up-front commitment fee of 0.5% to 1% of the total credit line; however, some banks waive this fee if the company's compensating balance is sufficiently high (in other words, you agree to maintain a

*Some of the categories have been adapted from Joan Ford, "A Dozen Ways to Borrow Money," in *The Best of Inc. Guide to Finding Capital,* (New York: Prentice-Hall Press, 1988.)

certain high cash balance in your accounts with the bank). There are three types of lines of credit:

—*Nonbinding*. The bank can cut off any further draw against your credit line if it deems sufficient adverse events have occurred in your business.

—*Committed*. Insert this word in the loan agreement, and the bank can no longer cut you off, even if your business runs into trouble (unless a specific clause is inserted, allowing the bank to do so). However, you will probably have to pay a premium to get the magic word inserted; expect the commitment fee to double. It never hurts to ask for this option.

Banks will require, for either of the above two lines of credit, that you "clean them up" (fully pay them off) for at least 30 days each year.

—*Revolving*. The revolving line of credit is similar to a revolving charge account. There will be an annual review and renewal involved, but probably no requirement for an annual "cleanup." The balance due is usually repaid in monthly installments of principal and interest.

I recommend you establish a line of credit with your bank as soon as your financial condition allows. Borrow frequently to your maximum credit level and pay it back fast. In this manner, your bank will be open to continually raising your credit line. Within five years, you could expect your credit line to equal 25% of your annual sales, and within ten years, it could equal 100% of your annual sales. Or, your bank may set a limit on your credit line based on a combination of inventory, receivables, and fixed assets.

• *Inventory loan*. This type of loan is made for the purpose of carrying seasonal inventories. It is usually reserved for established profitable businesses. The inventory being financed is used as collateral. Repayment is typically made in installments as the inventory is sold and the receivables are satisfied. The loan period usually spans a maximum of 6 to 9 months, and there must be an annual "cleanup" if the company plans to secure another loan the following year.

—*Floor-plan loan.* This is a version of inventory loans typically utilized by retailers of large-ticket items, such as automobiles, boats, etc. The lender obtains title to the specific floor-plan items until each one is sold, at which time the loan against that individual item is repaid.

▪ *Accounts receivable financing.* This type of loan is typically utilized by undercapitalized established companies whose sales are increasing. With this kind of loan, you pledge specific receivables as collateral, and the bank finances your invoices up to 60 days, for 60%–80% of their face value. In other words, when you invoice a customer, you can receive a loan for the discounted amount (60%–80%) from the bank. The loans are repaid as soon as the invoices are paid; this is usually handled by forwarding the receivables checks directly to the bank. The bank then takes its loan payment plus interest from the proceeds and credits your account with the balance. The cost for this type of financing varies widely (from 3 to 10 points above the prime rate), depending on location and the maturity of the company. Usually the contract is written for one year; however, some banks will work on a revolving format. Larger banks may specify larger minimum monthly receivable levels before a company can qualify for this type of loan. Some banks may just write the contract for a specific group of receivables.

—*Combination of accounts receivable and inventory.* Many banks will allow your company to combine accounts receivable and inventory lines into a single borrowing base. For example, your borrowing base might be limited to a maximum of 60% of your accounts receivable plus 50% of your inventory, with all of the accounts receivable and inventory pledged as secondary collateral.

▪ *Factoring.* Instead of pledging your receivables as collateral, under this form of financing you actually sell your receivables to a "factor," which may be a bank or a factoring company. The "factor" then assumes the credit risks and the collection responsibilities. There is a very high cost for this type of financing (typically 10 points over prime). The factor will assess this cost as a discount from your invoice and will refuse to factor any invoices it considers to be high-risk. This type of borrowing originally began in the garment industry but has since spread to a number of other industries.

▪ *Letter of credit.* The letter of credit is not a true loan but rather a guarantee of payment to help secure credit. When a vendor won't ship inventory on open account and you can't afford to prepay the order, ask if your supplier will accept a bank letter of credit (or LOC). Your bank issues the LOC, guaranteeing payment if you fail to pay. Your bank will charge you a fee of at least 1% of the amount guaranteed and will insist on a note, a compensating balance in your account, or some other asset as collateral. Don't expect to just walk in and pick up an LOC; your bank will want as much documentation and effort for an LOC as it does for a business loan.

Medium-Term Loans. These loans are usually for a period of one to five years and are utilized to finance plant expansion and equipment. For this category of loan, banks are very concerned about collateral and will probably require additional collateral from companies with perceived risk.

▪ *Term loan.* This type of loan is usually written for five years or the useful life of the asset it is financing. It is typically structured with quarterly payments of principal and interest.

▪ *Monthly payment business loan.* This is a variation of the term loan structured with monthly payments. You may be able to obtain an option with lower payments during the first two years. However, the bank may also impose certain restrictions on your company, requiring a certain level of working capital or the maintenance of a specific financial ratio (e.g., the current ratio) at a certain level. (Financial ratios are covered in Chapter 7.)

▪ *Equipment lease.* Larger banks may have their own leasing arm, while smaller banks may have an affiliation with a leasing company. Leasing a piece of equipment means a lower monthly payment than that required by a term loan. The reason is that with a loan your company retains title to the equipment, but when your company leases, the lessor retains title, which means at the end of the term of the lease (typically two to five years) you would have the option of (1) returning the equipment to the lessor, (2) renewing the lease for an additional period, or

(3) purchasing the equipment at fair market value. I'll cover more about leases under "Other Financing Options" later in this chapter.

Long-Term Loans. These loans are for five years or longer and are usually the hardest type of loan to secure. They are typically made for property acquisition, major expansion, and some start-up companies.

▪ *Commercial and industrial mortgages.* Use these when buying your building and property. Banks will usually loan up to 75% of the value of the building. These loans are usually written for five to ten years, but may be for as long as 25 years. Payment terms vary widely, depending on the amount of your loan and the perceived risk.

▪ *Real estate loan.* If you have sufficient equity and good financial standing, you can borrow against any real estate you own through a second mortgage. The bank receives all mortgage payments and passes on the amount due to the holder of the first mortgage. Environmental concerns are becoming a significant factor in the approval of these loans. Many banks are now requiring a Phase I EPA study to determine if any negative environmental impact exists. For example, if there is toxic waste or underground leakage, the new owners may also acquire the responsibility of a major cleanup, the cost of which may be greater than the price of the property.

▪ *Personal loan.* Bankers tend to believe your personal assets should provide much of the financing for major expansions or acquisitions, so you may want to consider a personal loan as part of your long-term financing plans. The idea is that you personally borrow from the bank and turn over the proceeds to the company as a "subordinated loan," which is repayable only after all other company debt is discharged. Or you may choose to invest the funds as equity, in which case they will increase the net worth of the company. In either case, your balance sheet will appear more attractive to your banker.

▪ *Asset-based loan or leveraged buyout (LBO).* The asset-based loan, or leveraged buyout (LBO), is only for an established company with sufficient cash flow to service the additional debt. An LBO is usually financed by a consortium of financial institutions. LBOs are typically handled by major brokerage houses or LBO specialists. I am discussing LBOs here because banks usually participate in them; however, I'll have further comments on LBOs later in this chapter at "Potential Financial Strategies."

▪ *Start-up loan.* This is probably your only bank financing alternative if you have a start-up company with little collateral. The bank will expect to see your own money in the deal, and because you probably lack sufficient collateral, your best bet is an SBA-guaranteed loan. There are two types of SBA loans:

> —*SBA-guaranteed loans.* The SBA can guarantee up to 90% of a business loan made by a participating bank. You can qualify for these loans even if you don't have sufficient collateral. However, you will have to complete an inordinate amount of paperwork, and you will probably have to pledge additional items such as your home for collateral. Once screened by the bank, 50% of all applications are approved by the SBA. The two primary reasons for SBA rejection are (1) no clear or believable repayment ability, and (2) lack of owner's equity; the SBA expects you to put up at least ⅓ of the equity. It will also require collateral from you as well as personal guarantees from each stockholder with more than 20% ownership. Hint: Look for a bank that participates in the Preferred Lender Program, and ask a loan officer there about an SBA loan; these banks don't have to go to the SBA for loan approval.
>
> —*SBA-direct loans.* The SBA allows you to apply directly for a loan if you have been refused by several banks. However, unless there is some mitigating circumstance, the odds are that the same concerns that prevented you from securing a standard bank loan may also sink your chances for a direct SBA loan.

Dealing With the Moneylenders

Bankers are lenders, not investors. They are in business to make a profit, but unlike investors, derive the profit only from the interest earned on your loan. If bankers are going to work with you, they need to understand you, your business, and the way you run it.

Your relationship with your banker will, in all probability, be a lengthy union, with its share of ups and downs. To achieve the most beneficial relationship, you had best begin courting a bank before you need capital. Tell your bankers all about your business. Provide them with financial statements and management reports. Invite them to business briefings and facility tours well in advance of your loan request.

This strategy will ensure your banker understands what you do and how well you do it before you need a loan, so you do not have to overcome this additional hurdle during the loan application process. Bankers are always focused on minimum risk and will want to see some type of collateral—the more perceived risk, the more collateral. So it pays to make yourself appear less risky in the eyes of your bankers by letting them get to know you long before you ask them for a loan.

The process of applying for your bank loan is a marketing task, so make sure that you are dealing with the most appropriate executive officer at the bank, that is, the one with power to make a decision regarding your loan. When in doubt, approach a higher-level bank officer before you approach a lower-level one.

To find out if you are talking to the appropriate bank officer, during your initial meetings subtly determine this officer's longevity at the bank as well as the chain of command. To whom does the officer report? What is the industry expertise of this lender? Does this individual have the authority (or influence) to get your loan approved? Is this officer competent enough to explain your company, your performance, and your loan proposal to others? Has this individual secured approval for other loans similar to yours? Remember, your loan officer is your in-house advocate; you want to make sure he or she has your best interests at heart. Does your loan officer show a genuine interest in your company? Is this person willing to be creative, suggesting modifications or alternatives more likely to gain approval of your loan request?

It might also be enlightening to inquire about the bank's current loan-to-deposit ratio. This ratio tells you a great deal about the bank's posture on risk, and thus about its willingness to lend money. If a bank in a smaller community has a ratio approaching 50%, you can bet it is aggressively seeking loan opportunities. In a larger city, a bank actively involved with loans may have a ratio as high as 60% to 80%. On the other hand, if you are considering several banks in your community and one of them has a ratio of only 28%, you can be sure that bank isn't very interested in making loans.

For an even better picture of the bank's risk profile, obtain a copy of the current balance sheet (balance sheets should be available at the bank and are also published in area newspapers). Look at the ratio of business (commercial) loans to other loans. If a particular institution's loans are 80% home loans (real estate), you know its focus is not on lending capital to businesses.

Once you are certain you are dealing with the appropriate officer and the right bank, schedule a presentation with the loan officer. At this meeting you must completely convince the loan officer of the credit-worthiness of your loan, so he or she can effectively champion your cause before the bank's loan committee. (I'll be addressing the specifics of how bankers analyze potential deals in Chapter 7.)

What should you be armed with when you approach your banker for this meeting? Unless you are applying for a start-up (probably SBA) loan, there is no need for a detailed business plan. The banker only wants to see a narrowly defined project plan; typical examples might include a plan for the expansion of your business or the addition of a new product line. In this 2- to 4-page project plan (which you can adapt from sections B, C, and H of your rough business plan), you must clearly define the "project" (as opposed to the "business"): the concise, specific purpose for which the bank funds will be used. State clearly why the funds are needed and what will be done with the money. Remember, it must not appear to be risky. The accompanying financials must clearly indicate the generation of enough additional capital over the period of the loan to permit repayment of the loan with a generous margin of safety.

You may want to have your accountant accompany you to the presentation. You should be making the actual presentation and show a clear knowledge and command of the financials, but it won't be a black mark against you if your accountant answers any difficult financial questions.

Even though you have done your homework properly, your loan may still be derailed by forces that are out of your control. What if, for example, the bank had just experienced losses from bad loans with two restaurant owners? If you show up trying to obtain a loan for a coffee shop, your loan application isn't worth the paper it's written on. The bankers will listen politely and then reject your request, no matter how solid your presentation, because top brass has bluntly stipulated, "Don't even think about bringing any more restaurant loans to committee."

The bank won't volunteer this information; if you want to find out the real reason your loan was rejected, you might ask several probing questions, such as "Has your bank had any bad experiences in lending to similar companies?" or "Would the bank be open to considering loans for this type of business?" If you sense a hesitancy, you might want to take your request elsewhere.

For fear of lawsuits, bankers may skirt the real issue of why they are denying your loan request. If a loan officer doesn't like your deal, it may be suggested that you need more capital in your business before the bank would be interested. If you get hit with a similar type of explanation, ask for clarification. Specifically what does the banker recommend you do to improve your application, and if you accomplish this, what are your odds for approval? If the bank seems anxious to help you correct deficiencies in your loan application, stick with it. Otherwise you had best take your business somewhere else.

When novice businesspeople apply for a bank loan, they tend to believe the only two possible answers to their loan request are yes and no. This is not the case. If your banker likes your business but appears unsure of securing approval for the amount of funds you are requesting, the reason may be that the credibility of your sales projections is in doubt. If you are confident of these projections, suggest the bank approve a staged loan: 50% now, 25% when your sales reach the projections indicated at month 3, and 25% when your sales reach the projections of month 6. However, if this proposal is approved, you should have a specific alternative financial source (other than the bank), just in case you fail to meet the interim sales projections. The bank may also counter your suggestion with an alternative staging scenario based on profits, cash flow, or some financial ratio it deems critical.

Fledgling companies tend to get hit with several noes before they finally secure their first loan approval. When you are hit with one of these noes, the way you respond demonstrates what type of businessperson you are. If you respond by cursing or by making an awkward exit, resolving never to do business with this bank again, what have you learned? Nothing. We all learn by experience, but we don't learn and we don't succeed by getting angry and burning bridges. Before you overreact, stop and think. The bank rejected you for a reason. What was it? Always use a no to gain additional information from your banker. What factors led to the bank's negative decision? Should you try to correct these deficiencies, or should you go elsewhere?

In fact, if you sense premature reluctance from your loan officer, don't ask for a final decision on your loan request. Explain you sense some hesitancy on the bank's part, and ask if there is something you should be doing to improve your chances for approval.

Your banker may indicate you need additional collateral or equity or may suggest you are asking for too much money. These responses probably indicate you need an infusion of equity capital into the business. Ask your banker how much additional equity would be needed to secure approval. Then raise the additional equity: Borrow against your home, from relatives, or by bringing additional partners into the business. Another alternative may be to rework the proposal, scaling down your plans and asking for less debt capital.

If the bank indicates a problem with the strength of your management team, you should ask for suggestions on what is needed, and even solicit recommendations to fill or replace any management positions.

If the bank reaches a firm no decision on your loan request, ask what action on your part would allow the bank to reconsider. If the bank's request is not feasible, then you must approach another bank. In this case, you should ask your banker one last sincere question: "Since it appears obvious we will have to pursue this loan elsewhere, could you make any suggestions to strengthen this proposal before we present it to another institution?" Listen to what your banker has to say, because chances are your loan may not secure approval from another institution until you correct this weakness.

Whatever the outcome, don't be too eager to jump ship and change bankers. You've probably spent a lot of time helping this bank understand your business. Can you really afford to take the time away from running your business to duplicate all this effort with another bank?

On the other hand, if you have patiently tried to work with your present bank and you sense it is no longer interested in doing business with you, then it probably is time to consider a trial separation. Unlike most marriages, you can secure a commitment from a new bank before actually divorcing the old one. However, if you still have a loan at the old bank, consider asking the new bank to assume this loan as well, so your old relationship is permanently severed, with no more alimony payments due.

Once you finally secure your loan, remember you have to perform to meet the loan commitment. Continue to provide your bank with monthly reports and financials, so they are always updated on your progress. If you have setbacks, let your bankers know and keep them appraised of the corrective action you are taking.

Equity Capital

The primary source of equity capital is an investor. This may be a wealthy individual, a company with discretionary capital, or a venture capital fund. The equity investor is focused on moderate, "prudent" risk. If the investor is a company, its involvement with your company may be minimal (for example, the company may want one of its executives to sit on your board). If your equity investor is an ex-entrepreneur or a venture capital firm, either one may expect to take a more active role in your company.

One of the overlooked advantages you have in raising equity capital is that usually the individuals you are dealing with have a great deal of business experience. For this reason, if they don't insist one of their people join your board, you should. You can readily utilize their expertise.

One of the reasons venture capitalists want an intimate involvement with your company has to do with the statistics of failure rates. In a typical venture capital portfolio of investments, 20% of the deals are a total loss; 50% of the deals ultimately become a "wash," breaking even; 20% probably average a 10-to-1 return on investment, and the other 10% become the real superstars. It is this final 10% that determines the success of a venture capital fund.

Even though venture capitalists know the odds are only 1 in 10 that any new investment will be a smashing success, they will never put a penny in your company unless they are convinced you will be one of their superstars.

Furthermore, an unfortunate transformation has taken place in the venture capital arena during the last several decades. As the cost of manufacturing technology has increased, start-up costs for new manufacturing companies have skyrocketed. As a vivid example of the change over time, consider this: When I started my first successful manufacturing company in 1970, I needed only $10,000 cash and a $50,000 bank loan to equip my facility with the "bare bones" basics. Little more than a decade later, when I started my next manufacturing business, I needed over $1 million worth of basic equipment before I could even open the front door.

As a result of these pressures, the vast majority of venture capital firms are no longer interested in investing in early-stage companies, preferring instead to concentrate on companies (and executives) with some existing track record. There's a logical reason for this: In companies with experienced management, the failure rate may be less than 20%, but with inexperienced management the failure rate is as high as 80%.

Because of high operating costs and the above-mentioned risk factors, venture capital funds will probably not be interested in your company unless you are already well established and are seeking at least $250,000. Therefore, most of you will be seeking your equity capital from private investors.

Vulture Capitalists

"Vulture capitalists" is an alias bestowed on professional venture capitalists by entrepreneurs who perceive that (1) professional venture capitalists unfairly insist on a larger ownership in the company than do other equity sources, and (2) venture capitalists are less patient, more prone to pull the plug and liquidate the company if the going gets too rough.

These perceptions are probably created by entrepreneurs who take deals to the venture firms that are perceived to be high risk (the higher the risk, the more equity the venture capitalists will demand).

When these same companies subsequently show significant problems, usually because of the lack of experience of the management team, the venture capitalists want to minimize their losses. The entrepreneurs would have been far better off mitigating the risk (probably with a stronger management team) before they approached venture capitalists initially.

If you have a corporation in a dynamic but fledgling industry, this is an option worth pursuing, provided you consider a few points.

- The best time to approach venture capital is after you have turned a profit. You can probably raise twice the funds for half as much equity at this point, because the perceived risk is so much lower.

- Usually, specific venture capital funds have certain preferred investment industries, about which they have accumulated a great deal of knowledge. Learn these industries. An excellent resource is *Pratt's Guide to Venture Capital Sources.** It is usually available in the libraries of most cities.
- At the same time, you should realize there is a vast difference among venture capital firms. Some of them are staffed by novices with no significant business management experience, who will base their decisions solely on your monthly financial statements and the pressure from their own peers to perform. You should avoid these funds like the plague, regardless of what they promise you.
- Research venture capitalists the way you would research your banker. Ask for recommendations from CPAs, bankers, and lawyers. Ask to speak to CEOs of other companies they have invested in. What is the maximum investment the firm can make in any one deal? You may need a subsequent round of capital, and you need to know the firm's financing ceiling. Find out the experience of the firm's management team. What kind of clout and business experience can it bring to your board? After all, you're looking for more than just finance people.
- Never approach venture capitalists as if you are in a hurry for capital. Even if you are impatient, you have to be cool. If they sense impatience or believe you are in cash trouble, venture capitalists won't touch you. They may even stall the deal for a while, just to make sure your company doesn't collapse.

If you perceive you're eventually going to need venture capital, consider approaching venture capitalists early (even before your product is ready and your plan is out of the rough draft stage). Explain you are not yet ready for venture capital, but you would like to interview them to determine if there would be mutual interest when you are ready to seek equity capital. Then go ahead and question them. Don't be afraid to ask for help (such as locating key executives or critiquing your plan), but don't try to bluff or lie to them. One fact you may want to learn up front: Have they invested in any competitive companies? If

Pratt's Guide to Venture Capital Sources, Stanley E. Pratt and Jane K. Morris, ed. (Wellesley Hills, Mass.: Venture Economics, Inc., 1990) is updated each year.

they have, be wary about showing them your plan, for fear it may turn up in the wrong hands.

However, having said that, I want to add that you usually don't have to worry about nondisclosure agreements with venture capitalists. For the most part, they are very honest and very ethical. Venture capitalists tend to form consortia to share the risk on various deals. If one of them is doing research on you, it will probably ask others what they know about your company. These professionals run into each other at board meetings (if they're part of the same deals, they're probably on the same boards), conventions, and while researching new deals, and they seem to pass information quite freely. Even so, although people you've consulted may talk about your deal in general terms with another venture capital organization, they are also extremely secretive about current deals they are working on. They will never discuss your proposal in detail with someone else unless they have your permission to do so.

If you try to "snow" a venture capitalist or behave unethically, word will get around fast; the venture capital world is small. Once this happens, you will be a persona non grata. (In fact, venture capitalists may even try to test your ethics with trick questions, as I'll be discussing in Chapter 7.)

Once you have members of a venture fund on your board of directors, don't be afraid to put them to to work. If you know they're going to be in the city of a major client, ask them to call on the client, if their presence could help. Ask them to accompany you on major presentations to large corporations to facilitate closing an important order. (They can effectively assure the customer of the financial backing required.)

A Smorgasbord of Equity Options

Now that I've discussed venture capitalists, let's review the potpourri of various other equity capital sources available to you:

- *Private money sources.* There are probably a number of wealthy individuals in your area with money to invest. They might be successful entrepreneurs who have "cashed out" the investment in their own company; these are sometimes called *angels,* because they are looking for new entrepreneurs to take under their wing. They will also want to be involved with the running of your company. Or they might be wealthy businesspeople with a desire to associate with a successful new company.

These private money sources don't advertise in the Yellow Pages. To find them, you will probably have to return to the same sources (e.g, CPAs, lawyers, bankers) I discussed when you were locating the other critical members of your team in the last chapter. These individuals are loyal and patient, and they give timely advice. You'll probably have to be referred to them, and if they are interested, they'll contact you.

When you meet with these investors, you will need a detailed business plan, showing how they will be able to "cash out" within five years. They will probably want the attorney to structure the deal so they can write off the losses if you fail. Most of these individuals have had significant business experience, and you would do well to recruit them for your board of directors.

▪ *Corporations.* Many corporations have elective capital available for equity investment in outside companies. Typically, however, these corporations invest in companies with sizable existing fixed assets, thus mitigating their investment risk. A very small number of corporations may be willing to invest in early-stage companies with experienced management.

▪ *Privately owned venture capital funds.* These funds vary broadly in size, expertise, investment policies, industries of interest, and the level of management support they will offer you. The very large funds are known as "deep-pockets" players, because they have very high investment ceilings. The remaining funds are probably interested only in regional investments. Their portfolio managers and executives are typically MBAs and ex-entrepreneurs.

Most of these funds have specific investment objectives. They might require the potential profits in any deal to be far greater than the inherent risks; for example, they might expect their earnings with a typical portfolio company to average 25% per year (over the life of the investment, because there will probably be losses in the early years). Due to the cost of investigating a potential deal (known as their due diligence effort), their minimum preferred investment is usually in the range of $300,000 to $500,000. They like to invest in industries in which they already have a good deal of experience and which they can track closely.

These funds typically form joint ventures with other venture capital groups, with one group being the lead investor, in order to spread the risk. And the more risk they perceive, the more stock they will want, along with clauses to protect them in the event that you or your team cannot perform.

Though they may indicate they're interested in early-stage financing, these funds are in fact generally interested only in later-stage funding. They will listen politely to start-ups and then probably tell you to come back and see them again in a few years (translation: when you have more experience and a positive cash flow and thus are less risky).

▪ *Quasi-public venture capital funds.* Most states now have state-supported or local business-supported venture capital funds to invest in fledgling companies within their borders. Usually their investment criteria are quite specific. To get specific information on the funds in your state, contact your state government's economic development organization (Department of Economic Development, Development Commission, etc.) in your state capital.

▪ *Seed capital funds.* These funds are very rare beasts. Some can be found in the private sector. Most are in the public sector. Seed capital funds focus on the earliest-stage companies, usually businesses involved with manufacturing that promise significant job growth that will benefit the area. Again, contact your state economic development organization for further information.

▪ *SBICs (small business investment corporations).* SBICs borrow the majority of their lending funds from the federal government or from banks. There are both bank-owned SBICs and privately owned SBICs. Many of the bank SBICs are staffed by ex-bank loan officers and tend to be very conservative. The privately owned SBICs tend to have the same goals and philosophies as do private venture capital firms.

Warning: SBICs are typically smaller (with shallower pockets) than private venture capital firms. If you know that your borrowing demands are going to be significant ($1 million or more), be sure that you have at least one "deep pockets" player (usually the larger privately owned venture capital firms). This player can in turn bring other smaller venture capital funds into the deal. (It's considerably harder for a smaller venture capital company to bring one of the majors into the deal; the majors like to take the lead.)

- *Commercial banks.* Many companies never consider a bank when they are ready for equity financing, because they fail to realize that commercial loan officers may offer referrals to private equity investors. Furthermore, many larger banks also have SBIC divisions, and the loan officer can arrange an introduction for you. This contact also has the added benefit of establishing your credibility for an eventual line of credit or other bank loans.

- *Investment bankers.* There tend to be two types of investment bankers: (1) those looking for promising young companies they can groom for an eventual IPO (Initial Public Offering), which they can handle—usually, these are affiliated with a major brokerage house; and (2) those looking for established profitable companies (probably with a minimum of $2 million–$5 million in annual sales) with owners who want to sell a portion of their equity.

- *Investment brokers.* These are not equity investors but instead they claim to know of potential investors for your business. Many are reputable; a few are not. They will demand a fee for their services, possibly with a portion up front. Investigate these brokers carefully before giving them your business. Check with the state, bankers, and even satisfied clients, before you sign anything. Even if you do enter into an agreement with an investment broker, do not make it exclusive. If they find you money, they receive a fee based on that money; however, if you raise any funds elsewhere, they are not entitled to any fee on these funds. Always proceed with caution with brokers until they have been thoroughly checked out.

- *Vendors.* If you need expensive machinery, consider approaching your vendors and offering them equity in the company in exchange for the equipment you need. If they perceive your company as having the potential for significant growth, they may jump at the opportunity, because they perceive you will be "locked in" to their equipment as you expand.

Other Financing Options

Now that I've covered the more common debt and equity sources, let's look at one last category of miscellaneous sources of funds:

▪ *502 Local Development Company Program (or 502)*. The federal government's 502 program offers local development companies (or LDCs) the opportunity to attract and retain small businesses. Your company may want to consider this option when you need a new facility or an expansion for an existing building. The LDC is usually a community organization—a subsidiary of the chamber of commerce or local economic development group—that applies to the SBA for LDC status. You initiate the process by making a presentation to your LDC on your company and the proposed facility.

If the LDC likes your presentation, it can borrow 85% to 90% of the needed capital from a financial institution, with the aid of SBA loan guarantees. The LDC raises the balance of the funds from other local sources, builds the facility, and leases it back to your company at prevalent leasing rates.

▪ *504 Certified Development Company Program (or 504)*. The federal government's 504 program is more flexible and broader in scope than the 502 program. Loans made under the 504 program are for land, buildings, improvements, machinery and equipment, and related costs (including legal and other fees). The interest rates offered under the 504 program are lower than those under the 502. Under the 504 program, a business approaches a certified development company (CDC; generally a financial institution) participating in the 504 program.

If the CDC decides to participate, the business must raise 10% of the desired loan amount. The CDC typically provides 40% of the loan amount of U.S. Treasury rates, because the SBA provides a loan guarantee. The CDC solicits the remaining 50% of the loan from a private lender (at current market rates) that is offered a first lien on the full value of the new asset, even though it only provides half the funds.

To take advantage of either the 502 or the 504 program, you need to know the LDCs and CDCs in your local area. The best way to obtain this information is to contact the business development specialist at your nearest district SBA office.

▪ *Small-Business Innovation Research (SBIR) Grants*. Federal agencies with R&D budgets in excess of $100 million must award a certain number of SBIR grants to small businesses. These awards are made once annually, and the application and award dates vary with the different agencies. Each agency solicits applications for awards in the following categories:

—*Phase I Awards.* Up to $50,000 for six months' research
—*Phase II Awards (after completing Phase I).* Up to $500,000 for two years' additional research

Phase I awards are typically given to finance feasibility studies for a product, not for the purpose of taking a product to market. Phase II awards will be granted only after the successful completion of a Phase I effort and final report; they are typically for fabrication and testing of prototypes.

Be advised that there are a large number of entrants and hence a low probability of winning an award. Furthermore, your probability of winning depends more on the stature of your scientific team than on the nature of your project.

SBIRs are not a vehicle to provide financing for your business. They can be used for new product research. In typical government fashion, you will have to account for all expenditures, and they must be for this specific research activity.

I recommend that SBIRs be viewed as providing additional capital for your research projects, not as a primary source of money for your business. With the extra effort involved, SBIRs cannot be used to provide your company with operating funds. SBIR grants are intended to help speed potential research for new products.

The SBIR application will ask for details about how you plan to use the award money. You are allowed to specify a small profit, but your application will be looked upon more favorably if you don't incorporate profit into your calculations.

The best way to increase your odds for winning is to affiliate with a credentialed principal investigator (this is your primary researcher; he or she is also referred to as a PI). The PI should probably be an academic (with scholarly experience in the area of your proposed research), because the review committees comprise predominantly academics.

The usual requirement is that the PI work with the company at least on a half-time basis during the period of the project. If the PI is a college professor, this may necessitate resignation or a leave from the university. If your PI cannot definitely make this commitment at the time of your application, consider specifying this academic as a contingent PI. That way, if your proposal wins and your PI is unable to take leave, you have the option of requesting approval for a substitute PI (possibly a graduate student currently studying under the original PI candidate).

To receive SBIR Program Pre-Solicitation Announcements, write to: Office of Innovation, Research & Technology, U.S. Small Business Administration, 1441 L Street NW, Room 500, Washington, D.C. 20416.

▪ *Leasing companies.* More and more leasing companies are willing to lease equipment to businesses; however, most of them prefer businesses that have been in existence for at least three years. You should be able to get the names of area leasing companies from your banker. The advantage of leasing is that it keeps you from tying up large amounts of capital for fixed assets when you can least afford it. Some leasing companies will even allow you to lease such items as computer software, which can be a considerable expense for a young company.

Make sure you are offered a true lease—that is, make sure the leasing company holds the title to the equipment and that you are allowed to return it or purchase it for fair market value once the lease term expires. (Otherwise, you will not be allowed to write off your lease payments as business expenses.)

The "Too Good to Be True" Deal

There are an incredible number of business con artists out there, preying on the enterpreneur trying to raise capital. *If a deal seems too good to be true, it probably is.* These folks promise you a "sure thing" for an up-front fee of several thousand dollars. The only sure thing is that they have your money.

Here is an example: A client came to me with a new business idea to cryogenically process scrap tires and plastics into usable material for a handsome profit. Rather than pursue conventional sources, he had contracted through a U.S. agent of a Canadian firm that claimed it would work with a European bank and a U.S. insurance company to fund his $10 million company. He had already paid more than $4,000 in processing fees to the agent and was told the money would be forthcoming within two weeks. One year later, he was destitute, but he still believed the agent would come through for him. For all I know, he may still be sitting by the mailbox waiting for his check.

Other danger signals: Beware if an agent "approves" your deal too quickly without checking on you or your references; if you are told during your first phone conversation that your project is certain to be approved; or if the agent can't give you a specific verbal or written procedure for the financing arrangement, including what you have to provide at each stage of negotiations.

My advice: If your financial advisors are leery of a potential finance scheme, and if the potential investors or brokers don't have impeccable references, stay away from it.

Some additional options of a more exotic nature that may be applicable to specific companies in certain industries and specific geographic locations will be covered in the "Financing Alternatives" section of Chapter 7.

Potential Financial Strategies

Getting your money is only half the battle. The secret to success is knowing how to use that money most effectively. Growth that is too fast kills as many businesses as does slow growth or no growth. Here are a few tips that will help you to steer a straight and profitable course for your business:

■ *For a young company.* Grow slowly as you gain experience. Creating a business is risky enough, so resist the temptation to grow too fast, thereby doubling the risk. Be a strategic thinker: Always have alternative strategies for potential worst-case scenarios. For example, what if you lose your major customer or the market dries up? What if a recession hits your industry? Always have a backup plan ready.

I suggest you prepare three sets of financials, based on three different scenarios: the best case (how you hope the business will grow), the probable case (how the business will most likely grow), and the worst case (what will happen to the business if nothing goes right). Then base all your business plan projections on the probable case. This strategy ensures that you have an alternative plan to fall back on (and that you have other projections ready in case investors ask you what will happen if you do better or worse than forecast).

Don't finance the company totally on debt capital unless you are convinced the business will show a profit immediately (and keep in mind that if you are wrong the company is out of business). It is far better to have a combination of debt and equity (and the more equity, the better your balance sheet looks). The more equity you raise, the easier additional loans are to secure.

Plan to have a sufficient buffer of working capital to cover contingencies. Remember, you don't have the capital to live "high on the hog" or to make wrong guesses.

If your company is a corporation, it is reasonable to consider selling stock to a few select private investors. But don't spin your wheels pondering options primarily applicable to later-stage profitable companies, such as going public thorough an IPO (initial public offering).

- *For a turnaround company.* If you are purchasing an existing company that has been losing money, your priorities will be different from those of starting a company from the ground up. Although you must be sure the market for the company is strong, you must first stop the hemorrhaging of the company by whatever steps are necessary and then build up the company's cash position. Equity capital is probably mandated in this situation, as is the re-establishment of customer and vendor confidence.

- *For an established expanding company.* If you wish to secure funding for the expansion of an established company, demonstrate an appropriate level of experience in your written plan by articulating an understanding of the barriers to expansion as well as the associated rewards. Present a history of your performance, complete with testimonials from customers and independent experts. If the company has sufficient assets, you might seek only debt capital, a combination of debt and equity capital, or venture capital.

- *For a mature profitable company.* Your financing strategy at this stage will depend upon management's goals. If management wants to raise additional equity, consider an IPO. If the goal is to "cash out," then secure the services of an investment banker to market your equity in the business.

If management wants to acquire the company from other owners, consider a leveraged buyout (LBO). The LBO is a transaction in which the buyers (usually a management team) borrow against the company's assets at extraordinarily high debt-to-equity ratios. The management team must be willing to put in additional equity as well. The company must be able to demonstrate sufficient cash flow in order to service the increased debt load. This mandates a review of possible scenarios to take into account all contingencies that could affect cash flow.

EXERCISE: Your Fund-Raising Strategy

In Chapter 4 you estimated your financial needs and subsequently modified them through your initial projections. Now it is time to turn these earlier estimates into reality.

You should combine the information you have gathered, along with your previously completed pro formas, to determine (1) how much capital you will seek and (2) what funding sources you are going to pursue. The completion of this exercise in your notebook should involve an extensive analysis and discussions with your existing management team, as well as conversations with a number of the sources I have discussed in this chapter.

When you have reached a decision on the above two points, update your tables from Section H of your rough business plan (Sources of Capital and Uses of Capital). List the different sources of funds as you now perceive them. Then list the application of these funds. Remember, you must be able to explain and defend your choices to potential investors.

Once you have arrived at a specific strategy for pursuing capital, it would be a good idea to test it before proceeding further. Assuming you will be seeking debt capital, go to a potential banker. Explain you are in the investigative stages of putting a new business proposal together, and you would like to air some early concepts to him or her for comment. Don't provide anything written at this point. Rather, give a verbal summary of the salient points, including the two tables. Then solicit the banker's opinion as to the probability of securing a bank commitment for such a proposal. And pay attention to any feedback you receive, positive or negative.

If you will also be seeking equity capital, you should repeat this tactic with your financial advisor and possibly one potential equity investor. They should be able to provide appropriate feedback as well.

These discussions will probably result in a modification to your strategy, which you should then detail in your notebook before proceeding.

Your Formal Business Plan

Perhaps you already have a stable, self-sufficient business. Maybe you are only raising debt capital. Possibly you are not raising any capital at all. If you fall into one of these categories, you may be tempted to skip this section. Before you do, please note the next key point.

Key Point: *The business plan is used primarily as a working document, not as a tool to raise capital.*

There are two goals for a business plan. The primary goal is for your plan to be a working document, the "business bible" for your company. It is a blueprint for the management team to follow, a document by which you can measure your progress. Your company will be faced with some tough decisions in the months that lie ahead, and the pages of your business plan should serve to help you in the decision-making process.

Essential to a strong business plan is the incorporation of the goals you defined for the company in the first chapter. These goals may not be explicitly stated in the plan, but their vital threads should be woven into the fabric of your plan. You and your board members must embrace this document as embodying the direction of your company's growth. Your investors must believe your company will not readily deviate from this plan.

The secondary goal of your business plan is to raise capital for the operation of your company. The majority of business plans never incorporate the primary goal, but only this secondary goal. As a result, they become only shallow sales tools that investors can spot a mile away. If potential investors do not believe you are committed to this plan or perceive you would deviate from it at a moment's notice, it will lose all credibility in their eyes, and they won't be interested in funding your business.

So, focus on the primary goal of building a business plan that is a solid working document. In that way, you will establish a level of credibility with investors that few plans achieve.

The Primary Goal

Your business plan is as important in bad times as it is in good times. I know this from firsthand experience.

In 1981 I sold my first company, which had become the leading manufacturer of agricultural monitoring systems, to an Australian conglomerate, at a very good price. As part of the deal, I agreed to remain with the company for several more years as president. At the time of the sale, my business plan called for the company to concentrate on a family of agricultural electronics products.

In retrospect, my timing for the sale was perfect, because during the next year the agricultural economy took a nosedive and remained depressed for the next six years. Sensing the severity of this farm recession, I modified the plan to concentrate on a shift into the general security market. Our products could be readily adapted to this growing market in both the U.S. and Australia, where they would be marketed through our parent company.

However, something happened that I had not foreseen. One executive saw an opportunity to expand his personal empire. Unknown to me, he made a strong pitch to the Australians to drop our standard product line and concentrate instead on contract manufacturing (assembling products for others). He had a large potential contract lined up in Chicago. As a result, in 1983 our parent conglomerate informed me our company would discontinue our standard product line in favor of contract manufacturing. I indicated I was not interested in remaining at the helm of a "job-shop" assembly house, so we parted company.

My successor took over executive duties. This manager had never formulated a strategic business plan and never understood the importance of it. He decided, without strategic planning, to change the direction of the company. Had he completed a marketing survey, he would have learned the competition was fierce (particularly from offshore companies), and pricing was cutthroat in this market. He would have also learned who the company's competitors were. The company could have developed a competitive advantage, with targeted strategies to secure other key customers.

However, the company did none of this. Instead, it plunged ahead with this one key customer, investing heavily in inventories and new equipment to fulfill this dream order, believing that somehow others were sure to follow. Unfortunately, the dream turned into a nightmare when the customer suddenly went into bankruptcy. Not only had management failed to put together a strategic plan, it hadn't even done a credit check on its only customer! Furthermore, they had no contingency plans for dealing with such a catastrophe.

From that point on, the company faltered, trying to secure one flash-in-the-pan product after another, and continuing to slide downhill. Still, management never considered developing a written business plan. The ship had sprung a major cash flow leak and was sinking, and management had to expend every effort to try to bail it out.

Management could have taken a few days to develop a crisis plan to provide a sense of direction but did not. After the parent conglomerate sank millions into the sinking ship, it finally sold the company to a successful executive in the contract assembly business. His organization had a definitive written plan, and after applying corrective surgery to the floundering company, nursed the remains of my old company back to health.

The moral of the story is this: No matter how small your company, no matter whether your star is rising or falling, your business needs a written plan of action. If you plan to be successful, you will need the stability and direction that a sound business plan offers.

The Secondary Goal

A well-prepared business plan serves not only as a guidebook for the company; but as your ticket of admission to the circle of potential investors. If it is to be used to raise capital, there are some essential elements your plan should contain:

- It should present a clear picture of your strategy. To achieve this, the plan should not be too complex or unreadable.
- It should convey a sense of what you expect to accomplish for the next five years.
- It should clearly focus on the benefits to the end user of your products and services, rather than on your product's features.
- It should focus more on marketing and the experience of the management team than it does on the specifics of your product (or service).
- It should justify, both financially and strategically, the means chosen to sell your products or services.
- It should clearly state the level of product development and market penetration already achieved.
- It should portray management as an experienced team with complementary business skills.
- It should contain believable conservative growth projections with appropriate documentation.

- It should indicate how potential investors will be able to "cash out," typically within five years, with an appropriate capital appreciation.

Grabbers

What do potential investors look for when they review a business plan? Believe it or not, your first challenge is to ensure they read the entire plan. Most equity investors have a stack of business plans on their desk. So how do you get their attention?

Think about the way you buy a new book to read when you are going on a trip. Chances are, you pull a book off the shelf, open it up, and start reading. If it grabs you, you keep it. If it doesn't, you put it back on the shelf and go on to something else.

Investors react the same way with business plans. If your plan grabs them in the first few minutes, they'll continue reading it. Otherwise, it will end up on the pile marked "return to sender," accompanied by a polite letter stating your plan is very interesting but doesn't fit their portfolio right now.

How do you develop "grabbers"? Here are some tips:

- The plan should be concise; some of the best ones are only 15–20 pages. If you try rewriting Tolstoy's *War and Peace,* investors won't be impressed.
- Investors like to see some evidence of significant customer acceptance, either through actual sales or product field testing.
- They will look for evidence of a strategic focus for the company (remember the primary goal of your plan).
- Investors want you to show clearly how they will make a profit by investing in your company.

One of the best ways to grab investors is with a well-written executive summary, which we'll discuss in greater detail in the "Basic Format" section of this chapter.

Turnoffs

There are certain elements of a business plan that are guaranteed turnoffs. If your plan contains any of these elements, you will never make it to first base with investors.

Here are some major turnoffs:

- *A plan that is too long.* Consider 40 pages to be the absolute maximum acceptable length. Beyond that, the plan will never be read.
- *An infatuation with your product (rather than a marketing emphasis).* This is guaranteed to label you a risky novice.
- *Financial projections that are out of touch with reality.* Only rookie entrepreneurs project sales to double every year; beyond a company's initial start-up, that rate of growth is unrealistic. This tendency to inflate growth projections is so prevalent among novice entrepreneurs that investors have given these projections a name; the hockey stick curve. Unless you have independent experts to corroborate your estimates, if investors see your projections result in a hockey stick curve similar to that in Figure 6-1, you probably won't see a nickel of their money.
- *A poorly written and edited plan.* Take the time to have an outside authority review your document for grammar, clarity, and spelling.

Let me tell you the story of an emerging company that failed to consider the importance of presenting a well-written business plan. It had developed an innovative machining technique utilizing laser tech-

Figure 6-1.   The typical hockey stick curve.

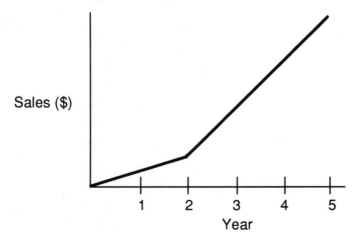

nology and had closed some impressive sales and achieved a measure of profitability. It was now applying for an expansion loan through a state economic development office.

The loan committee had already indicated a probable favorable response. However, the committee members wanted to see a business plan. So the company prepared a plan and submitted it. Based solely on that document, the loan was rejected.

What happened? The plan had been well written, but throughout the document the word *laser* was misspelled "lazer." The committee believed that if management didn't know how to spell the word that defined their business, it certainly didn't deserve the loan. And they were probably right. The company, by the way, never knew the real reason its loan request was rejected.

The Basic Format

Many investors will get their first impression of your business from your formal business plan. Make sure it is printed on quality bond paper and that it is visually perfect. The business plan conveys a number of subtle messages beyond the wording of the document. Something as simple as an ink smudge or a fingerprint on the first page will scream a silent message about your company's commitment to quality.

For favorable first impressions, form is as important as content. Your plan should be presented in some type of quality binder, and on the title page of each copy you should include a copy number. Furthermore, you should have a statement on the first page indicating additional copies are not to be made. These steps indicate you believe this to be a valuable document, that you have logged a copy out to the investors for consideration, and that you do not want the plan falling into other, unauthorized hands.

There are a number of ways to organize your plan. However, I recommend that your first draft be organized as follows:

- *Title page*. Critical elements on the title page include the name and address of your business, as well as a contact name and telephone number. Also include a statement prohibiting copying and a block stating "Date Issued " and "Plan ." Fill in these blanks with a pen when the copy is issued. Then keep a log of all outstanding copies. To repeat, all these actions emphasize this is a valuable document for your company.

▪ *Executive summary.* The executive summary is like a movie preview: If it generates excitement and expectations, people who experience it will want to stay for the entire show. To write the executive summary, start with the version you developed in Chapter 4 (Section A of your rough plan), modifying it to reflect any strategic changes you have incorporated since you developed your rough plan. To ensure that this section grabs the reader, include some subtle, unanswered questions. If the investor doesn't want to read on and find the answers, you've probably just lost a potential funding source.

Here are some examples of "grabber" text:

— "We will be marketing this product using an innovative new approach."
— "Our customer survey shows an intensifying demand for our new service."
— "This product addresses a unique and untouched aftermarket."

If such statements are not explained further in this section (and they shouldn't be!), investors will probably want to continue reading to discover further details. That's the point: You have "hooked" them.

Overall, this section should convey a sense of:

— *Scope (what you are doing).* For example: "We are in the computer marketing business."
— *Mission (where you are going).* For example: "Our sales and profits for the next five years are projected to be. . . ."
— *Intensity of purpose (why you will succeed).* For example: "Our unique leasing, training and warranty programs. . . ."

You would do well to review this section when the rest of the plan is finished, to ensure the key elements are present. Finally, have businesspeople from outside the company critique this page, to determine if it grabbed them as well.

▪ *Section 1:   The Company.* In this section, describe the company, its origins, and its expectations. Summarize the company's overall objectives so that the investor is left with a clear picture of where the company is going and just how it plans to get there. Define your distinctive competence, the chief factors that will account for your success. It had better sound believable; if it doesn't, it probably isn't, and investors won't believe it.

▪ *Section 2: The Management Team.* By discussing the management team in the section after "The Company," you are subtly emphasizing the importance your people will play in the accomplishment of your mission. In this section, include a brief description of each position, followed by the name of the person filling this position, along with a single-paragraph summary of the person's credentials and past accomplishments. If certain managers are currently working for other companies and do not want their names in print, include their initials only, with the following qualifier: "This individual is currently employed with a major company in this industry and has executed an agreement to join our company when financing is completed. Name furnished upon request."

If you still have holes in key positions for the management team at this point, don't try to hide the fact. Include a description of the unfilled position (and any specific requirements for the position) along with a statement similar to this: "We have interviewed six executives for this position but have been unable to select a sufficiently qualified individual. We would welcome the assistance of our financial partner in helping us locate the appropriate executive for this position."

Finally, include an overall organizational chart for the company, if you have a number of key management positions.

▪ *Section 3: The Market.* This section will be adapted from your rough business plan (Section C) from Chapter 4 and your marketing plan from Chapter 3. In this section, define the specific market to be served (clarifying the source of your data) and describe the benefits of the company's products/services to the end user. Indicate the projected size of the market for the next five years. You should leave potential investors with hard evidence that you have a clear idea of who will purchase your company's products/services and why.

▪ *Section 4: The Product (or Service).* Next, describe the company's products or services. If the company is selling a technical product, describe how it functions, and indicate whether or not it is currently on the market. If you have testimonials from satisfied customers, include them. Also detail any proprietary, patented (or patentable) features of the product.

Entrepreneurs love their products; however, it is a good idea not to get too carried away with this section. I recommend it be noticeably shorter than the previous section, indicating to the investors the management team realizes the priority of markets over products.

▪ *Section 5: Sales.* Having described the market in Section 3 and the product in Section 4 of your formal business plan, now disclose specifically how the company plans to approach its prospects and achieve its sales projections. The sales methods to be used should be clearly outlined and logically justified (if you have already achieved some market penetration, discuss this and indicate how this sales experience has been factored into your projections). You should also discuss and justify your sales costs and compare them with present industry practices. The reader must come away from this section convinced you have the right sales approach and that you will be successful in meeting your sales goals.

▪ *Section 6: Development (optional).* Adapt this section from your rough plan (Section D). The section should be relatively brief (a page or two) if your product development is well along. In general, the farther along the development process is, the easier it is to get significant funding. Why? Because investors like to see their money invested in manufacturing and marketing, rather than in development of a product not yet ready to be sold. High up-front development costs will probably inhibit most investors. On the other hand, engineering costs in support of manufacturing are usually accepted by the investors, because they translate directly into better products and increased profits.

If it is applicable, be sure to state the location of products currently in operation. Nothing turns off investors faster than someone trying to sell a "paper" product (meaning it exists only in the designer's mind and notebook). At least in the minds of investors, this is very risky business. Even if your product is not yet on the market, you must have some type of prototype to demonstrate.

▪ *Section 7: Manufacturing (optional).* Again, adopt this section from your rough plan (Section E). The section should cover the company's "make or buy" decisions (assemble in the plant or subcontract out) or the transition from "buy" to "make" when certain criteria are met. Keep in mind that investors will want to see a manufacturing process that is as inexpensive and efficient as possible, geared to maximizing profits.

A discussion of quality control may be appropriate in this section. This could lead into a discussion of anticipated warranty costs—how they will be allowed for and how they will be kept at a minimum.

- *Section 8:   Financial Data.* In this section, discuss the financial performance of the company (if any) to date. Include your previously prepared financial projections (income statements, cash flow statements, balance sheets) covering the next five years (monthly for the first two years, then quarterly thereafter; as an option, the balance sheet could be presented quarterly for the entire period). You may choose to present yearly summaries in this section and the detailed spreadsheets in the Appendix.

These pro formas should be realistic and the numbers justifiable. If potential investors have the feeling your numbers came out of *Alice in Wonderland,* that's probably where you'll end up looking for your financing. You may want to study financials from companies in similar industries to verify the credibility of yours.

- *Section 9:   The Investment.* Adapt this section from Section H of your rough plan. In addition, this section should detail the entrepreneur's expectations regarding the investment itself. Discuss how much capital is being sought and, if equity capital is desired, what percentage of current ownership it will purchase. Include your revised tables, Sources of Capital and Uses of Capital. You should also include a discussion of the company's projected value at the end of five years, along with the investors' projected return on investment (ROI). Your accountant will be able to provide data for this computation.

- *The Appendix.* The Appendix should include a compilation of miscellaneous material: detailed résumés, supportive material for the financial section, sales literature (if any), and other relevant company material.

Fine-Tuning

The body of your report should be composed by the best writer in your company. Don't argue about sharing the responsibility; this document is too important to be written by a committee. Write your plan as if you were talking to the potential investor. You must be able to convey enthusiasm but avoid artificial superlatives such as "fantastic sales" or "tremendous profits"; your financial projections should speak for themselves. Consider including some photographs of the management team working together or of the products being manufactured or being used in the field.

Assemble your completed plan in an attractive binder. To reinforce the appearance of an ongoing company, include copies of major purchase orders, letters from satisfied customers, and compliments from distributors.

EXERCISE: Your Full Business Plan

Armed with the pages of your rough business plan, your financial pro formas, and the details of the previous section, pause now and turn to your notebook to create the first draft of your company's plan. Keep in mind that the primary intent of your full business plan is not to raise capital but to create an operating document for your company.

Allow additional space at the end of each section for notes on revisions or additions which may occur to you at a later point in time. I suggest you do not strive for a final version of your formal business plan until you have finished this book.

Secrets of an Abbreviated Business Plan

The formal business plan you just developed contains all of the necessary elements to make it an effective operating document for your business as well as a tool to secure financing. However, if you are going to seek equity capital, I recommend you condense the plan into a unique format that will increase your odds of securing this form of financing.

The idea is to make your abbreviated business plan look similar to the investment analyses commonly reviewed by equity investors. This approach will definitely serve to set your plan apart from the majority of business plans received by these investors and will strengthen your presentation. Think of this abbreviated plan (roughly 15–20 pages in length, excluding the appendix) as your secret weapon. This abbreviated plan will quickly compose itself from the pages of your formal plan, with the exception of the first few sections, which have their foundation in typical stock offering documents. For those sections you will need the assistance of your lawyer and your CPA, who will provide the appropriate material and wording for the sections.

Here is my recommended outline for your abbreviated plan. To give you an idea of how a plan might read, I've inserted quotations based on our earlier example of the entrepreneur marketing a telephone screening device.*

TITLE PAGE: (same material as before)

EXECUTIVE SUMMARY: (same material as before)

THE INVESTMENT: (1 page)

> This section summarizes the details of the desired investment. If all funds are to be raised at once, you should indicate this. If not, show the different phases of funding. Have your business attorney assist you with this one, because it should include a description of the offering (what class of stock, convertible debentures, etc.), how many shares are being offered, and how much equity in the company (portion of ownership) the shares will purchase. The Sources of Capital and Uses of Capital tables are not included here. As a guide, this page is structured similarly to the investment section in a typical stock offering. For my fictitious product, this section would contain the following text:

> > The Company is seeking outside investors for equity participation to permit timely introduction of a new automatic telephone screening product. Funds will be utilized primarily for marketing, advertising, and product inventory.

> > Offering: $700,000 for 700,000 shares of common stock in SAC Corporation - No par value. This represents 37% of total outstand-

---

*Please note: The abbreviated business plan text examples are presented for illustrative purposes only. They are based on our earlier telephone screening device product, for which the fictitious SAC Corporation plans to raise $700,000. None of these passages is represented herein as legally appropriate for use in your state.

ing shares after completion of the investment, not including any issued or outstanding warrants or stock options.

Other additions to this section will depend on how you plan to structure the financing. Are there additional subordinated notes or convertible debentures? You and your attorney must make this determination.

RISK FACTORS: (2–3 pages)

This section should begin with a statement similar to the following:

> Purchasers of the shares offered should recognize that investment in the company involves a degree of risk and that the company's operating results cannot be accurately forecasted. No market for the shares exists. Among the risk factors an investor should consider are the following:

After a statement similar to the one above, list the risks involved in the investment, allowing a paragraph or so to summarize each risk. Some of the topics of risk will be very specific to your industry. However, many of them will be general in nature. If you are not able to define and articulate a number of serious risks for your company, you need to do more homework. All businesses, even the most profitable, carry a number of risks. Here are some ideas to get you started. Let's assume I am launching a business for the automatic telephone screening device we developed earlier. Here are some of my perceived risks:

The Product

This product will initially be manufactured for the company by XYZ Inc. of Chicago. At this time the product is technologically superior to other products on the market, but there is no assurance that the company can maintain technological superiority, thus diminishing the marketing advantage the company presently believes it has. In addition, offshore companies may develop and produce less expensive competing systems. The company has applied for a patent to protect the technology. However, there is no assurance the patent will be granted, or that, if it is granted, another company may not be able to circumvent the patent. Even though the unit has been thoroughly field-tested, there is no assurance that further development or modification will not be required in order to create market acceptability and adequate product quality.

Capital Needs and Operating Losses

The company will spend considerable sums on market development for the current product and further research and development for future products. It may not operate profitably in the first year or longer. The proceeds of this offering are projected to be sufficient to sustain the operations of the company until it is profitable. Conceivably, additional capital may be required. This additional capital may be obtained from investors who may purchase additional shares of the company at prices higher or lower than the prices paid by earlier investors.

Relationships With Other Organizations

The company's market program contemplates utilization of direct mail as the primary marketing method. Several organizations have expressed a high degree of interest in the product but will not issue a firm commitment until the final version of the product is demonstrated.

Competition

The company's staff is small and the financial resources are limited. Should a large competitor from the telephone industry elect to enter the market, this action could put the company at a significant disadvantage.

Limited Management

Although principals have extensive experience in associated industries, they have not had experience in this specific niche. Additionally, the number of executives in the company is small and death, disability, or departure could result in short-term reduced performance. The vice-president of marketing for the company is presently employed by another corporation and has indicated that he will join the company upon completion of the funding. He has executed a letter of agreement to join the company at that time. However, if he does not join the company, completion of the company's planned activities for market development could be delayed.

Limited Operating History

The company is a newly organized corporation in the earliest stages of development. The company's product and services are a relatively new concept in the telecommunications industry.

Limited Transferability of Stock

The shares have not been registered under the Securities Act of 1933 as amended and will not be transferable unless they are registered or an exemption is obtained. The shares may require registration under State Securities Law before they may be resold. Consequently, there is not likely to be a secondary market for the shares for a considerable period of time and a purchaser may not be able to liquidate his or her investment.

Although these statements appear to be negative, they indicate to potential investors that you understand the risks involved in your business, which in turn gives you more credibility in their eyes. Once again, risk is part of business, and investors expect that any investment they make will have some risk associated with it. By discussing these risks up front, you are showing investors that you are an experienced professional, not a starry-eyed entrepreneur.

SUMMARY OF SOURCES AND USES OF FUNDS FOR THIS INVESTMENT: (½ page)

This is where you present your Sources of Capital and Uses of Capital tables, along with a summary paragraph.

DILUTION: (½ page)

Your attorney can prepare an appropriate statement similar to the following:

As of December 31, 19XX, the company had 1,200,000 shares of common stock outstanding at a net tangible book value of $1 per share. Net tangible book value per share represents the amount of the company's tangible assets, less the amount of its liabilities, divided by the number of shares of common stock outstanding. Dilution represents the difference between the offering price per share and the net tangible book value per share as computed in the event of completion of this offering.

Upon completion of this offering, if all offered shares are purchased, the company will have an aggregate value of 1,900,000 shares of common stock outstanding at a net book value of $1,900,000 or $1 per share. The purchaser of the common stock in this offering at a price of $1 per share to the new investor will experience no immediate dilution in net tangible value of $1 per share.

CAPITALIZATION: (1 page)

Your attorney and your CPA can assist you with this page. Figure 6-2 shows a typical format.

THE OPPORTUNITY: (2–3 pages)

Extract this section from the full business plan sections The Market, The Product, and Sales. Briefly describe the industry, size of market, and rate of growth. Point out the segment you intend to attack and show why this niche represents a solid opportunity. Introduce the product or service. Compare your product/service to the competition's. Identify potential problems as well as the most critical competitive issues affecting your target market. Discuss strengths and weaknesses of your product, and describe your marketing program.

THE COMPANY: (1–2 pages)

Extract this section from the full business plan's section The Company. Summarize your company's history and formation. Communicate the company's mission statement, purpose, and/or objectives. Why is the company uniquely suited to provide the product or service within this niche? Why will the company succeed in the execution of this plan?

THE PEOPLE: (1–3 pages)

Extract this section from the full business plan section The Management Team. Briefly describe your key executives, their

Figure 6-2. A typical format for the capitalization element of an abbreviated business plan.

As of September 30, 19XX, the company capital consisted of 10,000,000 authorized shares of common stock at $0 par value, of which 1,200,000 shares have been issued and are outstanding. This offering of 700,000 shares at $1 per share, assuming the sale of all shares at a value of $700,000 and giving no effect for options and warrants, will result in the following adjustment:

Stockholders Equity— December 19XX	Outstanding (unaudited)	Adjusted (unaudited)
Common stock, no par value per share; authorized 10,000,000 shares; 1,200,000 issued and outstanding shares (as adjusted 1,900,000 shares, assuming the company reaches its subscription goal)	$1,200,000	$1,900,000
Total stockholders' equity	$1,200,000	$1,900,000
Book value per share outstanding	$1.00	$1.00

Holders of shares will be entitled to one vote per share in the election of directors and on all other matters that may be submitted to a vote at a meeting of shareholders. Cumulative voting is not permitted and holders of shares do not have preemptive rights to subscribe for and purchase their pro rata portion of additional shares of the common stock of the company that might be authorized or sold in the future.

Related Transactions

John Doe, president of SAC Corporation and developer of the product, in exchange for the assignment of the rights to these developments, received 1,000,000 shares of common stock of the company.

ABC Partners, a financial consulting firm, will receive a professional fee of 5% of the total capitalization of the company. ABC Partners has the right to convert one-half (1/2) of the total professional fee into warrants to purchase common stock of the company at a rate equal to one-half (1/2) the price per share paid by the investors.

The contract of the president of the company contains a provision for the president to receive a stock option up to 95,000 shares of common stock that will represent a maximum of not more than 5% of the shares of the company. The exact number of options on these shares is dependent upon the performance of the company.

responsibilities, and their past accomplishments (not just past titles). Emphasize those achievements that relate directly to the new company: not résumés, but a concise paragraph summary of each (utilize the paragraph from your previous draft). Include the names of adjunct team members (company attorney, CPA, banker, other key company personnel, and consultants). Also include your board of directors (or advisors) as it currently exists.

THE FINANCIALS: (number of pages as required)

Extract this section from the full business plan section Financial Data. Include pro formas from full plan for five years. Highlight start-up costs and operating deficits. Include key operating ratios and compare to typical ratios for your industry (you should be able to obtain this information from *RMA Annual Statement Studies,* * which should be available through your banker).

THE APPENDIX: (same material as before)

EXERCISE: Your Abbreviated Business Plan

You could elect to use your full business plan as your investment tool. But if you do, you risk having your document look like all the others that come across the investor's desk. If you are planning to secure equity capital from sophisticated investors (in which case it's especially important to have your plan stand apart from the others), I strongly recommend you complete this exercise.

To do this exercise you will need the assistance of your lawyer, as well as data from your CPA, for the sections The Investment, Risk Factors, Dilution, and Capitalization. However, feel free to begin work with a first draft on these sections. The intent in the remaining four sections of the plan (The Opportunity, The Company, The People, and The Financials) is to condense the information so that your presentation is concise.

The primary intent of this special version of your plan is to secure capital, but the plan must still contain the thrust and vision of

---

*Published and updated annually by Robert Morris Associates, One Liberty Place, Philadelphia, Penn. 19103.

the full business plan you will be using as an operating document. And like your full plan, this one should be attractively packaged. Keep it short: If the main body contains more than 20 pages, you should carefully review the material again to ascertain if any additional condensation is appropriate.

The purpose of this exercise is to create the first draft of your abbreviated business plan. After reading the rest of this book, you may glean additional insights that will prompt you to make revisions.

The Never-Ending Story

Your business plan, despite all your effort, is not completed at this point. In fact, it will never be completed; it will continue to undergo a metamorphosis as your business and its needs change. As your company grows, you should take the time to review and revise your plan at least annually.

Over time, the format of your plan will begin to change. For example, as you grow you will probably add a section on strategic planning, to include specific dates to accomplish certain milestones, so that you will know if you are behind (or ahead of) schedule.

Your business plan is a valuable tool. As you grow and consider expanding in different directions, refer to it regularly. Is your contemplated expansion in line with the goals you established in the plan? If so, great. But if it is not, then you have two choices: Either (1) modify your expansion to be in line with your plan or (2) modify your plan to include this new direction. The selection of which path to follow should never be made hastily, but only after sufficient assessment to ensure you are proceeding in the right direction. Many young companies arrived at the gate labeled "success" only to be locked out because management decided erroneously to expand in a new direction—not because it really made strategic sense for the business, according to the company's business plan, but merely because it excited top management. Instead of analyzing their options, they sought out those who would validate their desires, and rejected the rest. (Incidentally, this error is by no means reserved for novice entrepreneurs. Ted Turner's acquisition of the MGM film library, which he pursued at a high cost just because he wanted it, ultimately put his entire cable empire in serious jeopardy).

*   *   *

All businesses need a written business plan, regardless of whether they're just starting and even if they're not trying to raise capital. The business plan serves as both a working document and a fund-raising tool.

Yet when it comes to raising capital, your business plan is only a "product," something you have created. And just like the other products you plan to sell in your business, without the best marketing program this product will sit on the table, gathering dust. Now that you have developed your plan, the next step is to figure out how you're going to "sell" it.

7

Winning the Finance Game—The Finish Line

Selling Your Plan

At this point, you have developed everything necessary to win the entrepreneurial race—almost. You should by now have a solid formal business plan and an appropriate strategy to market your product/service. What is missing is the right game plan to successfully raise the capital your company needs. Which brings us to Level VIII:

LEVEL VIII: Develop a Marketing Strategy to Obtain Financing for Your Company

In order to develop an effective marketing strategy, you must analyze the marketplace of potential investors just as you evaluated your consumer market in pursuit of your marketing plan. Your goal is to determine who are the most likely "buyers" and why they would participate in an investment in your company.

If you have an established profitable company with tortoise growth, your focus may be on debt capital. If you are riding the whirlwind of an established company with jack rabbit growth, you may be looking at both debt and equity.

If you have a start-up company, chances are your first priority is to secure equity financing while keeping your debt capital sources appraised of your progress. The debt portion of your capital requirements should then follow with less effort once you have shown the ability to raise your required equity. However, if you have elected to raise

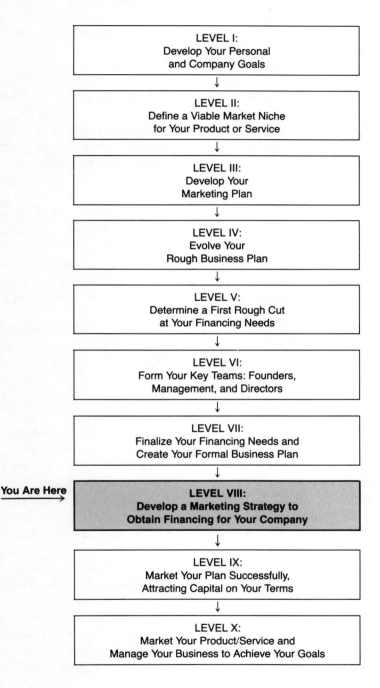

both equity and debt from the same people, both efforts should be pursued simultaneously.

The Equity Funding Obstacle Course

Thus far you have created a business plan designed to pique the interest of potential investors. However, an equity investor doesn't peruse your plan and then hand you the money any more than a movie studio hands a featured role to a new starlet. There are four major obstacles you must overcome on your path to victory.

Your *first obstacle* will be to survive the initial review of your plan by equity investors, who will be reading the plan to evaluate its soundness. Most plans are weeded out at this initial stage because of some major weakness. For some reason or other, the investors don't believe you can achieve the results your plan proclaims. And if they don't believe the written document, no amount of persuasion on your part will convince them otherwise.

Most venture capitalists will just return your plan at this point with a polite note saying, "Sorry, we aren't interested." If this happens to you, you must try to determine why. Call the investor and ask for recommendations to strengthen your plan before submitting it to other investors, and listen closely to what you hear; you will need to correct any deficiencies in the plan before pursuing other investors.

If your plan overcomes the first obstacle, it means that potential investors are interested enough to invite you to make an oral presentation. This is your *second obstacle*. At this point, investors will have a number of questions (including some loaded ones) to fire at you. They will want to know more about the personalities and capabilities of your management team. On the basis of your oral presentation, they will form a conclusion about your team's integrity as well as its capability to accomplish your plan.

The investor's perception of the caliber of your team (even if it consists of just you) is more important than what is written on paper. No matter how carefully you constructed it, the scenario typed out in your plan probably will not happen exactly as proposed, any more than the plan of a battlefield general will proceed exactly according to expectations. Investors need to know that your management team is committed to the battle that lies ahead, even if circumstances change.

This does not mean that your team has to be "perfect." A small weakness will not scare off investors, as long as you haven't tried to hide it. Investors can probably help you overcome a minor deficiency. And if you have indicated unfilled positions on your management team, you can actively solicit their help to fill these management positions with top-notch people.

If after your oral presentation the investors still like what they see, a *third obstacle* lies ahead as they begin their due diligence process of investigating you, your team, and your company in depth. This due diligence effort generally consists of four phases: market research, management team assessment, product investigation, and financial analysis.

The investors will perform some form of limited marketing research. If you performed your marketing research well, they will check out several of your results and probably accept the rest. If you did not do a thorough job, their marketing analysis may take much longer, adding another six to eight weeks to the process.

As part of this process, they will be checking out the members of your management team as well. They will be interviewing your references in detail, and if they find any past skeletons someone tried to hide, you can kiss their money good-bye.

The investors may utilize outside consultants to study your product, in an effort to determine whether there is some weak link in the technology or the product cannot be mass-produced in a cost-effective manner. (If you are already an up-and-running company, their effort in this area may be minimal.)

Finally, they are going to conduct a thorough analysis of your financial projections (I will discuss this activity later in the chapter). Even though you may have proposed a specific combination of debt and equity, they may believe a different ratio is appropriate or perhaps an infusion of capital in stages, as certain milestones are reached. Keep in mind you are dealing with financial specialists; it's wise to listen to their recommendations.

At this point, one to three months have passed since your would-be investors first read your plan. If you survived the due diligence effort, they have an idea what the final structure of the financing arrangement should look like, and so do you. The trouble is, their idea and your idea are probably different. Therefore, you must overcome the *fourth and final obstacle,* negotiating the final structure of the deal.

There will probably be some give-and-take on both sides as you try to work out what is best for the financial health of the company.

Equity Capital Myths

The people who provide equity capital do not broadcast their desires to invest; they and their dealings tend to be shrouded in secrecy. Because of this environment, a number of myths have sprung up around the subject of equity investors, myths we would do well to dispel at this point.

   1. *"Equity investors aren't interested in early-stage companies."* There is a widespread perception that equity investors, particularly venture capitalists, avoid start-ups like the plague. Although it is true the majority of venture capital firms prefer later-stage deals, some of them will look at a start-up business if the company has an experienced management team. On the other hand, there is some truth to the myth: There are very few venture firms that *specialize* in early-stage companies, and these tend to be located in technology centers in only a few states. (For an early-stage company, equity investors want to be located in close proximity because of the additional interaction required.)
   Regardless of the stage of your company, it never hurts to talk to professional venture capitalists. It's not likely they will invest in your start-up company, but you can always ask, and, in the process, lay the groundwork for a future relationship.
   Only a decade ago, venture capitalists invested a great deal in early-stage companies. Why have they migrated away from most early-stage opportunities? Because venture capital firms raise their capital primarily from institutional investors, and the institutions want less risk. A decade ago, the risks of investing in early-stage companies were far less than they are today, because of the greatly increased costs of the technology needed to get a manufacturing business off the ground. With such high start-up costs, even potential winners represent far less profit than they did ten years ago. It's simply not worth the venture capitalist's effort to take the risk of investing in a high-cost start-up. The payoff is no longer great enough. Still, if you have a start-up company with a strong management team, venture capital is worth a try. But if you don't have the credentials to interest professional venture

capital, you should head for the source I recommend for the majority of new companies: individual equity investors, wealthy individuals in your local area. They will be able to provide both capital and business experience.

2. *"Equity investors are looking for some mysterious ingredient my plan doesn't have."* There is no mystery about what equity capitalists are seeking, but plenty of myths. In fact, they are looking for specific elements in a sound business plan. They aren't just looking for technology-driven opportunities; they are looking for unique companies that have the potential for rapid growth and substantial profits.

Equity investors know these companies will require experienced leadership to cope with the stress and rigors of riding the growth curve. Therefore, they are also looking for sound and experienced management. But as we mentioned previously, if they like the essence of your deal and you still have a critical management slot to fill, they can help you find the right candidate to fill it.

One of the best ways to gain investors' attention initially is with a sound, well-written business plan that generates a sense of excitement. By now you should be armed with such a plan.

Timing is everything. Since investors are looking for a healthy company to invest in, they will be highly skeptical of an entrepreneur trying to raise money fast and will wonder whether this company already has one foot in the grave. Your best bet is to approach equity investors as far in advance of your critical need as possible.

Remember, equity investors are seeking an average return on their investment of at least 25% per year. Note I said *average*. They expect you will probably lose money the first one or two years, but then your performance must make up the deficit. If you think 25% each year seems exorbitant, consider this: Instead of lending you their money, they could deposit it in a bank and probably earn 10% or better, with no risk. Because they know they will lose money on over half of their equity investments, you need to be able to make up the difference!

Furthermore, once experienced equity investors commit to a deal, they realize their investment is not a one-time event. They expect to be called upon to make additional investments in your company, as the growth of the business requires.

3. *"No equity investor will meet with a novice entrepreneur like me."* There is a common misperception among entrepreneurs, espe-

cially novice entrepreneurs, that equity investors will not visit with them. Nothing could be further from the truth. For the individual equity investor, you will probably have to be introduced through someone else in the finance world. However, if you have played your cards right and have developed a solid business plan, it should be an easy task to get CPAs, bankers, and attorneys to arrange introductions for you.

Professional venture capitalists, even though harder to win financing from, are easier to see. Although you could still arrange an introduction through the above sources, you could also send them an introductory letter and follow up with a phone call requesting an appointment.

If potential equity investors ask you to send a plan before meeting them, explain that you would like to visit with them to determine whether the "chemistry" is right before you send your plan. Your intent here is not to make a full presentation but to offer your credentials and a brief idea of your plan. The one-page description you developed for your team search might make an excellent enclosure for your letter. At this stage you are trying merely to whet their appetites.

Once you get your foot in the door, you are not home free. For every 100 business plans a venture capital firm receives, its management team probably reads 20 of them through completely, considers 10 of them to have potential, considers 5 of them seriously, and ultimately funds 1 of them.*

Private equity investors fund a higher percentage of the deals they review (between 10% and 20%); however, they look at fewer deals. Nevertheless, if you are invited to present a deal to a private equity investor, your odds are considerably better that your deal will be accepted than they would be if you were visiting a venture capitalist.

Don't be discouraged about the seemingly high odds against securing financing. This book will provide you the ammunition to put your proposal at the top of the heap.

4. *"Equity investors will want to take control of my company."* The intent of equity capitalists is not to control your company but to make a profit on their investment. They would like nothing more than to give you money, leave you alone, and see you meet your projections and reward them with profits. Unfortunately, fate intervenes: If only

---

*Based on a recent HTC Group survey of selected venture capital firms.

50% of your assumptions go according to plan, you have performed well. Things rarely go according to plan.

If you keep asking for more money to bail out the boat because rocks keep punching holes in the bottom, sooner or later investors are going to ask why you keep sailing onto the rocks. Accordingly, they will want a clause to replace you if they believe the ship is in danger of sinking and you still insist on steering for more boulders.

Even though investors will want to include covenants in the deal that allow them to replace you if you can't perform, at the same time they will probably insist on an employment contract, to ensure you will stay with the company for at least five years.

The younger a company is, the less experienced management it has, or the more risk the investors perceive, the larger share of owner-ship equity investors will demand, in order to protect their investment. If you have an established profitable company, you may be able to raise $1,000,000 for only 25% ownership, whereas the same company at a nonprofitable stage may require 50% ownership to raise only $500,000, because the perceived risk is greater.

If your company is in the high-risk category, don't panic if the equity investors seek 60% (or more) of the company. This may be what it takes to get the deal done. First try to get them to consider other options, possibly additional debt instruments in lieu of a portion of the equity. If they remain firm and if they don't have a reputation for taking over companies (which you should already know because you checked their reputation out with other investors, CPAs, and bankers), then they are saying you are a higher risk, and they need additional compensation for that risk. As long as you believe your sales goals will be achieved, you should insist on a buyback clause in the investment agreement, which gives you the right to repurchase the investors' shares over the next five years, subject to specific sales/profits criteria, if you wish controlling interest again. It's as simple as that.

5. *"It will take forever to get my money from an equity investor."* It is true that the equity investor will not sign a check for you immediately after you shake hands on a deal. If you have everything lined up perfectly, you may be able to secure funding from an equity investor in as little as two months, but the average deal probably takes twice that long.

The myth that equity investors take "forever" to come up with the money you need probably was generated by entrepreneurs who hadn't done their homework before approaching the investors. If, for example, you have made some poor assumptions in your marketing plan, investors will spend time checking out the details you should have taken care of previously, and this could add several more months to the fundraising process. If any other part of the plan has not been thoroughly researched, equity investors will take their good old time with their due diligence efforts to ensure they are protected.

If you present investors with a plan that is thoroughly researched, you should receive your money in a reasonable period of time, a matter of a few months. If you have been trying for a year and still don't have money after pursuing a number of financing sources, don't blame the investors. The odds are there is something seriously wrong with your proposal. That's why it is critical along the way to ask potential investors what you can do to improve your proposal.

Loaded Questions Investors Ask

During early meetings potential investors are not only focusing on your company's prospects; they are also trying to ascertain certain critical facts about you: What makes you tick, how honest you are, how ethical you are, and how committed you are to this deal. Obviously they will not ask you about these issues in a point-blank manner. Rather, they will subtly ask you some "loaded" questions. Some of these questions may be offhand or casual, asked while you are walking down the hall or driving to a meeting. They may seem trivial, but they are far from it. Your answers may well make the difference between receiving funding or a polite "no" from the investors.

Following are some examples of the loaded questions investors might ask. Their questions might be worded differently, but the intent of the questions will be similar. Try your hand with each of the following questions. Only after you have formed your own response should you read my comments. In each case, one of the investors is speaking informally to an entrepreneur whose deal is being considered:*

Jim, I am truly impressed with the background and experience of your managment team. Individuals of your caliber would have no problem securing excellent positions in industry, would they?

*These questions have been adapted from an example in Richard M. White, *The Entrepreneur's Manual* (Radnor, Penn.: Chilton Books, 1977), pp. 214–216.

If you agree with the investor, you may have created a serious blunder. Now the investor might begin to wonder if, when the going gets rough, you will throw in the towel and leave for one of those cushy, secure jobs, leaving the investor high and dry. This is one reason that equity investors want you "tied into the deal," meaning they expect you to put a hunk of equity into the company as well, equity you would forfeit if you fled. Second, they are going to want you to execute an employment agreement guaranteeing you will not move to a competitive company for the next five years.

Here's another loaded question:

Sharon, you have an excellent track record as a business manager. I have a unique proposition for you. I have another company we have already funded that is starting to grow and really needs a top-notch CEO. If we aren't able to put your deal together, would you be interested in this challenge? It comes with a package including annual compensation of $90,000 plus a performance bonus, hefty stock options, an executive car, and country club membership.

You are being tested to determine your commitment to your own company. If you would sell out to the highest bidder, then why should any venture capitalist risk an investment in you? Respond to this one wrong, and you will never see this investor's dollars. Here's another one some entrepreneurs set themselves up for:

Rob, in our study of your plan, we see that you have budgeted starting salaries for the two top officers of $60,000 annually. Yet your résumés indicate you are both earning around $35,000 in your current positions. It seems to me you are trying to use our deal to give yourselves a significant raise.

Oops! Something this obvious could blow your whole deal. Besides, would you really be foolish enough to give the investors additional stock in your company just to finance your salary? *Additional fringe benefits and perks should come out of profits, not investment monies.* If you really belive in what you are doing, you should be sacrificing significant salary until there are profits to cover it.

Don't try to counter by saying, "because that's what our counterparts in this industry are being paid" unless you (1) already have their experience and (2) are already showing profits that are typical for the industry. I strongly suggest you set your starting salaries in close proximity to what you were making before you ventured out on your own. You want to show your commitment to investors. Budget appropriate increases as the company shows a profit, and you won't be placed in the awkward position of having to field this one.

Beware of this loaded question:

> Kathy, in our investigation thus far we are very impressed, with the exception of one of the members of your management team. We believe your company is seriously weak in the marketing area. Before we could agree to provide funds for the company, you need to replace this person with a strong marketing executive. How do you feel about this?

This can be a tough one, because frequently the investors are not trying to trick you; they may have a very real concern about a weakness in a key managment area. Unless you correct this perceived deficiency, they are not about to invest in your company. They probably have some candidates lined up for you to interview.

However, if you are positive that you have an extremely qualified person in this position, then this is probably a trick question. The investors are trying to measure your confidence in (and commitment to) your management team. After all, if you don't have confidence in your own team, then why should they?

How would you answer the following loaded question?

> Larry, what do you plan to do when you retire?

As strange as it may seem, some entrepreneurs lead their companies energetically through the tough start-up phase, only to become complacent and flounder when they start to make money. Investors will probably test your sensitivity to this tendency by asking questions like the one above. If you indicate by your response that you are currently interested in retirement, equity investors may not be interested in you. I would suggest that your best response is to tell them you are not interested in retirement now because you are focused on ensuring the continuing success of your company. Add a closing comment that maybe you'll start worrying about retirement in another 25 years.

Here's another trick question:

Jerry, before our meeting on your company's proposal, I have a small favor to ask: I have a cousin who is a supplier to your industry, and I'd appreciate it if you could see that he gets at least a small part of your business. If his quotes are a little high, just tell me what the others are bidding, and I'll see that he matches it. That way we can help him out without it costing you anything extra. Okay?

Investors must believe you are ethical. At some time during your discussions, they will devise a test for your ethical standards. This test can take many forms, some subtle and some not so subtle, such as the question above.

If you agree to this request, you are a dead duck. If investors think you are even slightly unethical, they will not touch your deal with a ten-foot pole. If you are ethical, just respond with the answer that you know is right.

Watch our for the trick question hidden in this monologue:

Chris, I envy you. You've created something our society really needs, and you are growing an exciting company. I sit here riding herd on our investment money, putting it in and taking it out of companies, while you guys have created something from nothing. I sure wish I was in your shoes . . .

Listen politely, but if you ever agree that money isn't an important commodity, you've just lost the investor's interest. After the monologue is over, you had better tell this individual that, although he or she is entitled to that opinion, your two organizations obviously have serious philosophical differences concerning money. Because you are focused on money as an important commodity, perhaps you should be looking elsewhere for financing, for an investor who shares your philosophy. That response should put this issue to bed.

During your continuing dialogue with potential investors, you should remain aware that they are continually evaluating the enthusiasm and commitment of your management team. Prior to each meeting, you should psych your team up, review your objectives for the meeting, and prepare the team to handle any loaded questions that might arise during the session.

Appetite-Whetting Strategies

I've discussed many ways in which you can develop a strong case for your plan before investors. Now I want to talk about some special tech-niques you can use to achieve an even greater competitive advantage. Some of them can only be used in specialized cases, but if they work for you, use them. All is fair in love and war, and sometimes, securing investors's money is a lot like war.

These approaches can improve your chance for equity financing because they can make the equity investor want to participate. These creative strategies can give you the inside track to "yes," but they do require some early-stage planning for effective use.*

1. *Bring potential investors in early.* Bringing potential investors into your deal at an early stage is an excellent technique with a high success rate for securing funding. It can succeed with both venture cap-ital and private equity investors.

The idea is that you target the investors prior to launching the com-pany. Visit with them during the formative stages of your business, inviting them to advise you from the conception stage. Include them in the screening and selection of your management team. Let them cri-tique your business plan, and allow them to participate in key deci-sions. You might offer them a seat on your board, as well as a "right of first refusal" on first-round equity financing. Because they have been working with you since inception, when the time is right for equity financing they will probably be ready to play.

Another twist is to initiate this strategy by personally interviewing a number of potential equity investors. Instead of asking them to choose

---

*Several of these techniques have been adapted from *ibid.*, pp. 231–233.

your company, you are turning the tables and conducting an interview for the purpose of determining which of them you will select. You should conduct this screening process as if they were going to be an integral part of your management team. Ask penetrating questions to ascertain what they could contribute when problems arise. When you make your selection, continue to work with this group during the development phase, keep them appraised of your progress, and let them know well in advance when you will be submitting a plan.

If you already have an existing business, it is obviously too late to bring in potential investors during the conceptual stage. However, if you anticipate the need for equity capital in the future, you should still consider approaching potential equity investors well in advance of your planned expansion. Solicit several of them to advise you in your marketing research, business plan development, and pro forma financials. When you are finally ready to pursue equity capital, you are assured of their interest in your plan as well as their understanding of your markets. Thus, you are guaranteed serious consideration from these investors.

2. *Leverage partial commitments.* If you are trying to raise $800,000, and you receive a commitment from one investor for $200,000 subject to a commitment for the balance, get a commitment letter from the investor. Then use this letter to attract other investors and possible SBA loans. If you get another investor to commit $100,000 on the same basis, add that investor's letter to the pile. Having commitment letters to show potential investors establishes far more credibility that just telling them you have commitments.

3. *Use investors as a test site.* This strategy is not always applicable, but when it is I've seen it work miracles. I've seen companies manufacturing innovative office products and new telephone electronic message systems lend prototypes of their newly developed products to venture capital firms for evaluation in their offices (caution: this is only effective if the prototypes work well). If the product is a time/money saver for the firm, and if it is backed by a strong plan, the firm will probably want to invest.

4. *Play the celebrity game.* Try to attract a well-known figure to your board—an ex-governor or senator, a Nobel prize winner, or high-profile business executive. Keep in mind you are not just looking for "glitter." You want a board member who can contribute expertise to the

company. This strategy won't guarantee funding, but because equity capitalists are also human, this key personage may sway a close vote on financing your company to a "yes," because the investors want to rub shoulders with your celebrity.

5. *Seek investors when your company is profitable.* I mentioned this in passing during an earlier section, but it is worthy of special attention. If your company is already profitable and if management is experienced, you represent far less risk to potential investors. Therefore, your company will be more appealing to them, and you will be able to raise far more money for far less effort and equity. One way to achieve this posture is to scale back your start-up plans and initially finance with an SBA loan and several private equity partners until your company is profitable, then expand with the help of venture capital. In that way, you will be able to maintain the lion's share of ownership.

6. *Develop a prototype.* This strategy is always applicable if you have a product as opposed to a service. With a functioning prototype to observe, investors will be interested. Without it, they will be turned off fast. Ignoring the need for a prototype is one of the most common "sinkholes" for early-stage entrepreneurs trying to raise capital. I strongly recommend you do not approach any professional organizations for equity until you have at least a demonstrable prototype. Otherwise, you lose credibility, and fast. If you do not yet have a working prototype, your company is at the stage known as "pre-start-up" or "seed." Equity capital funds for seed stage companies are almost nonexistent. If you don't have a rich uncle, your best bet would be to secure an SBA loan coupled with several private equity partners until you build a prototype, at which point you will have advanced to the start-up stage and can approach major equity investors.

But What If It's a Banker?

Thus far in this chapter we have focused primarily on equity investors. However, part of your plans may include a bank loan. Many of the same points discussed in this chapter are equally applicable to bankers. As I discussed previously, if you are pursuing a start-up or an SBA loan, the banker will want to see the complete business plan as well. Otherwise the banker will be looking for a narrower *project* plan. If you are not using bank financing as part of the package, you should at least consider securing a line of credit with your bank to borrow against (the improved financial position you realized from securing equity financing will help you in seeking a line of credit).

Assuming you are trying for an SBA loan to supplement the equity capital portion of your package, the banker will be looking for many of the same elements as the equity investor is: a sound marketing program, an experienced management team, and a viable business plan.

The banker's perspective is usually different from that of the entrepreneur. Think of your business as a tree: Most potential borrowers spend their time pointing out the beautiful leaves, the majestic branches, and the solid trunk. What the banker is looking for is evidence of the strength of the root system supporting the tree. The banker wants to see stability, integrity, and a good reputation. Both the banker and the equity investor must be comfortable with your contingency plans: What if you walked out with their money today, launched the business, and a week later you were hit by a wayward truck and were killed? How would the business survive?

Your Stage and Your Sources

The current stage of your business will probably define the most likely sources of capital. Most novice entrepreneurs believe that an initial injection of cash is all they will need. They fail to realize that as they start to grow their company will require additional cash infusions to keep pace with the growth. The stages of company growth are reasonably well defined:

▪ *Seed financing* (highest risk). A company at this stage has little more than a concept to sell. Even if your product is based on a product similar to that of another company, as long as *your* product is only in your head and on paper, your company is at the seed stage. Money at this stage is typically for the purpose of developing a prototype and verifying the theory of operation and product profitability, along with appropriate marketing research. Probable sources of funds at this stage are personal loans, funds from individual investors, or the rarely seen seed-capital fund.

- *Start-up financing* (high risk). A company at this stage has a prototype product or service and requires financing to produce the product or service, as well as for market development and acquisition of additional key personnel. Probable sources of funds at this stage are start-up bank loans, individual equity investors, and a very few venture capital funds.

- *Second-Stage financing* (medium risk). A company at this stage has achieved initial market penetration and is generating significant cash flow (hopefully positive). Funds are usually required for operating capital. Probable sources of funds at this stage are additional bank loans and/or additional equity.

- *Third-Stage or expansion financing* (lower risk). A company at this stage has probably achieved an impressive track record, and additional funds are needed to keep up with significant growth. Probable sources of funds at this stage are additional bank loans and professional venture capital.

- *Fourth-Stage or mezzanine financing* (lower risk). With a company at this stage, the next financing options may involve going public through an initial public offering (IPO) or a merger or acquisition with another company in the industry. Funds are required to carry the company through to the next stage. Probable sources of funds at this stage are additional bank loans and professional venture capital or corporate investors.

- *Initial public offering*. At this stage, part of the company is sold to the general public. The equity raised is used to expand company operations. Some of management's shares of stock can be sold.

Once you have an established company on the road to profitability, here are some additional suggestions for funding sources:

- *Company operating profits*. The soundest (and cheapest) source of capital. Use this for bonuses, salary raises, management perquisites (perks), capital equipment, product development, expansion, and a portion of all other capital uses.

- *Additional debt capital*. Use this source to cover seasonal cash flow shortfall and/or conservative market expansion; it can also be used for low-risk operating capital (e.g., funds to expand an established business), accounts receivable and inventory financing, and equipment and real estate purchases.

▪ *Additional equity capital.* Seek these funds for rapid growth, significant market expansion, or moderate- or high-risk operating capital (e.g., funds for launching a new product line).

EXERCISE: Reviewing Your Fund-Raising Strategy

Now that you understand some additional realities of the capital marketplace, you may want to revise the fund-raising strategy you formulated in Chapter 6. Here are two rules of thumb by which to evaluate your strategy:

1. If you have an early-stage company and if you are looking for $100,000 or less, try for a combination of your own equity, an SBA (or other start-up) loan, and one or more local private equity investors.
2. If you are looking for $300,000 or more for a high-growth, high-profit company with experienced management, you are a definite candidate for equity investors and possibly a candidate for venture capital.

In either case, your company's best strategy will probably be a combination of several of the financing options I have discussed. If you have not already done so, you should contact the network you have now established (bankers, CPAs, etc.) along with the SBA, the small business division of your state's economic development organization, and the nearest Small Business Development Center (SBDC) to complete your list of alternative capital sources.

Once you have created your list of alternatives, you can review it along with your previous strategy to ascertain if any adjustment is warranted. Consider which one or combination of these alternatives represents the best strategy for your company. You may also want to contact several of these sources before finalizing your strategy.

Chances are you have an early-stage company and thus will be approaching investors with a somewhat anemic balance sheet. A "yes" from investors won't be based solely on what you have written in your plan; it will also be based on *you*. Whether or not you secure funding will depend on how effective you are at marketing yourself and your plan to potential investors. Which brings us to the next Microgenesis level.

LEVEL IX: *Market Your Plan Successfully, Attracting Capital on Your Terms*

Identifying Financiers' "Hot" Buttons

The most effective way to deal with investors involves understanding how they think, and what elements of a potential deal can "turn them on."

Bankers Only

Mark Twain once defined his philosophy of bankers in a single sentence: "Bankers will loan you an umbrella when the sun is shining and then want it back when the rains come." It is true that bankers are focused on absolute minimum risk, but Mark Twain was overstating the case a bit; they do want to be of service to their clients. To accomplish both of these potentially conflicting purposes, bankers will lend smaller amounts to new companies until they have accumulated sufficient collateral (which reduces the bank's monetary exposure) as well as longevity (which reduces the bank's statistical risk). SBA loans do not violate this statement, because the SBA steps in to provide additional collateral and to absorb some of the additional risk. If a start-up business has strong management and raises significant equity capital, banks may perceive early-stage risk to be sufficiently mitigated and may substantially increase the company's loan ceiling.

For a start-up loan, your banker will want to see a full business plan, but for continuing loans to existing business clients, your banker will only need to see a project plan. The project plan focuses only on

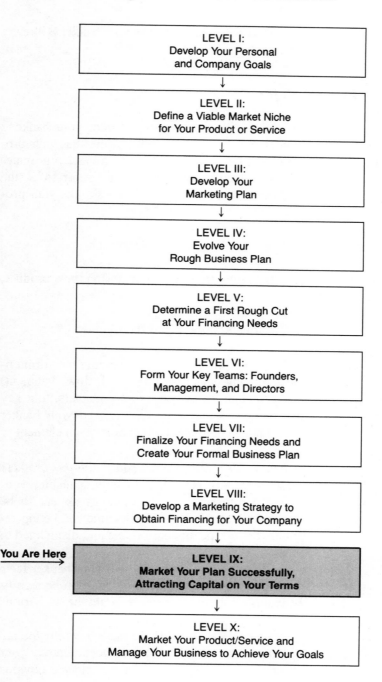

LEVEL I:
Develop Your Personal
and Company Goals

↓

LEVEL II:
Define a Viable Market Niche
for Your Product or Service

↓

LEVEL III:
Develop Your
Marketing Plan

↓

LEVEL IV:
Evolve Your
Rough Business Plan

↓

LEVEL V:
Determine a First Rough Cut
at Your Financing Needs

↓

LEVEL VI:
Form Your Key Teams: Founders,
Management, and Directors

↓

LEVEL VII:
Finalize Your Financing Needs and
Create Your Formal Business Plan

↓

LEVEL VIII:
Develop a Marketing Strategy to
Obtain Financing for Your Company

↓

You Are Here →   **LEVEL IX:**
Market Your Plan Successfully,
Attracting Capital on Your Terms

↓

LEVEL X:
Market Your Product/Service and
Manage Your Business to Achieve Your Goals

the specific activity requiring financing, because your banker is already familiar with the company.

The 3 + 4 + 3 + 3 Method

Regardless of which of these categories you fall into, your banker's analysis of your proposal will be extensive. To ensure that your proposal trips the right triggers, I recommend that you review your material from the banker's perspective, utilizing what I refer to as the 3 + 4 + 3 + 3 method. If you touch all thirteen bases solidly, your proposal should have a strong shot at approval:

First Group (3). Your proposal should clearly state:

1. Why the requested funds are needed (expansion, new product, etc.)
2. How these funds will be utilized, in detail
3. Why you believe this proposal is not risky

Second Group (4). Your proposal's accompanying pro forma financials (balance sheet, income statement, and cash flow statement) must be credible. When the banker analyzes your financials, four key elements will be investigated to ensure credibility, and your banker must be left with a strong affirmative feeling regarding each element:

1. *Can management achieve the forecast sales with this project?* If your forecast sales are perceived to be reasonable, your banker will feel comfortable; if the numbers appear to be clearly overoptimistic and not based on sound marketing research, your banker will feel uncomfortable and disinclined to lend you money.
2. *Are the forecast project costs reasonable?* If your banker feels that you have estimated costs poorly and there will be significant cost overruns, your loan request could be in serious trouble.
3. *Will the project be completed within the projected time frame?* If your plans are well thought out and documented, your banker should be content. But if you have neglected obvious

contingencies and have made outlandish assumptions, your banker will be very nervous about lending you money.

4. *Will the project generate adequate positive cash flow to repay the loan?* If your banker is comfortable with the first three elements and believes you are running a frugal operation, you should pass this point; however, if you failed any of the others, or you are perceived to be wasteful in your spending practices, you may fail here as well.

Third Group (3). Your banker will apply three tests against your proposal for the purpose of ensuring a low risk factor:

1. *What collateral is pledged for this loan?* You had better have sufficient unencumbered assets to pledge against this loan. Otherwise, you are wasting your time in requesting a bank loan (except for an SBA-guaranteed loan, which can mitigate this requirement).
2. *What is the extent of your proposal's earning power?* Previously you were ensuring adequate cash flow to service the loan. However, your banker must also be convinced there is sufficient cash flow to repay the loan with a generous margin of safety to cover the unforeseen contingencies that inevitably develop.
3. *What is your management team's experience?* Your proposal must give the lender a feeling of confidence in your management team's business ability and integrity (even if the team consists of you alone).

Fourth Group (3). Presenting your proposal to the bank is clearly a marketing task, because the purpose of your effort is to sell your banker on three major factors:

1. Your proposal
2. Your company
3. Yourself

If your banker has a problem with one of these last three factors, it could scuttle your application. On the other hand, if your bank has firm confidence in all three of these factors, the loan committee will tend to look more favorably at a weak balance sheet.

If you pass solidly on all thirteen key points, you should probably have your loan approved. If this is your first major business loan, you may be overwhelmed by the multipage loan agreement. I strongly urge you to read every word of the agreement and any ancillary documents. If you have any questions or you would like more time to study the material, you should inform your banker that you want your attorney to review the document. Don't worry. Unlike the deal offered by the high-pressure car salesperson, this one won't vanish in the next 24 hours.

Learn from John's experience: John, a young electronics entrepreneur with an existing company, was experiencing cash flow problems but was still able to get a badly needed loan for operating capital. He was so excited when the loan officer placed the loan agreement in front of him that he signed it, took his money, and left. He was on top of the world.

Ninety days later, when the bank reviewed his latest financial statement, he was called in for a meeting. There was a specific clause in the loan agreement prohibiting any use of the proceeds to pay debts incurred prior to the date of the loan. Almost half of the funds advanced had been used to pay old debts, because John had never bothered to read the agreement. The bank called the note, and the company was sold. To this day, John doesn't think he did anything wrong. But he violated his signed commitment, and as a result he no longer has a company. It's hard to fault the bank. After all, from the bank's perspective, if John had violated one obvious requirement, what other rules had he overlooked in the running of the business?

In a mid-1980s survey by *Inc. Magazine,** bankers were asked for the major reasons they rejected small-business loan applications. The most frequently cited reasons were too much debt, too little equity, lack of collateral, inability to demonstrate repayment potential, and inadequate financial information.

In the same study, bankers were also asked for major problems in dealing with small businesses. The most frequent responses to this question included too little equity, inadequate records, incapable management, and inadequate financial knowledge.

---

*Adapted from data reported in Jay Finegan, "Are Bigger Banks Bad for Small Business?" in *The Best of* Inc. *Guide to Finding Capital* (New York: Prentice-Hall Press, 1988).

Finally, when the bankers were asked for the characteristics of the *ideal* small-business borrower, their most frequent responses included adequate equity (capitalization), experienced management, sound financial practices, timely, well-prepared financials, and a positive profit history.

Equity Investors Only

Equity investors will never be as excited about your product or service as you are, because investors and entrepreneurs are not motivated by the same forces:

- You want a successful, dynamic company and the recognition that comes with it. You accept their capital as a necessary ingredient to attain this goal.
- They want to make money, and they accept an investment in your company as a means to that end.

Never lose sight of the above point. Investors invest in you because, *and only because,* they expect to make money. You probably will show losses during the first two years, but your overall equity growth should *average* at least the aforementioned 25% per year for equity investors to be interested. But beware: If you project a growth curve that is too rapid, equity investors will pass off your projections as pipe dreams. You must be able to defend your sales projections on the basis of sound market research (and if you can get some of this research and analysis performed by unbiased third parties not affiliated with your business, this will lend additional credibility).

If you have done the previous exercises well, you have arrived at a business plan that equity investors will accept as your company's "business bible." If you have not, they will perceive it to be only a sales tool to attract their money and they will not be interested.

In looking at your plan, equity investors will determine a rough estimate of the probable value of your company five years from now. A quick and dirty method of computing this value for purposes of your equity presentation is as follows: Take your projected net profit after taxes at the end of year 5. This figure represents that year's contribution to the company's equity or net worth. Let's assume your net profit in year 5 was $450,000. Then the investor may compute several estimates of the potential value of your company at the end of year 5.

- For a conservative estimate, the investor may multiply net profit times a factor of 10 ($450,000 × 10 = a conservative valuation of $4,500,000).
- For a desired estimate, the investor may multiply net profit times a factor of 20 (450,000 × 20 = a desired valuation of $9,000,000).
- If you are in a high-growth industry, the investor may multiply net profit times an even higher multiple (even 50 or 100) to yield a best-possible valuation.

However, for all payback computations, your investor will probably opt for the conservative valuation figure. Here's how it works: In the above example, let's assume you are expanding a business known as the ACME Company. You are seeking $400,000 in new equity, and you are willing to give up 30% of your stock. An equity investor may judge that your company could conservatively be worth $4,500,000 in five years. The investor's portion of your company would be worth $1,350,000 (30% of $4,500,000). That's an appreciation of the investor's equity over the five-year period of 238%, or an average of 48% per year. It could also be viewed as an investment growth of 3.38 to 1 (computed from the ratio 1,350 to 400).

As we mentioned earlier, most private equity investors like to see at least 25% annualized growth. Thus, this typical investor would probably look favorably on the above example of 48%. However, a typical professional venture capitalist is probably looking for a minimum investment growth for an early-stage company of at least 5 to 1 over a five-year period, or an average annual return of 80%. Therefore, this deal may not interest professional venture capital firms.

Keep in mind that the numbers in the above paragraph are only guidelines. I suggest you always ask your potential equity investors (whether individual investors or venture capitalists) what is the rate of return they expect in their deals. Then you'll know if you are in the ballpark for serious consideration.

Even though a new company or an expansion represents risk, the equity investor must be left with no doubt your company will succeed. If any doubt exists, the equity investor will pass, at least for the time being.

To gain this necessary feeling of confidence, an equity investor ideally wants to see a strong business plan, experienced management, convincing financials, and an element of something unique in your deal. Rarely do equity investors participate in companies that appear to be mere clones of other businesses. They want to see sizable growth and large profits, and this mandates creativity.

Equity investors also want a comfort factor with the market analysis as well as your proposed marketing plan. You can expect them to challenge you to tell them why your selected sales method is better than others, and you'd better have a solid answer.

Don't try to snow equity investors. If you don't know the answer to a question, admit it. Then tell them you will get the answer for them, and do so in a timely manner.

Equity investors don't expect you to know everything, but they do want to see honesty, commitment, and integrity. You would do well to have references who can attest to the strength of these characteristics in you. If you have had past failures, don't hide them. Explain them and tell the investors what you have learned from them. Show me an entrepreneur who has had one success, and you have probably found a person with more luck than knowledge. Show me an entrepreneur who may have had a couple of failures, and you've found someone who has amassed a great deal of business knowledge.

Financing Alternatives

Are there any "surefire," quick, and easy techniques to bypass any of the above hassle? No, and if you meet someone who tells you there are, you had better watch out. However, there are some unique ways to finance a business that I have seen used with some success, but they still require considerable effort. Here are a number of them for your consideration:

Private Offering of Nonvoting Preferred Stock to Customers

If you have any customers who have expressed an interest in an investment, you might offer them this option as a way of raising funds without giving up control of the company. You could set the stock to pay monthly or quarterly dividends. As an example, you might set up this class of stock with a dividend payment based on a 16% annual interest rate plus a 3% share of net earnings. Also, you should consider offering the shareholders a guaranteed "buyback" plan, whereby after two years the company would repurchase an individual investor's stock on the shareholder's demand, paying par value on 7% of the shares each month over a period of 14 months. Your attorney can outline the ramifications of this approach for your business and help you determine whether or not it is appropriate.

Equity R&D Partnerships

Several areas of the country (usually in the vicinity of major cities) have active equity R&D partnership funds. These funds can facilitate a partnership between your young company and the equity partner (or partners). Equity investors who participate in these R&D partnerships are typically in the higher tax brackets and are able to use the early losses of the partnership as deductions against ordinary income. Later, when profits appear to be forthcoming, the partnership interests are converted to equity in a new corporation, based on a formula set when the deal was first negotiated. Because of the offsetting early-year deductions, investors in R&D partnerships may be willing to accept as much as 50% less equity in your company than they would under a conventional venture capital deal. Most of the Big Six accounting firms have specialists who can fill you in on the applicability of this partnership to your business.

An Existing Shell Corporation

There are a number of inactive corporations that still have assets (in many cases, cash) and shareholders. Investors and brokers are generally aware of the existence of these corporations. If you find a suitable one, your attorney can negotiate a deal whereby your company is merged into the shell corporation, and you acquire the corporate assets. This is a quick and relatively easy way of forming a corporation without going through the hassle of a public offering. However, you also acquire all the shareholders and reporting procedures that come with the package (see the list item below on public stock offering for additional comments). And if there are any skeletons in the shell corporation's closet, you inherit those as well.

Sale-Leaseback of Assets

Although we covered equipment leases in Chapter 6, the topic of sale-leasebacks is worth noting as a specific alternative way of raising capital. Should your company have any recently purchased assets or other assets of significant value, you may want to investigate the sale-leaseback as a method of generating capital for your company.

Under the sale-leaseback mechanism, you sell an asset to a leasing company, receiving cash for the market value, and you sign an agreement to lease the asset for a number of years. At the end of that time, you usually have the option to renew the lease, purchase the asset for fair market value, or return the asset to the leasing company for disposal. This is a useful alternative for solving near-term cash problems.

Zero-Coupon Bond

Also referred to as a zero, this is a debt instrument designed to free the borrower from having to service the debt through periodic cash payments. With a zero-coupon bond, no payment is due until maturity, which could be as high as 25 years. The borrower acquires the funds interest-free, but at a substantial discount from the face value of the bond. For example, a five-year, $3 million zero might net the company $1.9 million. The company will then owe the bondholder the full face value, $3 million, at maturity.

A zero is usually utilized by companies with an existing equity/asset base and an experienced management team. The more risk perceived by the lenders, the more bonus kickers the lenders will ask for, such as stock warrants and convertible debentures. Check with your attorney or CPA regarding the appropriateness of zero-coupon bonds for your business.

Public Stock Offering

Be careful here. A public offering may sound like a great deal, but this strategy brings with it a great deal of time, expense, and headaches you may not be able to afford. Once you have stockholders, they won't just give you free rein; you will have to concentrate on satisfying them *and* running your business at the same time. If you still want to consider this option, you will need a strong enough plan to convince an investment banker to participate. Here are some points to consider before pursuing a public stock offering:

- What is your objective? If it is to acquire capital for expansion, acquisition, or debt repayment, I recommend you consider other options, because potential buyers will be harder to convince. On the other hand, if your objective is to increase your company's equity, going public may be the best way.
- You can't arbitrarily set a price for your stock. The stock price will be determined by your balance sheet. You should have earnings of at least $1 million per year to avoid a low price per share on the offering.
- If you are seeking only $1–$2 million, locate a local investment banker with a single office and around a dozen brokers who deal with individual investors.
- If you are seeking $5 million or thereabouts, locate a regional investment banker with a number of offices in your area of the country.
- Nothing is free. Between legal and other expenses, plan on *up-front* fees running at least 10%–15% of the amount of the offering. Furthermore, count on delays in getting your money, because these inevitably occur.
- Try to secure a "firm" or guaranteed underwriting rather than a "best efforts" underwriting. "Firm" means the underwriter will buy any shares not subscribed to by the public.
- For a creative twist, consider selling subordinated debt at the same time as your stock offering. This should minimize the expenses associated with putting both individual programs together.
- Once your business becomes a publicly held company, your actions are the concern of every stockholder. When a required report shows the company doing poorly, irate stockholders will be calling you; because they are owners, you will have to take the time to deal with them.
- You must deal with all the required reports for publicly held companies, disclosing many items previously kept confidential (such as salaries).
- Your ownership position could be diluted, and you may lose control of the company.

Your Financials Under the Magnifying Glass

Odds are you are not a financial whiz. Yet you have assembled a set of financial projections for your business that will be scrutinized and judged by financial experts. An experienced financial analyst is like a good psychiatrist—he or she can evaluate your financial projections and tell you more about yourself than you ever thought possible. This analyst will judge your business experience level, your financial expertise, and your propensity for risk taking, all from the tests and analyses performed on your pro formas.

Because of this, you would be wise to ensure that your financial projections deliver the right message. In this section, I'm going to discuss some of the actual tests that will be performed on your projections. There is always the temptation to bypass the management decisions, goals, and strategies you have already formulated, and simply "rig" your projections so they pass these tests. However, if you do this, you risk everything, because this type of approach is so obvious, it will be spotted immediately by a trained professional investor, and your plan will immediately be placed on the "return to sender" pile.

Let's take a look at some of the ratios investors will use to analyze the soundness of your business. The majority of the numbers used in the following examples came from the pro forma income statement and balance sheet examples in Figures 4-1 and 4-2.

A term that investors utilize frequently is *liquidity*. Liquidity may be viewed as the ability to pay your bills. It is one of the primary considerations of sound financial management. When an investor asks, "How liquid are you?" the question really is "What is the sum of your cash and those assets that can be readily turned into cash, which could be utilized to pay your debts?" The first few ratios I'll discuss are various measures of liquidity.

Current Ratio

The investor will examine your *current ratio*. This ratio answers the question, "Does the company have sufficient current assets to meet current debts, with a reasonable margin of safety against possible losses?"

The current ratio is defined as follows:

$$\frac{\text{Current assets}}{\text{Current liabilities}} = \frac{554,250}{262,400} = 2.11$$

Note that investors prefer a minimum ratio of 2.0. If your ratio is lower than this, you should do one or more of the following to raise it: Pay off some of your debts; replace short-term loans (less than one-year) with long-term loans; raise more equity through outside investment, or plow profits back into the business.

The data for the current ratio can also be expressed as a whole number. It is then known as net working capital, which is computed as current assets minus current liabilities. In our above example, net working capital = $291,850.

Bankers like to study this number over a period of time, to assess your company's ability to withstand unforeseen financial crises. If there is a concern, your bank loan may be tied to a requirement to maintain net working capital above a specific minimum amount.

Acid Test Ratio

One of the best measures of liquidity is known as the *acid test ratio,* or *quick ratio.* It is defined as quick assets divided by current liabilities. What are quick assets? The assets you own that can be turned into cash quickly. Quick assets are determined by subtracting inventory from your current assets, because inventory is difficult to convert rapidly into cash. In computing the acid test ratio, you are asking the question, "If my sales should suddenly vanish overnight, could I still meet my debt obligations?"

The acid-test ratio (or quick ratio) is computed as follows:

$$\frac{(\text{Quick assets})}{\text{Current liabilities}} = \frac{(\text{Current assets} - \text{inventory})}{\text{Current liabilities}}$$

$$\frac{554,250 - 209,870}{262,400} = 1.31$$

You should strive for a quick ratio between 1.0 and 2.0. Bankers will want to see a ratio of 1.0 or greater. In general, the higher perceived risk they see in your business, the higher they would like to see this ratio. Their focus is on prudence and safety.

On the other hand, if this ratio is too high, it also indicates poor management, because you have idle cash lying around. Equity investors will not tolerate that situation. It is in your best business interest to keep the business strong and trim, rather than cash fat, so strive for a happy medium, probably no higher than the ratio in the example above. Remember, if you have too much cash, you are not making this resource work for the company.

Like the previous ratio, the quick ratio can also be expressed as a whole number, referred to as net quick assets and computed as quick assets minus current liabilities. In our example above, net quick assets = \$81,980. This is an approximation of the immediate cash you would have if you were forced to liquidate.

By the way, notice that last word, *liquidate*. This does not translate to "go out of business." What it means is "turning the assets of your business into cash," which you may do periodically with some of your assets even if you aren't going out of business.

Inventory Turns

If your company is involved in manufacturing and/or distribution, investors will want to determine how fast your inventory is rotating (how quickly old product is being sold and new product is being restocked). This rate of turnover is called *inventory turns*.

There are several accepted ways to compute this figure, which is calculated for a specific period of time (month, quarter, year). One commonly used method is to divide your cost of sales by your average inventory, where average inventory is determined by adding the starting inventory for the period and the ending inventory for the period together and dividing by 2. Here is an example:

$$\frac{\text{Cost of sales}}{\text{Average inventory}} = \frac{608,300}{196,210} = 3.10$$

In the above example, you are "turning" your inventory 3.10 times per period. Obviously you want this number to be as high as possible, but in certain industries seasonal fluctuations are to be expected. Most manufacturing companies fall into the 3–6 range; however, some well-managed companies are able to achieve a figure of 20 or better.

If you track inventory turns on a monthly basis, you will be able to spot negative trends before they become serious problems.

Sales/Fixed Assets

This is a ratio of particular interest to equity investors. By comparing your *fixed assets* to your *net sales,* they can determine how leverage-conscious you are (in other words, how well your fixed assets are contributing to sales). Owning your building may seem like a good idea, but if your company is young and growing and this transaction doesn't contribute to sales and profits, of what value is it?

$$\frac{\text{Net sales}}{\text{Fixed assets}} = \frac{1,104,330}{348,300} = 3.17$$

A typical range for this ratio with a growing company is between 5 and 10.

Fixed assets represent one category upon which bankers and equity investors differ. Bankers prefer bricks, machinery, inventories, and property. They want to ensure that your company has adequate collateral for future loans. They also believe these assets represent barriers to your competition, barriers other companies will have to match in order to compete effectively. Following your banker's desires will increase your fixed assets and therefore reduce this ratio.

Equity capitalists, on the other hand, don't want to see your money tied up in buying buildings and equipment. They want you to leverage your money by leasing buildings and equipment, as well as maintaining minimum inventories and subcontracting out a portion of your production effort. This strategy frees up more of your capital for marketing activities (after all, would you rather have buildings or profits?). Following this strategy will decrease fixed assets and thus increase this ratio.

The best strategy for you probably depends on the stage of your business: At an early, unprofitable stage, you had best focus on using your dollars for marketing, while at a later profitable stage, you should begin to accumulate fixed assets.

Profit Margins

There are three *profit margin* ratios you should be intimately familiar with:

Gross Profit Margin:

$$\frac{\text{Sales} - \text{Cost of sales}}{\text{Sales}} = \frac{\text{Gross profit}}{\text{Sales}}$$

$$= \frac{496,030}{1,104,330} = .45 \text{ (or 45\%)}$$

(Most companies should ensure that this margin is above 50%.)

Operating Profit Margin:

$$\frac{\text{Operating profit}}{\text{Sales}} = \frac{161,780}{1,104,330} = .15 \text{ (or 15\%)}$$

Note: (Operating profit = Gross profit - Operating expenses).

Net Profit Margin:

$$\frac{\text{Net profit}}{\text{Sales}} = \frac{107,420}{1,104,330} = .10 \text{ (or 10\%)}$$

If any of these ratios is too low (or too high) compared to the average in your industry, expect to have your sales figures, your cost of sales, and your operating expenses challenged by investors. This does not mean that you are wrong, but you had better have valid reasons (based on sound research) for deviating from the norms.

Return on Investment

For equity investors (as well as business owners), one of the most useful measures of profitability is *return on investment* (or *ROI*). This is normally computed as:

$$\frac{\text{Net profit}}{\text{Investment}} = \frac{107,420}{280,000} = .38 \text{ (or 38\%)}$$

The above net profit figure is for the period being computed (year, quarter, etc.), and the investment figure is the total investment in the company to date. The resultant percentage figure indicates how much investors "earned" on their investment in your company during the period. In a similar manner, you can also calculate return on sales (sales as the denominator) or return on equity (equity as the denominator) if desired.

Now that I've presented a number of ratios, let me qualify my comments by emphasizing that these ratios and their desired ranges are only rough guidelines. You may run into trouble when potential investors compare your ratios with typical ratios for your industry.* You should have already asked your banker to provide you with the ratios for your industry prior to submission of your plan. If your financials represent a serious deviation, you will be asked to justify your results. Because your numbers should be based upon the strong foundation you developed during the previous levels, you should be able to produce your data, analysis, and assumptions for the investors. If your logic is sound, potential investors will likely accept it.

Eight "What Ifs" and How to Handle Them

1. *What if you are trying to close a deal, but you appear to be at an impasse with the investors?* Listen to what they are saying. Then swallow your pride for a minute, put yourself in their shoes, and try to determine if their approach makes strategic sense. All too often, inexperienced enterpreneurs believe investors are trying to take advantage of them, when they are actually making a very reasonable offer. They may be asking for more because, with their experience, they perceive greater risk than you do, and let's face it, you are not an unbiased source!

A novice company executive came to me for advice on raising debt capital for his new company. He had been trying to secure an equity loan (a loan where you sweeten the deal by offering stock options as an enticement for lending the money) for more than a year, without success. He was armed with a good product but a weak plan. He believed funding to be imminent and did not want to rework his plan.

I suggested several strategies for him to pursue. Of particular difficulty was the fact that he did not want to sacrifice more than 25% equity, even though his company was in the start-up stage.

---

*Most often they will use the *RMA Annual Statement Studies* as a guide. This volume is published and updated annually by Robert Morris Associates, One Liberty Place, Philadelphia, Penn. 19103.

Three months later he announced that a Chicago venture capital firm had offered him a $200,000 loan to be paid back as $1 million at the end of five years. If you put a pencil to those numbers, you'll find this is in line with our previously discussed venture capital guidelines for risky start-ups. Here was a venture firm willing to participate in this executive's business without asking for any equity. Yet this man turned down the firm's very reasonable offer without talking further. As a result, he is penniless today, with a paper company that never got launched, and still blaming the investors for his mistakes.

2. *What if you have an established business, are looking for an equity loan or loan guarantee, but your potential investors believe your projections are overstated and want a larger equity kicker as a result?*

- One option (discussed previously) is to accept the investor's terms but insist on an equity buy-back clause in the agreement. As long as you perform according to your projections, you will be entitled to repurchase shares from the investor at a preset price per share, until you achieve the percentage ownership you originally proposed. A possible corollary is to have additional nonvoting stock issued to the investors (thereby they enjoy financial rewards but not control) or to retain the option, not to repurchase the investor's stock, but to acquire additional shares subject to your performance until your percentage ownership reaches your target.
- Another option eliminates equity ownership for investors but guarantees them profit sharing. Configure the deal as a revenue-participation certificate (or RPC). Think of an RPC as a royalty on revenues. It must be structured by your attorney so as not to appear as a dividend. Here's how it works: Let's say your investor wants 20% ownership of your company in exchange for a loan or guarantee. Simply translate that desire into 20% of your projected pretax profit on sales. If projecting average pretax profit was $500,000, the investor would receive $100,000. The RPC should run for a specific period of time that is acceptable to both parties.

3. *What if an equity investor likes your start-up deal but insists that you invest $10,000 of your own money in the deal?* The investors

expect you to be at some risk along with them. This can be a problem if you have no funds and no ability to raise any. If you cannot provide cash for your share of participation, consider one of the following:

- If you truly believe your projections, offer the investor this alternative: The investor receives 100% of the equity in the company, and you receive an option to acquire 51% of total authorized shares in 5–10 years, at 150% of the investor's cost, with the funds going to the company. This option could be adjusted downward in price, e.g., to 100% of investor's cost if it is exercised earlier, or it could be placed on a sliding scale subject to the performance of the company.
- Here's another option: The equity investor loans you $10,000, with your company's stock and the product pledged to the investor as collateral.
- Alternatively, sign over all rights, including products, patents, and trade names, to the company.
- Offer a personal guarantee against the investor's note (with your home or other assets as collateral).
- Offer to provide a guarantee to the investor to the extent that retained earnings fall short of projections. If they fall short, you pay investor.

4. *What if the investors insist on total control of the board of directors?* Enterpreneurs are very uneasy about giving up board control. If your management team consists largely of novices, the investors may insist on it. Otherwise, try the following tactic: Set the size of your board of directors at five people, with the investors receiving two of the five seats. Your investment agreement should then list "events of default" (such as default in payments on debentures, loans, or provisions of the agreement; bankruptcy; judgments; failure; or loss of key executives). If written notice is given and these faults are not corrected by management within a specific time frame, the investors have the right to appoint an additional two members to the board, giving them control.

5. *What if you and the equity investor disagree on the amount of equity to be offered in exchange for financing?* One way to limit the equity an investor receives is to structure the deal with the equity capital being infused in monthly (or other periodic) installments over a period

of time. These are to be exercised at the entrepreneur's option, with a block of shares reserved for the investor. Whenever management asks for additional capital, the company must give up additional equity. This structure (similar in many ways to a bank line of credit) gives management a strong incentive to achieve positive cash flow rapidly. It also discourages management's purchase of unnecessary equipment, because managers won't want to sacrifice the additional shares of stock required for the additional capital.

6. *What if you are seeking an investment for fixed assets?* A potential alternative that will help you to retain equity is to have the investor purchase the equipment and lease it to your company, rather than providing the capital for the company to do so. This option is also attractive to the investor because if the company defaults, the investor recovers the assets with far less hassle.

7. *What if an investor appears concerned there may be some serious, unknown, or undisclosed liabilities in your existing business?* These liabilities may be sufficient to discourage any investment. For example, let's say one of the assets in your company is a building that you purchased. This building and your company are currently located in a little town of 2,000 people in upstate New York. It's a $10 million building, and if your company goes belly up, it's unlikely that anyone else in that small town will buy the building. This potential liability, if it is not overcome, could easily cause an investor to utter a polite no.

One way to overcome such a potential liability and protect the investor is to create a new corporation free from the encumbrances of the present company. This will take some effort on the part of your attorney as well as concurrence from your creditors, but if it keeps the company from going out of business, it may be a good alternative for all sides.

Here's how this scenario works: Your attorney forms a new corporation that holds title to the assets transferred from the old corporation, but none of the liabilities. These assets are cleanly transferred in exchange for some consideration (which must be satisfactory to both owners and creditors). Thus investors can rest easy. The skeletons in the old closet are replaced with a new closet.

8. *What if earlier lenders have all the traditional assets and entrepreneur's guarantees (and possibly all the shares of the company) tied up as collateral?* Consider having the new investor purchase all other

critical but unencumbered assets of the company as security. This is accomplished at the time the new loan is entered into. The investor then contributes these assets for use by the company.

For example: Purchase the sole right to use the company's name, exclusive rights to all patents, exclusive rights to the customer list, full distribution rights for the product, and any improvements to the product.

The investor should also grant the entrepreneur the right to reacquire these assets for the same sum paid for them by the investor, after the loan has been repaid.

A Few Fiscal Fragments

Remember that your relationship with your financial partners is not a passing thing. You are probably going to be partners for years to come. In general, as long as you meet projections or can adequately explain deviations and take corrective action, your partners will let you run the business. In addition, equity investors are usually willing to give you help when you ask for it.

If you have solid financial controls, investors will be impressed, because there is always the concern that some member of the management team might run off with some of their funds. Eliminate this concern by requiring that company checks always be signed by two members of the management team: you (so you maintain control) and another management team member. Have your bank print two signature lines on your checks, along with the words "Authorized Representative" above the signature lines.

Mix your capital sources. Don't put all of your eggs in one basket. What if you do a deal with a single venture capital firm and suddenly the firm is sold or management changes? The firm's attitude toward your company could change as well. An added advantage of having more than one capital source is that, through each one, you will generate additional business contacts that might be beneficial down the line.

If you go the venture capital route, select venture capital firms that can bring power and experience to your board of directors. Many venture capital firms may offer not only their own people but also well-known corporate executives who are affiliated with the venture firm.

Think Frugal

An important part of your plan and your operating philosophy that is so important is what I refer to as the TF factor. TF stands for "Think Frugal." I strongly recommend you always manage your young company as if you are in financial trouble. No company ever got hurt by doing this, but corporate graveyards are filled with the carcasses of those companies that got slaughtered by living "high off the hog." TF will ensure that you maximize profits, and may help provide buffer funds for emergencies.

Potential investors should sense TF permeating your company. Raises and upgraded office equipment should be financed out of profits, not with equity or debt capital. If you are considering a new piece of capital equipment, are you asking questions like: What is the payback (when do the savings offset the acquisition cost)? Does it make strategic sense now, or am I purchasing it too soon (only because I want it now), possibly jeopardizing the company if a downturn occurs and I don't have the cash?

Here's an example of what can happen when you don't employ the TF factor. In 1987 a young company in the business of supplying unique chemical solutions secured a large contract with a major pharmaceutical company. Based on the strength of that contract, company management secured a state economic development grant to expand the plant capacity. As part of the expansion, the company's top executives went on a buying binge and purchased several custom cherry desks at a cost of several thousand dollars each. Three months later the pharmaceutical company discovered a cost-effective method to replace these chemical solutions, and the major order with the young company was canceled. Would the money spent on the extravagant office furniture have saved the company? Probably not, but it could have kept the doors open for another month while the company tried to find alternative customers for its product.

Whenever you authorize company dollars to be spent or working time to be invested, you are using up valuable assets of the company. Before you do so, always assure yourself this specific investment is the soundest use of those assets. If you could easily secure board approval for your action, it's probably correct; if not, it probably isn't. When in doubt, visit with a board member or one of your outside mentors.

Closing the Deal

When you finally hear investors utter that magic word "yes," realize that "yes" may *not* mean the deal is done. It could mean, "Yes, we are interested in participating, but only for a specific amount and only if you get additional investors to commit to the remaining amount of equity." In this case, have them issue a commitment letter to you. This letter may be useful in obtaining the commitments of other investors.

It could mean, "Yes, we are interested in looking at you further and don't want you talking to any other investors until we give you a decision." Be careful about this one. You are putting all your eggs in one basket. If their due diligence takes another 6 to 8 weeks, can you really afford to wait? If investors approach you with this response, tell them you will be glad to give them a right of first refusal but you are going to pursue other avenues as well, and set a specific date for their response in writing. If they remain adamant, they are probably very interested. In this case, consider giving them one week to make their decision about whether or not to invest. If they balk at this, ask them for an option payment up front, perhaps 10% of the amount you are seeking, as a short-term loan. In return, you grant them an option to participate up to the full amount of the investment. You'll need your attorney to draft the option. Having to advance you these funds ensures that they will accomplish their due diligence in a timely manner.

Finally, a "yes" response could mean, "Yes, we will do the deal." Great, but don't expect the funds tomorrow. Typically, the negotiations to determine the staging of cash injections, how much money you are going to invest, the division of company ownership, employment agreements, and drafting of the investment agreement could easily require another 30 days, so make sure your company is covered for that period. If things are really tight, you may want to ask the investors to help you secure a short-term bank loan for the interim period.

One more caution about securing financing: Always beware of greed. A friend of mine (a wealthy gentleman farmer who has invested wisely in several start-up companies) summed up the pitfalls of greed in the negotiating process in this way: "Bulls make money and bears make money, but pigs get slaughtered!" His advice: When it comes to putting the final package together, don't be pigheaded, but be flexible and work with your investor to strike a middle ground deal.

In the final analysis, it's probably up to you to say the final yes, but never say it too quickly. Be willing to yield, but only if your counterpart does as well. If you will be negotiating on a key point (say stock ownership percentage), prior to the meeting you should know both your starting position and your absolute minimum (or maximum, as the case may be) that you will retain or give up. Using this as your baseline figure, work together to achieve the best compromise you can.

The best deals involve give-and-take on both sides. If two parties walk away from a concluded deal with one party feeling great and the other party feeling shafted, it probably wasn't a very good deal. On the other hand, if both parties leave the table with a feeling akin to "Boy, that was tough. I had to give in some areas I would have preferred not to, but all in all we struck a fair deal," then you have probably struck an excellent bargain.

After you have concluded your deal with a handshake, follow up with a letter to the investors summarizing all the salient points agreed to. Then be prepared to sit back and wait. It will probably take your attorney and their attorney up to a month to get the investment agreement and other documents in order before you can have the actual "closing," where the funds will finally be transferred to your account.

* * *

Once you have your money in hand, you are ready to tackle the next major part of this book, which is the process of sowing the right seeds to ensure the successful growth of your business.

Part

Two

Growing Your Business

Beyond Financing

Chapter
8

Marketing Magic

You have run a good race and achieved your financing goals. But don't start celebrating just yet. Think of the capital you've raised as a full tank of gas for your business. With it, you can start your company moving in the right direction. But if you don't continually replenish the gas, you run the risk of having your company lose momentum, cough, sputter, and drift to a stop.

Your next challenge is to ensure that your company continues to generate fuel, to keep it running in top form. That won't happen by accident. It will require a solid marketing strategy and effective management techniques. That's what the final Microgenesis level is all about.

LEVEL X: Market Your Product/Service and Manage Your Business to Achieve Your Goals

Developing a Sharper Image

People choose to eat at a certain restaurant because of that establishment's reputation. The same thing is true in business. People do business with companies on the basis of the reputation of those companies. Your business is no exception. Therefore it's wise to cultivate the proper image for your company and begin to establish a strong reputation from the start.

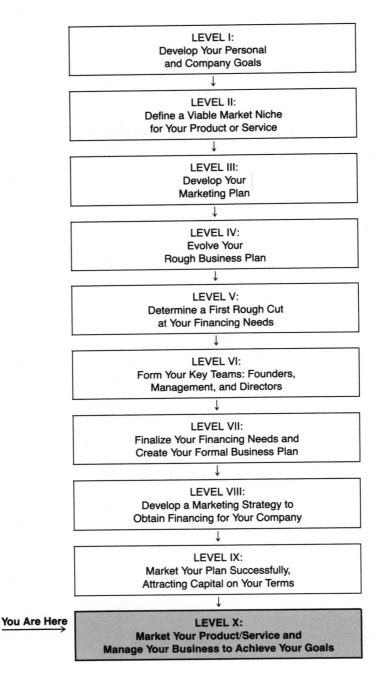

LEVEL I:
Develop Your Personal
and Company Goals

↓

LEVEL II:
Define a Viable Market Niche
for Your Product or Service

↓

LEVEL III:
Develop Your
Marketing Plan

↓

LEVEL IV:
Evolve Your
Rough Business Plan

↓

LEVEL V:
Determine a First Rough Cut
at Your Financing Needs

↓

LEVEL VI:
Form Your Key Teams: Founders,
Management, and Directors

↓

LEVEL VII:
Finalize Your Financing Needs and
Create Your Formal Business Plan

↓

LEVEL VIII:
Develop a Marketing Strategy to
Obtain Financing for Your Company

↓

LEVEL IX:
Market Your Plan Successfully,
Attracting Capital on Your Terms

↓

You Are Here →

LEVEL X:
Market Your Product/Service and
Manage Your Business to Achieve Your Goals

Developing Your Image in Print

How do you begin to build the right image for your company? Unless you are in retailing, most of your potential customers will probably never see your building. But most of them will see your product literature, your business cards, and your stationery. If your printed material looks "schlocky," if it is of poor quality, potential customers will expect your company and your merchandise to be the same.

Even in lean times it is important to spend money on quality marketing literature. This doesn't mean you have to spend thousands of dollars on a slick four-color brochure. But it does mean that you must at the very least develop a high-quality black and white flyer or other piece of marketing literature. Bite the bullet and have photos taken by a professional with fine-grain film. You can usually find a young professional photographer just starting out who will charge a reasonable rate and yet give you the quality you need.

Also be sure to have good-quality business cards and stationery printed. In many cases these will provide the first impression customers will have of your company. Spend a little extra money now to have your printer, a designer, or an advertising agency design a unique letterhead for your business. Then have it printed on heavy paper (I recommend 24 lb. stock); the extra weight gives a subtle suggestion of high quality. Furthermore, never list just a post office box for your address, unless you want to portray the image of a boiler-room operation that might vanish overnight. Always include a street address, even if it's your home. Once you have your business cards, always carry them with you. You never know when you will need them. I have been asked for my card at parties, grocery stores, and even in a movie theater.

Developing Your Personal Image

Leverage your printed look with a personal appearance tour. Look for opportunities to make presentations on your industry and your products to area civic groups and business meetings. When you make your appearances, keep in mind that the way you dress is important. You want to portray the image of a successful executive with a successful business, even if you are still struggling.

Contact the business editors of area newspapers about writing an article on your company. Radio stations sometimes conduct programs that honor local industries; try to get on their calendar. Contact your chamber of commerce, business development groups, financial organizations, and your area SBA office for other public relations ideas.

The Importance of the Receptionist

Key Point: *Your receptionist is one of your most important team members, providing first-time callers or visitors with their initial impression of your company.*

No discussion of image can be complete without mentioning the importance of selecting a top-flight professional receptionist. The receptionist, in brief exchanges with customers or would-be customers, conveys the image of your company, whether you like it or not. The person chosen for this critical function should be thoroughly professional, enjoy interacting with people, and must always sound cheerful and helpful over the phone, *even at times when she or he doesn't feel like it.*

I learned this the hard way. I hired an attractive, pleasant receptionist who did a fine job, except when she was under stress (which is often in a young growing company). Then she became a bear. I admonished her to guard against this, but to no avail. One difficult day she answered a call from our largest customer with the greeting "And what the hell do *you* want?" It was the last phone call she ever answered for our company.

I suggest that as part of the interview process, you have a trial telephone dialogue with receptionist candidates. Observe how they respond to inquiries from irate "customers" as well as happy ones. Observe their grammar, demeanor, and how reassuring and helpful they are in dealing with the customers.

Never underestimate the importance of the receptionist. If you want to cut costs, do it in other areas. You get what you pay for; if you strive to save a few dollars by hiring a less experienced or less professional receptionist, I guarantee you will lose thousands of dollars in potential customers who will take their business to a more professional company.

The Importance of Packaging

Many entrepreneurs spend years developing a high-quality product, then pay little or no attention to how they package it. This can doom sales of even the best of products. Poor-quality packaging, whether of a product or service, conveys to would-be buyers an image of poor quality. If you skimp on the packaging, your product will be guilty of poor quality by association. Never mind that your product might be the highest-quality product ever offered in your market; if your packaging is lousy, most potential customers won't bother opening it to see what's inside.

The Power of Advertising

During a sweltering summer in the late 1940s, I launched my first business venture: a lemonade stand on the west side of Main Street. As timely as my product was, traffic all but ignored my enterprise, and I netted only 30 cents the first day.

The next morning, I put up a sign down the road: "Quench Your Thirst—Ice Cold Lemonade 500 Feet Ahead!" I netted $12 that day, a whopping 4,000% increase in sales. That is how I learned my first lesson in the power of advertising.

Just because you have a fantastic new company or product, customers will not necessarily beat a path to your door. (Remember the proverbial "better mousetrap.") It is up to you to get the message out to potential buyers about the great new products or services you have to offer.

Getting the Words Right

George Plimpton once interviewed Ernest Hemingway for an article in the *Paris Review.* He asked the great author how much time he spent in rewriting his works. Hemingway replied that it depended on the book and told Plimpton that he had rewritten the last page of *A Farewell to Arms* 39 times before he was happy with it. George Plimpton wanted to know what was it that had him stumped. Replied Hemingway, "Getting the words right."

Putting the right words (and getting the right look) on the printed page so that potential customers will dial your phone number is a difficult task. We entrepreneurs tend to be lousy ad writers, but we try anyway. We believe we understand our product better than anyone, so we tend to write copy loaded with product features. The trouble is, we never answer the potential buyer's real questions. Buyers don't care much if our new widget has five control knobs, ten operational modes, a U.S. patent, and hundreds of transistors crammed into a single integrated circuit. They want to know how this product will help them be more efficient, save money, or experience more enjoyment out of life.

I was so proud of the first brochure I wrote on my MinAlert monitoring console. The product had some terrific features, and I explained them all in the brochure. Then I took these terrific new marketing materials to a major trade show. Potential buyers stopped by our booth, picked up a brochure, looked at it, looked at it again, looked at it some more, and then laid it back on the table and walked on.

The literature didn't really interest them, because I hadn't bothered to answer their first question, which was "What will this product do for me?" Furthermore, the brochure did not ask potential buyers to take action and contact us. Even if potential buyers had been interested, we weren't making it easy for them to do anything about it.

When I threw that brochure away and created a new one addressing the needs of my potential customers, my next trade show was totally different. The brochures went like hotcakes. This was an expensive lesson I am sharing with you so that you can develop effective literature the first time around. No small business can afford the luxury of throwing away thousands of dollars worth of worthless literature.

The best way to create excitement in your literature is to have a professional write the text. This person will need to spend a lot of time picking your brain first, in order to fully understand your product or service and what sets it apart from your competitors' offerings. If, like most entrepreneurs, you cannot afford this option initially, then choose the best writer in your organization to write the text.

As you compose your brochure, never forget that your customers are not interested in what your widget does; they want to know how your widget will solve their problem. Visualize each of your potential customers wearing a giant sign that reads, "What will it do for me?" If you answer that question in your marketing materials, you are on the right track. And remember to include a strong call to action in your materials. Urge the customer to contact you right away, and include your phone number and address in a prominent spot in the ad or brochure.

Where to Advertise

In Chapter 3 you developed a clear understanding of your market. Now you must decide what advertising media best suit your business: newspapers, magazines, trade journals, radio, TV, telemarketing, or direct mail. Don't overlook any of these options, but don't select one just because it's cheaper. Select it because it's the best one to reach your potential customers.

For starters, you might determine what magazines your potential customers read by attending trade shows and observing which publications are exhibited at the shows. Ad agencies can also help you find the right publications, and going through them usually won't cost extra because the agency receives a commission from the publication.

How often should you advertise? Running an ad once is a waste of money. People will rarely respond to your pitch the first time around. It's the repetitive nature of your ad that will get their attention. Whether you are advertising in written, audio, or video media, if you are faced with a limited ad budget, a large number of small ads is better than a small number of large ones. While this can be expensive, each medium will quote rates based on multiple insertions, which are cheaper.

The Purpose of an Ad

Except in the case of mail-order literature, the purpose of an ad is *not* to close a sale. That comes later. The purpose of a typical ad is to generate sales leads, to expose consumers to your product or service, and turn them into potential customers.

The first goal of a written ad is to catch the reader's attention for three seconds. Only if the ad succeeds in "hooking" the reader in the first three seconds will the reader spend another 5–10 seconds to read parts of the ad in more detail.

All too often, we become so enamored of our own ads, of seeing our own product in print, that we tend to believe others will react with the same enthusiasm we feel. They won't. To realize how other people read ads, think about the way *you* notice ads when you browse through a magazine. Rarely do you give even the most striking ad more than a few seconds' notice. Neither will readers give *your* ad, no matter how striking, more than a few seconds of their attention. So you'd better use those few seconds well.

I chuckle when I see ads and brochures that feature prominent photos of the management staff followed by the caption "Here is our team of experts to help you." You can bet the executives featured in the ad were hoodwinked by their ad agency. It was easy to sell them on the ad because it appealed to their egos. But it's doubtful that such ads serve their major purpose: generating leads.

The challenge in your ads is not to show what a fine-looking management team you have, but to get the reader's attention, to make the reader interested enough to want to learn more about your product or service.

Your ad has the opportunity to convey one or two points, nothing more. The point of the ad is not to spell out everything about your company and your product; it is rather to get the reader interested enough to seek additional information. Because of this, the ad must have a strong "call to action," telling the reader where to call or write for that additional information. The call to action may be in the form of a mail-in coupon or a toll-free telephone number.

You should tailor your ads for the particular market segment you are targeting. Don't try for a general, broad-based ad. If you're putting your ad in a journal for homemakers, then make sure that your ad is aimed at homemakers.

Figure 8-1 is an example of one of our ads that was particularly effective. The left side caught the reader's attention, and the right side could be read in 10 seconds. Where is the "call to action?" If this ad ran in a national magazine, we dropped our toll-free telephone number into the bottom right-hand corner. If a dealer ran this ad in a local newspaper, our phone number was replaced by the dealer's name, address, and phone number.

A Word About Direct Mail

If you are going to choose the direct mail approach, plan carefully. This technique may seem to cost more, because you will be sending a bro-

Figure 8-1.   Example of an effective ad layout.

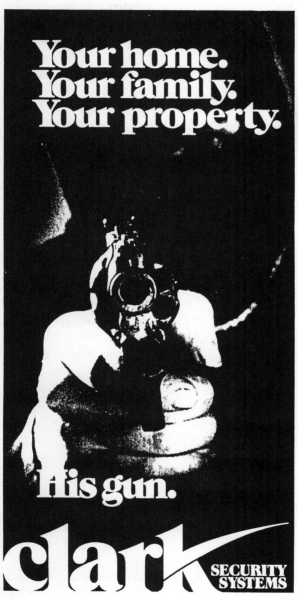

Sentinal™ **scares away trouble before it stares you in the face.**

Sentinal is the home security system that stops crime before it happens! Its buried magnetic sensor detects vehicles as they enter your driveway.

Sentinal's console turns on indoor or outdoor lights and or sounds an outdoor siren. Frightens away intruders fast when you're home or away.

It also turns on lights automatically when you drive home at night for your safety. Affordable and easy to install, it comes with a one year warranty.

Get Sentinal before crime gets you.

chure or other mailer to every person on your mailing list. However, you can purchase lists from magazine publishers or list brokers that include only the names of people with specific demographic profiles, thus ensuring that your message will be targeted to the proper audience. For example, you could request mailing labels only of families with parents who are between the ages of 30 and 45, who have a joint income of more than $50,000, two high school kids, and a boat. The big challenge is to make sure your literature gets read when it is received. If you go with direct mail, I recommend you hire an advertising agency with a direct mail specialist to develop your material for you. This will cost you money in the short run, but it will save you money in the long run.

Getting the Most From Your Advertising Dollars

Advertising in print can be an expensive proposition. Here are some helpful hints to secure magazine advertising coverage at bargain basement prices (or even free):

Salvage Space. Let's assume that on your small budget you will be placing ads that are ⅑ of a page in size. Have you ever noticed that magazines sometimes run public service ads for the Red Cross, the American Heart Association, or some other worthy nonprofit organization? Are they being civic-minded? Guess again. These public service messages are inserted at the last minute as replacements for advertisements that paying customers canceled. You can take advantage of these cancellations, too, by asking if the publication has "salvage space." If you contact the magazine's advertising manager directly and if you have an ad ready to go on a moment's notice, you can probably negotiate a "salvage space" rate as low as 10%–20% of the usual cost of that space. The disadvantage is that you won't know which issue the ad will appear in until the last moment; therefore I suggest this strategy be utilized in addition to your usual ads.

Island Space. Before you place a standard ⅑-page magazine ad, you might want to consider paying slightly more for ⅑-page island space. Standard ⅑-page ads usually run three to a column in the first and third columns. The second column is reserved for text.

By purchasing island space, your ⅑ ad will appear in the middle of the page, surrounded only by text. This definitely attracts more attention.

Press Releases. In addition to paid advertising, you might be able to get some free advertising. One way to do so is by contacting publication editors with a press release on your product or service. If possible, include pictures taken with customers using your merchandise or of employees working in your facility. If your product or service is unique enough, the editor may even be interested in a feature story. Better yet, write your own article so that you are listed as the author, to begin building an image as a recognized "expert" in the industry. Study several issues of the publication first, to be sure that the magazine will consider your type of story.*

Small is Beautiful: Marketing Tips for the Little Guy

Most small companies worry too much about their big, powerful, better-established competitors. In truth, the David of your small company has the potential to slay the Goliath of your larger competitors.

One reason is that being big usually means being slow. Most of the larger companies in your industry will have extremely slow reaction times. It may take their marketing managers 6 to12 months to learn you exist, another 6 to 12 months to track how you are doing, and another 6 to 12 months to figure out what to do about you. This means you probably don't have to worry about them for 1½ to 3 years. During the early stages of your business, your major competition will probably come from the lean and hungry smaller companies like yourself.

Big also means inflexible, and inflexibility can hurt the customer service function. It is far easier for a small company to respond to unique customer requests than for a large company, which generally is laden with standard operating procedures and a limited number of product options. Large companies may offer standard styles, sizes, and colors, and if the customer wants something else, the companies too often exhibit a "take it or leave it" attitude.

---

*For additional ideas and recommendations on publicity, the reader is referred to "*Do-It-Yourself Publicity.*" See the "Recommended Reading List" at the end of this book.

Here's where the small company can gain market share. If customers want a different color, style, delivery schedule, or other option, they will often turn to a smaller company, which has the flexibility to give them what they want without charging them an arm and a leg extra for the service.

When customer needs change (and they will), your small eager company can react far more easily to these changes in the marketplace than a large bureaucracy can. Making changes in a big company is like kicking an elephant, while making changes in a small business is like kicking a gazelle; the small business can adapt almost instantly.

A final word about being small: Don't let price be your discriminator. You don't have the resources to compete with the giants if they decide to sell their competing products at a loss in order to force you out of business. Let them fight over price while you emphasize quality, durability, a stronger warranty, or some other customer-oriented feature.

EXERCISE: Capture Your Thoughts on Marketing

This chapter has covered a number of marketing and advertising topics. If you haven't already done so, I would suggest that you jot down how specific marketing themes apply to your product or service. (How can you develop a sharper company image? What marketing technique should you be using?)

Competitive Research

Just because you shouldn't worry about your larger competitors doesn't mean that you should ignore them. Many entrepreneurs spend plenty of time studying their competition in order to develop a sound business plan, only to ignore the competition when they have the money to start competing with them! Don't fall into this trap. You must continually monitor the activities of your competitors so that you will know how to respond effectively to them, and so you won't be caught off guard by an unforeseen product announcement.

Monitoring the competition means more than knowing what products competitors are offering. You must also know where they are headed. Old competitive data is as valuable as yesterday's newspaper.

Continue to gather information on your competitors by sending for their product literature and getting copies of their annual reports, as well as by talking with dealers, distributors, and salespeople. Identify your key competitors and determine their strengths and their weaknesses. At least once a year, write up a brief analysis for your files on *each* competitor, then review these files to spot trends over the long term, to help make intelligent decisions during your annual planning sessions.

The Sales Process

Marketing is a critical function. But you should always keep in mind that all marketing efforts must be focused on the ultimate goal of selling the product. And to sell a product or service often requires you to overcome sales resistance on the part of the potential buyer.

> **Key Point:** *Your business will not be successful unless you sell your product or service. Because it is human nature to resist sales, the majority of all your orders will be closed only by overcoming this sales resistance.*

Underestimating the Sales Process

Never underestimate what it takes to make a sale. We entrepreneurs are enamored of our products, and sometimes we forget that not everyone else will automatically feel the same way about them. Customers have to be sold.

When novice entrepreneurs begin calling on major customers for the first time, they tend to underestimate the hurdles they are about to confront. I want you to conjure up a vision of old Ebenezer Scrooge at his worst. Now imagine you have just walked into the buyer's office and Ebenezer is sittiing across the desk from you. Scrooge has already had a hard day and has taken lots of grief. Now a new supplier (you) shows up. Scrooge scowls at you, peering over his half-spectacles, and grunts the following greeting: "Look, I don't know you. I don't know your company. I don't know your company's product. I don't know your customers, your record, or your reputation. Why should I buy anything you have to offer?"

There is no need to panic and run out the door at this point, although many an entrepreneur has been thoroughly shaken by such Scrooge-like characters. The best strategy is to pause, take a deep breath, and answer Scrooge's questions. Remember, he is like any other potential customer in that he is really thinking about a single question: "What will your product do for me?" If you can effectively answer that question, you will be close to making the sale. Show him why your product will make him look good and earn a handsome profit for his company, and he may eventually give you the opportunity to prove it.

Selecting Sales Reps

If your business is in distributing or manufacturing, sooner or later your company will need a field sales force. Because most of you will not be able to afford the luxury of a full-time field sales force initially, you will start out using an independent sales representative, that is, a sales "rep" who acts as your agent. Here are some facts you should know:

A sales rep usually represents products (known as lines) for an average of 6 to 20 companies like yours (these companies are referred to as principals). Reps don't buy and stock products; they act on your behalf to secure orders. A rep calls on customers (referred to as accounts) in a specific geographic territory. Reps have to be great salespeople, because they work on commission only.

There's an old saying that "a rep sells what sells"; in other words, reps give most of their time to the lines that are the easiest to sell. Most reps want a written rep agreement for their territory. The agreement will give them the exclusive rights to market your product in *their* territory and receive commissions on all your sales in their territory.

It's the squeaky wheel that gets the grease. Companies that contact their reps frequently (probably every week) to see how many calls the reps made for their company during the previous week, will probably get more than their fair share of the rep's time. If you prescreen your leads before you send them to your reps, so that the reps receive only solid "warm" or "hot" leads, they will spend more time working for you than for larger companies. (We'll discuss this technique later in the chapter.)

If you understand and utilize the points made in the previous paragraph, which are ignored by most other companies, large and small, you will have a head start when it comes to winning the lion's share of your rep's time.

However, your rep's time isn't enough: To be effective, your rep must also win orders for your company. It isn't your rep's responsibility to develop an effective sales presentation, it's yours! To gird your reps for effective battle in the marketplace, you must arm them with three high-quality essentials: literature, techniques, and training.

In order to be sure that your reps will actively represent your company to potential customers (as opposed to just carrying your literature in a briefcase), you must furnish them with effective marketing techniques proven to work with your product or service, along with attractive, professional sales materials.

Then you must train your reps well. Reps need to feel that they know more about your product than the people to whom they are trying to sell it. This may seem elementary, but it is often overlooked. Without adequate training and motivation, the best rep in the world is useless. Nothing is worse than an occasion when a customer asks your rep a question he or she can't answer.

To make sure your reps have all the information they need to serve your customers effectively, they must have access to all departments within your company. When one of your reps is in the office of an angry customer and you are not available, the rep must know whom to call to get action. You may believe the rep is *your* representative, but he or she is also a customer's advocate. No rep wants to alienate a potential customer (and hence lose a potential commission).

Sales reps demand full responsibility for their accounts. If you bypass a rep and go directly to the customer without letting the rep know, you will embarrass him or her. When the rep visits the customer the next time, and the customer has a question or comment relating to a meeting with you (that the rep knows nothing about), your rep will feel foolish, not to mention angry, and perhaps even inclined to begin focusing on products other than yours.

If you have such a low opinion of a rep that you bypass him or her, it's time to find a replacement you can work with. Otherwise, always keep your rep in the loop. For example, whenever you write to a customer, send a copy of this letter to the appropriate rep. When you ship an order, send a copy of the shipping notice to the rep. When you have a packet of material to send a potential customer, consider sending the material to the rep to deliver to the customer. Your rep will not only be making another sales call; he or she will also be fulfilling a need to be part of your sales team.

Sales reps can be a boon or a bane to your business. Make sure you choose the best ones. How do you find them? By talking to other business executives. Ask for their recommendations for the best reps to use. Talk to their reps for recommendations. Call or write to your area rep association. It won't be long before you have a number of qualified candidates.

Once you have a group of candidates, interview them using the same procedures you used to interview candidates for your management team. Your primary interest here is in the size and volume of business the reps handle for their existing customers. Ask to talk to some of their customers as well.

Generating Sales Leads

Often companies use the number of leads generated as the measure of success or failure of an ad. The organization may count the number of coupons clipped and returned for information, or the number of phone calls received in response to the ad.

This is fine, as far as it goes. The problem is that you can have all the leads in the world, but if you don't turn them into sales, the marketing campaign was a failure, no matter how big a stack of returned coupons it generated. In spite of this rather obvious fact, the majority of companies relying on lead generation techniques do not have an adequate system for transforming those leads into sales. Often, leads are simply passed along to sales reps, and that's the end of it.

When you receive sales leads, what do you do with them? If you don't have a procedure in place for dealing with them immediately, it's time to develop one.

Don't make the mistake I did: In 1978 my first company created an exciting new product called Sentinal. (It is featured in the ad in Figure 8-1.) Sentinal could detect vehicles pulling into a driveway. It would sound an alarm in the home or business and turn on outside lights for five minutes whenever a vehicle approached.

The product was so new that we had received our brochures from the printer just hours before leaving for our first trade show of the season. We took all but a few brochures to the show. The brochures were attractive and included a coupon on the back that would-be customers could clip and send to us for more information. The product was a success, and we distributed every copy of our brochure at the four-day show.

Before we returned to the office, our sales department had already received several of the returned coupons. However, because the product was so new, we hadn't briefed our sales personnel on a procedure for handling the leads. When they received several mail-in coupons that said, "Send me more information on 'Sentinal,'" they didn't know what to do. So they went to the literature room, spotted the remaining Sentinal brochures, and sent this brochure to these people.

Can you imagine how angry *you* would be if you had seen a product you wanted to buy, had clipped the coupon on the brochure advertising the product, mailed it the very same day you saw it at a trade show, then received in the mail the following week the identical brochure from which you clipped the coupon? Not surprisingly, I received a number of hostile calls from irate people as a result of this scenario and lost a number of sales. Believe me, I never made that costly mistake again.

Some companies have a system of keeping a copy of the lead in a file, sending a copy to the field, and requiring the sales rep to report back on the status of the lead. But where is the incentive to make the field salespeople follow up, particularly if the lead is clearly a dead end?

Whether an ad generates a hundred leads or a thousand, most of them will be worthless. If all of these leads are sent out to the field without being qualified, the salespeople will start contacting the leads—until they wise up. Because most of the leads will turn out to be dead ends, the reps will soon learn to let the leads sit, but inform *you* that the people weren't ready to buy.

Large companies as well as small ones are guilty of failing to qualify leads. This presents a golden opportunity for a small company to get a jump on its larger competitors who don't do a good job of qualifying leads. The small company that sends to the field only those leads with a real potential of being turned into sales will win the time and devotion of reps who are also representing larger companies.

You should view each lead you receive as if it were a pancake hot off the griddle. If you allow it to just sit there for a while, it will "cool off," and its value will then be practically worthless. Yet this is exactly what most companies do, spending large advertising budgets generating leads, then letting them sit there and turn cold. Later, these same businesspeople wonder why they aren't closing sales.

When you receive a lead, act on it immediately. Before sending it to the field, have someone contact the lead by telephone and qualify the potential buyer. By "qualify," I mean determine the category of the lead. Leads can be grouped into four categories:

1. *Dead*. The dead lead doesn't remember your product and claims to have no interest at all. Maybe the person already purchased a competitor's unit. Perhaps his or her spouse sent in the request, or the person circled the wrong number on a bingo card. In any event, the dead lead is not worth your time. Discard it.

2. *Cold*. The cold lead is not a buyer. It might be an inquisitive student or professor who wants information for a file. It might even be a competitor (with some practice you can learn to sniff these out). Send product information as a courtesy (unless the lead is clearly a competitor) but don't bother following up.

3. *Warm*. The warm lead was intrigued by your product but is looking at a possible purchase in the future. Send marketing literature to these leads and have a sales rep call on them. Warm leads liked your product, and a good salesperson might be able to create the sense of urgency needed to move them into the "hot" category.

4. *Hot*. The "hot" lead is a person with an identified need for your product who wants to place an order *now*. Send literature to these leads immediately and have a sales rep call on them soon to close the order. "Warm" and "hot" leads, by the way, include all those who call or write to you to inquire about a product. Send them literature and a sales rep fast.

It has been estimated that up to 95% of warm and hot leads will result in a sale if handled properly, while less than 2% of all other leads will. Prescreening may cost you in time and money, but the payoff is big. By being sent only warm and hot leads, your field sales reps will realize that leads your company sends them will probably result in an order. As a result, they will follow up more promptly than they would with the typical leads they receive, because your leads have credibility. The result? Fat commissions for them, and more sales for your company.

Closing the Sale

Think about how you decide to buy any major item. You hesitate about making a commitment until you are absolutely certain you want the product, which often means when the salesperson convinces you that you want it.

The sales rep on the other end of the buying transaction must keep in mind this natural sales resistance and plot a strategy accordingly. If your company has done a good job of marketing your products or services, sales should follow, but not automatically. In general, the more your product or service costs, the more sales resistance you will have to overcome.

Here are a few tips I've learned about closing the sale. Try starting with small talk, which seems casual to the potential buyer, but which is intended to determine critical information about the person. How confident is this person? How flexible? How decisive?

After you have the answer to these basic questions, try to determine the customer's needs as they relate to your product. Let's say you sell console television sets. You might ask, for example:

How long have you had your color TV?

What do you like most about it?

When you do decide to buy a new one, what will you be looking for that you don't have now?

Then, talk about some satisfied customers (by name) and tell how they have enjoyed their purchases from you.

It's the rare customer who won't have any objections to the sale. Knowing this, try to draw them out, getting them on the table now. For example, you might ask:

Why haven't you purchased a new TV yet?

Once you know the customer's objections, you can deal with each of them casually, by focusing on how your product will overcome the objections.

Then it's time to try some early closing techniques.

John, what features would you want on your new console television? If I had it available in a 27-inch stereo model or a 42-inch projection model, which would you prefer?

Finally, it's time to go for the jugular. Make an offer the customer can't refuse, and you should have the order.

But never forget, the sale doesn't end with the order. If you continue to provide unequaled service after the sale, you can expect repeat sales down the line, and this is the foundation of a solid business. I know a TV dealer who gives new customers a bottle of champagne when they purchase a new console TV, and he follows up with a call a week later, asking how they are enjoying the new TV. And if there is any little problem, this dealer makes sure it gets fixed, fast and free.

To help make sure more sales will be forthcoming, keep your name in front of the customer. One of the easiest ways to do this is by starting a monthly newsletter. Simpler still, send your customers birthday cards each year, along with an annual thank-you card on the anniversary of their product purchase. Chances are, when they are ready to deal again, they'll be back to see you. And send others to you as well.

I could write volumes on the sales process. There are hundreds of effective sales techniques. You would do well to spend time with your sales reps, watching them in action and helping them to refine their techniques. I also heartily recommend that you read *Zig Ziglar's Secrets of Closing the Sale,* written by one of the best-known sales closers around.*

Removing the Barriers to Buying

Sometimes companies make the buying process so difficult that you have to wonder if their secret goal is to go out of business! You have probably, at some time or other, called a company to inquire about a

*Zig Ziglar, *Zig Ziglar's Secrets of Closing the Sale* (New York: Berkley Books [paperback], 1982.).

product, only to be met with a disinterested receptionist on the other end of the line, who puts you on hold, then transfers you to someone else in the company. But this person does not have the information you are seeking, and so you are shuffled once more to another department, then to another, and maybe yet another, until finally you are put into contact with someone who has the information you want and promises to mail you an informational packet, which never arrives.

Strive to make buying, or even seeking assistance, from your company a pleasant experience. When customers call to place an order, the experience should not only be easy and pleasant, but effective. That means the order must be taken accurately. Nothing upsets a customer more than calling in a special order and receiving the wrong merchandise. After taking the order, your staff member should read it back to the customer. Errors can be corrected for pennies at this stage, but will cost far more to correct later, after the order has been shipped.

If a customer calls for a quote that must be mailed, try to respond the same day. If this not possible because of the effort involved, then send a letter to the customer (with a copy to your rep) that same day, thanking the customer for the request and stating when the requested information will be sent. Then make heads roll if that date is not met.

Whether talking to the customer face-to-face or by telephone, use the pronoun "we" in all cases, except when you are discussing problems. When you say "we" will do this, it gives customers the feeling of a team working for them in the home office. However, when a customer calls in with a problem, have the employees handling the call use the pronouns "I" and "me" so that customers perceive that the employee is taking a personal interest in their problems (more on customer service in Chapter 9).

EXERCISE: Summarize Your Thoughts on Sales Technique

How can you apply these sales topics (reps, sales leads, closing, barriers) to improve the success of your business? Weave your answers into a new plan of action for your own sales force.

*   *   *

Now that your company is well established and sales dollars are starting to flow, it's time to turn your attention to the management of the business. As your company grows, you must refine your management skills in order to deal effectively with the agony and the ecstasy of that growth, the subject of our final chapter.

Chapter
9

Developing Your Management Style

You probably didn't start your business out of a desire to manage other people, but here you are just the same. Effective, innovative management may well be the key to the ultimate success of your business. If your sales take off because of a strong marketing program but you have ignored the management side of the business, you will soon find your company in deep trouble.

To hone your management skills, let's examine the notion of management, including some traditional management techniques and trouble spots, and focus on the meaning of managing for success.

Leading vs. Managing

Typically we entrepreneurs tend to be good leaders but poor managers. We're great at leading the charge, but we are lousy at training our subordinates to manage their troops in our absence. How do you rate as a manager? If you've had management experience, what does your track record look like? Have you been able to turn a profit in tough times? Are your employees willing to give you all they've got? Do they remain intensely loyal, even when your company's ship is sailing through stormy seas? Are you loyal to them in troubled times?

I believe that being a good leader is far easier than being a good manager. I've seen many a natural leader attempt the transition to management, only to flounder in the process.

To lead is to show the way by going in advance. To manage is to administer, supervise, co-ordinate, and direct others, to give them appropriate freedom to produce results, and then to consolidate their results into a unified accomplishment.

To manage well is to manage so that your business continues to grow with the minimum number of people (and dollars) required. A critical part of managing well involves delegating some measure of responsibility and accountability to those being managed, grooming them for the day when one of them may step into your shoes.

To determine if you're the typical leader-but-not-manager type, just look at your style: Are you, rather than your subordinates, pursuing major accounts? Do you assign your subordinates relatively trivial tasks, or do you turn them loose on major projects? Do you keep all of the major responsibilities for yourself, or do you share them? If you tend to want to control everything in the company and retain all authority and responsibility, you will need to develop your management skills, for the most critical aspect of effective management is learning how to delegate.

You can't afford not to delegate. Young, emerging, and expanding companies tend to be understaffed. If you are spending your time managing your managers, then you are utilizing your staff to the maximum, but if you are only leading them, reserving all of the major responsibility for the company's business for yourself, then they are not much more than glorified gofers, and you are underutilizing this important and scarce resource.

Learning how to manage effectively, learning how to delegate responsibility, is critical if your company is to run smoothly. Effective management allows your company to operate in a proactive mode rather than in a crisis mode, anticipating problems rather than reacting to them.

EXERCISE: *Your Managerial Abilities Inventory*

To find out what kind of manager you are, I suggest you take a personal inventory of your managerial abilities as you perceive them. There are no "right" or "wrong" answers in this exercise; it is simply meant to give you a better understanding of your skill level.

On a new page in your notebook, draw two columns. Label one "Managerial Strengths" and the other "Managerial Weaknesses." Then list as many items as you can in each category. (Be honest; if you can't come up with several weaknesses, you had better keep trying, because even the best managers are weak in some area. If you don't identify your weak areas, they are guaranteed to come back to haunt you.)

Once you have completed this activity, you should strive to run your business in a manner that takes advantage of your strengths, while also working to improve your weaknesses.

Flexible Management

Particularly if your style is more oriented to leading than managing, you may wonder how you can go about turning your subordinates loose on major projects or in other ways delegating responsibility to them, when some of them might not yet be capable of doing the job on their own. To help you along, if you haven't already done so, I would strongly recommend that you read the book *Leadership and the One Minute Manager.** The book will help you to learn how to delegate, as well as how to get your management priorities straight.

If you want to be effective, you must take a different view of management, learning to serve those who work for you, rather than vice versa. Your employees' job is to be responsible for their actions, while you must be responsive to their needs, providing them with the resources and coaching needed to develop them into effective managers.

The best way to find out how effective you are as a manager is by asking your subordinates how they perceive your abilities. If they are not afraid to give you an honest answer, you can learn a valuable lesson from them. It is impossible for you to be thoroughly objective about your management style. By getting feedback from those who work for you, you'll get a more balanced view of your management strengths and weaknesses.

*Ken Blanchard, Patricia Zigarmi and Drea Zigarmi, *Leadership and the One Minute Manager* (New York: William Morrow & Company, 1985).

Management is a skill that requires time and practice. While it may be time-consuming to develop your managers (not to mention your own management skills), believe me, you will spend much more time cleaning up their messes if you don't help them to develop as they go.

This need not be an overwhelming burden. Not everyone needs the same amount of management training. Inexperienced or new employees require more direction than do more experienced workers. Furthermore, just as some people are born leaders, some are born managers, and they are a priceless resource for your business. If you have a born manager in your company, assign the management development process to him or her as much as possible. After all, the best way for employees to learn how to manage effectively is to be around a pro.

Management Control Systems

No matter what the size of your business, you need to have management control systems in place—sets of procedures designed to ensure that your company functions smoothly and efficiently. They need not be complex; some of them can be as simple as requiring two senior managers to sign all company checks. But as your company grows, your systems are likely to grow in complexity along with it. Let's take a look at some basic management control systems.

The Triumvirate of Control Systems

In the process of starting my first business, I wore all the hats: management, marketing, engineering, administration—you name it. As my business grew, I continued trying to be everywhere, but there came a point when this just wasn't possible.

I am a "walk-around" manager. I have always roamed through the manufacturing area of my companies several times a day, to visit with the troops, to show them I cared about their needs. When my first company was small, this was an efficient management technique, because I could uncover potential problems long before they became serious. However, when the business had grown to 50 people and I still "walked the assembly line," there was the potential for problems.

In a company of 5 people, we were like family, but in a company of 50 people the environment had changed. To most of the workers, I was "Mr. President," the person of authority. So when I casually mentioned in passing, "I wonder if we could improve productivity by changing the work flow to this new technique," my employees took it as an order and, after I left, shut down production and rearranged the assembly line.

As a result, my crusty shift supervisor came into my office, closed the door, placed her arm on my shoulder, and said, "Scott, we love to see you out there, to know that you care. But if you want to get any work done, you had better learn not to say anything out there that even remotely sounds like a directive!" She was absolutely right, of course, and a good set of control systems would have prevented this problem.

If you have good control systems in place, they will continue to provide guidance whether or not you are walking the floor of the factory. Your control systems should be strong enough to permit the company to continue operating reasonably well even if you were suddenly to suffer a debilitating illness. A good set of control systems will act as your silent sentinels, ensuring that your directives are followed even when you're gone.

The three basic control systems that I recommend you develop and implement for your business are (1) Management by Objectives (MBO); (2) Management by Exceptions (MBE); and (3) Management by Motivation (MBM).

Management by Objectives (MBO). Management by Objectives (MBO) involves defining a set of specific objectives that help all employees to focus on meeting company goals. Using this system, managers define in writing the company's major objectives and communicate them to every employee. (To keep the key objectives of my second company in the minds of my employees, I had them painted on a large sign and posted in the employee break area.)

All employees must perceive that management openly embraces these objectives; they must be sincere. If one objective is "to save every dollar possible in the operation of the company," but the employees see you drive up in a new Cadillac, it's unlikely they will give their all to meeting the objective.

The strength of MBO lies in the fact that it forces a singleness of purpose on a fledgling management team, even in the midst of the other crises that inevitably arise. It is the anchor that calms the boat in the midst of the storm. Another advantage of MBO is that it focuses on results, not on the number of hours employees work or on political posturing.

EXERCISE: Establish Your Own MBO Objectives

Try developing some management objectives for your own company. On a new page in your notebook, write the heading "Management by Objectives for XYZ Company." Then list as many MBO objectives as you can for your business. Examples might include "Achieve sales this year totaling $650,000"; "Sign up 20 new major customers during the next year"; or "Become the most successful company of our type on the West Coast, in terms of return on sales." Make sure the objectives are specific and measurable. Leave room in your notebook to add additional MBO objectives as you think of them later.

Management by Exceptions (MBE). Management by Exceptions allows your managers to ignore routine ongoing operations until a problem is encountered. In a typical manufacturing or service company, the vast majority of each manager's time is spent making routine and predictable decisions. This is a luxury you can't afford, and this wasted time stifles the efficiency you need in order to remain competitive.

MBE controls serve as warning flags that let managers know when they must take action to solve a problem or halt a negative trend. For example, MBE controls may be set up so that when more than 8% of your products fail final inspection the first time or more than 5% of your orders are shipped late, it is time for the manager to take action. As long as the company is operating below these danger points, operations can continue without your intervention.

MBE is particularly important for manufacturing businesses. Among other things, it is a useful tool for keeping track of inventory. For a manufacturing business, running out of inventory can be devastating. Not having a critical five-cent part on hand can prevent a company from completing and shipping a $500 product. If the company is shipping several of these products each month, you can see how the dollars quickly add up.

When my companies were small, I monitored every problem and potential problem area myself. As my companies grew, I continued to monitor problem areas, often taking time away from more important tasks (such as marketing) to do so. This preoccupation with monitoring potential problem areas, even when a problem did not exist, diverted my most valuable asset, my time.

MBE controls helped me to get out of that unproductive mode. We simply developed a warning flag to alert me if things got out of hand. As long as 95% of our products were shipped on the promised date, I would not get involved. If delays exceeded that figure, the warning flag was raised and I would then be notified.

As your company grows, you can use MBE controls to increase the efficiency of your management staff. To establish an MBE environment, you need to become skilled in recognizing what areas need to be monitored, and at what levels the "warning flags" should be established. Then your management team will be freed up to concentrate on more productive activities.

EXERCISE: Initiate Your Own MBE Controls

Try your hand at developing some MBE controls for your own company. Write the heading "Management by Exceptions in XYZ Company" on a fresh page in your notebook. Then list potential "warning flags" for critical areas within your business. Examples might include: "Notify the president if a shipment is late or if the stockroom is out of stock on any item" or "Secure the president's approval on any purchases over $200 or any checks above $100." Leave room in your notebook to add additional MBE flags as they occur to you later.

Management by Motivation (MBM). Management by Motivation (MBM) is a system for rewarding individuals or groups for their performance in meeting the company's objectives. MBM controls are utilized to add "muscle" to MBO and MBE controls. To be most effective, MBM should recognize achievement openly and compliment all those who are responsible.

When you set up MBM controls in your business, make sure that the controls are relevant to the particular group they are addressing. For example, the MBM control "If we achieve sales of $500,000 this year, every employee will receive a bonus of one week's pay" is probably not appropriate for the entire company, because manufacturing workers have little control over meeting this goal. However, this goal would be an appropriate MBM control for the sales department. Rewards should be established only for those goals over which workers have control.

An MBM control for the entire company should consist of a goal that all employees can have an influence in meeting. For example, you might establish the following MBM control: "If we achieve an assembled system failure rate of less than 1%, total annual sales of $500,000, and a bottom line profit of $20,000, every employee will receive a bonus of one week's pay." With this MBM control in place, even your production workers perceive that they have a hand in achieving the goal.

When you utilize MBM controls that can potentially reward a group of employees, you must continually inform the group of their progress toward meeting their goals, or the MBM control will have lost much of its value as an incentive. Using the example above, you might post monthly progress reports and abbreviated financial statements on the bulletin board, with a summary of progress to date. If the company falls behind, you should schedule department meetings to discuss what each department can do to ensure that the goals are met.

When applicable controls are in place, each department will police itself. If some employees see others not doing their fair share, they will let the deficient workers know it, because their actions (or failure to act) are affecting everyone's bonus!

EXERCISE: Developing Your Own MBM Controls

Now it's time to consider developing some MBM controls for your own business. At the top of a new page in your notebook, write "Management by Motivation in XYZ Company." Then list several MBM controls that you could install in your company. An example might be "An employee bonus of one week's pay will be authorized if our operating profit goal of $200,000 is met for the entire year."

Now that you are familiar with MBO, MBE, and MBM, which ones are you *least* comfortable with? These are the ones that you should concentrate on the most, until you are equally comfortable with all three. The reason is that your company needs all three control systems in place to function with maximum efficiency. Furthermore, when you understand all of the techniques, you can respond intelligently when your financiers ask, "What sets of controls have you installed in the company?"

The idea is to achieve an ideal balance within your company, a combination of MBO, MBE, and MBM controls that will bring out the best in your people in terms of performance, profitability, and employee satisfaction.*

Other Control Systems

In addition to the three sets of controls reviewed above, there are certain other controls you should establish to ensure the smooth operation of your company. These include committing all procedures to writing in the form of a personnel manual (this will start small but will grow with the company). This manual should address policies (such as vacation, sick days, wage reviews, bonuses) and company guidelines (approval for travel, cash advances, trade show rules, expense reports, invoices for payment, advertising, capital equipment, etc.). Such controls reduce the risk of serious personnel and financial problems, and they will impress investors as well.

If you don't think it's important to put personnel policies down on paper, take a lesson from my friend Sarah. Sarah started a small service company a while back. She recruited experienced managers to fill her key positions. The company was launched in the spring, and she told the managers they would have two weeks' paid vacation each year.

Because of inevitable start-up crises, no one was able to take a vacation for the first eight months of the company's existence. During the last week in December, Sarah informed the employees during a staff meeting that because they had not used their vacation, they would lose it at the start of the new year. Not surprisingly, Sarah had a mutiny on her hands. Her managers threatened to quit; she refused to give in and

---

*For additional detail on the topic of MBO, MBE, and MBM control systems, the reader may wish to refer to pages 17–22 of Richard White, *The Entrepreneur's Manual* (Radnor, Penn: Chilton Books, 1977).

called me for advice. Sarah swore she had told her employees there was no vacation carryover. But her employees indicated that she never discussed carryover with them.

I informed her that, although she may have intended to clarify this issue, it was apparent that she never did. I told her that she had two choices: reinstate her managers' lost vacation days or lose most of her key staff. I recommended that she save face for all concerned by declaring a one-time vacation bonus for all founding managers. Then I suggested she should create a personnel manual immediately. She did, and the problem was resolved.

Managing for Success

Key Point: *To be successful, you must take exceptional care of your customers through superior service and quality; and you must constantly stay in touch with the needs of your employees.*

Successful business executives strive to take care of their customers. They also go out of their way to create environments in which their employees can flourish.

Quality and Service

One way of taking care of customers is by providing them with high-quality products and services. Many managers fall into the trap of thinking that quality is an added expense. But by cutting corners on quality, you gain absolutely nothing. In fact, in the long run skimping on quality will actually cost you money. The pennies you may save initially will cost you dollars later in lost time to handle complaints and correct problems, and possibly in lost customers.

In addition to providing quality, successful managers also provide their customers with top-notch service. It's fortunate that most business managers continually make the assumption that their relationship with their customers stops with the sale. This provides you with a golden opportunity to surge ahead of your competitors by maintaining a strong relationship with the customer after the sale. Even as a small company, you should maintain a customer service department to provide service after the sale.

Here's how one of my suppliers excelled with customer service and won a loyal customer—my company—in the process: Shortly after my first business really started to expand, this supplier failed to deliver 1,000 new cabinets on time. I had customer orders and systems already assembled, but no cabinets in which to mount them. I was furious, because I was losing sales. I swore I would change suppliers as soon as I could.

The cabinets finally arrived four weeks late, along with an invoice for $6,500 across which the supplier had scrawled, "Sorry for the delay. These first 1,000 are my treat!" When I called him for an explanation, he informed me this shipment was free because he had failed me this time, but he wanted the opportunity to prove it would never happen again. Because of this act, this supplier kept my loyalty over the years. What did it cost him? $6,500. But ultimately he gained tens of thousands of dollars in revenues from our continued business relationship.

I learned a lesson from my supplier. I soon began to provide all of my monitoring consoles with a lifetime guarantee. My guarantee allowed the buyer to exchange a previously purchased console for a factory-rebuilt console at any time, simply by paying a $20 shipping and handling fee. This applied even if the buyer's console had been struck by lightning and melted into a blob.

My cost was around $60 per unit, and I looked at it as an advertising expense. I usually received a letter of thanks when the new console arrived, and I was sure this customer was telling all his friends how he got a new system for only $20. Not a bad investment for either of us.

Another customer service strategy is to provide a toll-free telephone "hot line" that delivers important information to customers. You might also run local workshops or develop a monthly newsletter to keep your name in front of the customer. The possibilities for serving your customer are limited only by your imagination.

It's tough to win a new customer and just as tough to keep that customer with the onslaught of competition. Remember that a happy customer will buy from you again and tell others of your fabulous service, thereby gaining for you the positive reputation your company needs. Whatever you spend now in keeping your customers happy will pay off in big dividends later, in the form of repeat sales and referrals of new business.

Staying in Touch With Your Customers

Are your customers happy with their purchases? Most companies never bother to find out. They believe that if they do not hear from customers, this is a sign that everything is fine. In fact, they could be very wrong. By calling your customers after they've purchased products from you, you get the chance to resolve any complaints they might have (and you should move heaven and earth to do so). If they are satisfied with their purchases, you have reinforced in their minds what a terrific company you are. Either way, you will put yourself ahead of your competition by staying in touch with your customers.

I maintain that a satisfied customer will tell others about your company for several months after making a purchase. A dissatisfied customer whose problem is not solved will complain about your company for a few years. An initially dissatisfied customer whose problem is courteously and speedily corrected will sing your praises for life.

If you have a local business, one way to stay in touch with customers is to hold annual customer-appreciation days, offering discounts to established customers. If you have a regional or national business, I suggest you establish a customer advisory board, selecting several customers to serve on the board and help you to plan for new products. This is an excellent way of ensuring that you keep directly in touch with the marketplace, and a way to build even more customer loyalty.

The important point is to let your customers know that you value their business and their loyalty. If you convey this to your customers and provide them with superior service as well, you can bet they will return the favor by referring other potential customers to your company.

Staying in Touch With Your Employees

As you grow, it is equally important that you stay in touch with your employees. Companies often tend to drift from their employees as the business grows in size and complexity. This is a major mistake. How can you expect your employees to be dedicated to the company if you show by your actions that you no longer have time for their concerns, their input, and their well-being?

It's unrealistic to think that you can spend much individual time with employees as your business grows in size. But no matter how large your company grows, you can still convey to them, by your attitude and your actions, that you are wholeheartedly supporting them. This means, among other things, that you must treat all of the employees (and customers) with integrity and respect. If your employees see you berating someone else in the company, they will wonder when it will be their turn, and you will have lost their respect. If they overhear you lying to a customer to get an order, they will wonder if you can be trusted.

Integrity: An Essential Ingredient

Integrity doesn't just apply to your employees and your customers. To be a winner, you must show integrity in all of your personal interactions. You must practice integrity with suppliers, investors, the community, and even with the competition.

Here's an example of integrity in action: Say you have a serious cash flow problem because payment is late in coming from a major customer. Because of this, you probably won't be able to pay all your bills during the current month. If you are a manager with integrity, you won't wait for your vendors to call and ask why you haven't paid them, and you won't try to buy time by telling them "the check's in the mail" unless it is. An executive with integrity will call suppliers before an invoice's due date, explain why the payment will be late, and tell them when the vendor will receive it. This approach will work 99% of the time.

I know this from personal experience. A customer of mine went bankrupt early one month, still owing my company $30,000. I had no recourse but to stretch out my payments to suppliers until receivables caught up. This meant delaying payments to some suppliers for 45 days.

My initial reaction was typical. If I just clammed up, I thought, maybe my suppliers would forget about my overdue bills until I could pay them. But I knew this would not be the case. Furthermore, these were my business associates, and I owed them the courtesy of an explanation.

Even though my invoices weren't due for another two weeks, as embarrassing as it was, I called my major suppliers. I explained my problem and the delay in payment it would cause. I indicated to all of them that they could charge me interest if they wished.

My vendors couldn't believe I had called them in advance of the due date. All but one let me know they appreciated the early warning and indicated they would give me the time I needed. Several even expressed concern over my difficulty and asked if they could help by extending payments further.

Only one vendor, a supplier from Long Island, was irate. He insisted on immediate payment. Somehow, I scraped the cash together and made his payment. Then, as soon as my cash flow recovered from the deficit, I found an alternate source and notified my Long Island supplier he was being terminated. When he asked why, I reminded him of his earlier treatment of me when I was in trouble. Because I was a major customer, he tried for three years to get me back, but to no avail. When lightning strikes and my business is injured, I don't want to be surrounded by fair-weather friends.

Don't lie to people you deal with, don't play games, don't avoid tough decisions, and don't pass the blame on to someone else. If you want to gain the respect of your employees, make sure the buck stops with you. For example, sometimes you will have to terminate people who have meant a lot to you, and no matter how long you've been in business it never gets any easier. Just remember that an executive with integrity won't delegate this unpleasant duty to a subordinate just because the executive wants to avoid a difficult situation. Remember, if these people have worked hard for you, even if things didn't work out they deserve the courtesy of hearing from you why they must leave.

I once failed in this area. I had an employee who had worked hard in the stockroom when my first company was small. But the company grew beyond him, and he made several costly errors without realizing what he had done. When we finally decided to terminate him on a specific day, I used the excuse of a bank meeting to delegate the task to my vice-president. He didn't want to face the issue either, so he handed the task to our purchasing administrator. As a result, this employee, who believed he had given his best to the company, was informed of his termination at the last minute by a third-level employee. I regret my lack of integrity in that action to this day.

Praising and Reprimanding

Treat your employees as adults; treat them as partners; treat them with dignity; treat them with respect. Treat them, not your cash or your equipment, as the primary source of productivity gains for your business. It's the least expensive way to ensure the continued success of your business. This is a tough order, particularly as your company grows and faces a continual stream of new challenges and crises. Nevertheless, you must not let the stress of such a situation affect your treatment of your employees.

Above all, make sure that you reprimand and praise your employees properly, in a productive manner that will reinforce the employees' value to the company.

When I must criticize a subordinate, here is an approach I use that might work for you. It is quick (three or four minutes) and surgically to the point, but most importantly, it is constructive rather than destructive.

First, always conduct the reprimand sessions in private. Call the errant employee into your office and get right to the point ("Jerry, I want to discuss your late report"). The worst thing you can do when you must reprimand someone is to try and stall until just the right moment to deliver the bad news. There is no right moment. You both know what's coming, and stalling only increases anxiety and the potential for argument.

Describe the unacceptable activity, and be factual rather than judgmental.

[*Judgmental*:] Jerry, I can't tolerate your late reports.

[*Factual*:] Jerry, your last two late reports cost the company lost sales of $5,000.

Then pause for a few moments of silence.

Encourage the employee to tell his or her side of the story by asking open-ended questions ("In your opinion, Jerry, why did this happen?"). Then listen carefully to the response: Is your employee accepting responsibility or just providing excuses? If your subordinate does not agree there is a problem, it won't be solved. So ask the employee for some probable solutions. Then you both should jointly agree on the most appropriate corrective action.

Finally, conclude the meeting by restating your employee's value to the company. Have the subordinate summarize the agreed-upon solution in his or her own words, to make sure you both have come to the same understanding. Schedule a follow-up meeting if necessary.

As managers we are quick to reprimand but slow to praise. Yet the simple act of acknowledging a job well done is essential for maximum productivity in your business. We all like to be told when we've done a good job. Praise makes us work just that much harder.

Praising, unlike reprimanding, should usually be done publicly, before the appropriate staff members, and also in private on a one-to-one basis. The point is to let the employees you are praising know that their actions have benefited the company and that you truly appreciate their efforts.

Avoiding the "Good Guy" Image

Too often, new managers try the "good guy" approach to management, believing that an easygoing style will elicit the best from workers. Unfortunately, this approach usually works only as long as things are rosy. I recommend that you adopt a style that combines an easygoing attitude with fairness, firmness, and flexibility. Being fair means that you do not take advantage of employees, that you do not ask anything of them you would not ask of yourself. Being firm means that when you assimilate all the facts and make a decision, you are not easily swayed. Being flexible means that, while you may be firm, you are also open to employee ideas if they have merit.

Motivating Your Staff

As an entrepreneur, you are driven to make your company succeed. You are willing to work long hours and take calculated risks in order to achieve success. Because of your drive, you look at others on your team working long hours alongside you, and you probably assume they are driven by the same force that motivates you.

If so, you are wrong. Few if any of your employees are entrepreneurs. They may work hard, but they are not driven by the same force that motivates you. They believe in working hard to achieve a certain level of management and comfort. Once they reach that level, they will likely practice risk avoidance and not rock the boat, so they can maintain what they have earned. This attitude isn't bad, but you must understand it exists and motivate your people accordingly.

To inspire employees to high performance, you need to instill confidence, pride, and commitment in them. Furthermore, you must make sure you keep them satisfied. Most new companies ignore employee satisfaction, because they don't see it as contributing to profits. Nothing could be further from the truth! If employee satisfaction is not continuously addressed, morale suffers, productivity drops (therefore products cost more to manufacture and/or sell), and employee turnover increases (resulting in additional costs to hire and train new employees). The environment you create within your company will determine how motivated and committed your employees will be. Following are some ideas on how to develop a productive and satisfying environment for workers.

Develop a Review/Appraisal System That Fosters Employee Growth

Foster within your employees a willingness to further develop their business skills for the good of the company. An innovative way to do this is with the employee review process. Typically management overlooks this area, and it is a golden opportunity with which to inspire your people.

Here's how it works: Have your supervisors meet every six months with each individual employee. At these meetings, the supervisor and the employee jointly agree on a set of performance goals for the employee for the next six months. These goals are prioritized according to their potential contribution to the success of the company. Some of these goals may be short-term (to be accomplished within the next six months), while others may be longer-term (with some progress expected during the next six months). The goals are then written down and initialed by both the employee and the supervisor, with a copy going to each.

Six months later, employee and supervisor meet again to discuss the employee's accomplishments toward meeting these goals. A statement of accomplishment is written and placed in the employee's file, along with a new set of goals for the next six months.

Salary reviews, which are handled separately, are given on an annual basis in conjunction with every other performance review. Salary increases are tied to the employee's performance in meeting the goals set forth in the biannual management/employee meeting. This process instills in employees a feeling of being contributing members of the team and inspires them to work harder to meet their goals, knowing their salary increase depends upon it. An added benefit of this system is that the supervisor can steer the goal-setting process to ensure that the employee develops the experience necessary for promotion within the company.

Practice "Letting Go"

Delegating can be a difficult task for company founders, but there comes a time when you must begin to pass responsibility and accountability on to others. It might be tough at first to fight that tiny voice inside that says, "I know that I can do it better and more efficiently if *I* control it." But it's better to listen to the other and wiser voice that continues ". . . but I *must* give them the responsibility and the experience if my company is to grow and prosper."

To make the task of letting go less painful, take it in small steps. Start by giving your subordinates the right to make decisions and to commit the resources needed to achieve a goal you both agree on. Delegate an entire project to them, and let them take full responsibility for carrying it through.

If you have trained your employees well, delegating should be a far less painful process than you might think. Many entrepreneurs have been flabbergasted to find that the tasks they finally delegated were carried out more efficiently by their subordinates than by themselves!

Use Company Logos and Slogans

If your company is relatively new and not yet steeped in tradition, a slogan or a logo that communicates the history and/or vision of the company can become a point of pride for your employees. If it is sincere, they will readily share this pride with others. Slogans and logos help employees to identify with the company, thereby reinforcing their sense of belonging and contributing to a worthy establishment.

You might have T-shirts, jackets, coffee mugs, and other items emblazoned with the company logo or slogan. Then give them out as awards for excellence at company athletic events and company picnics and parties, where you foster group cohesiveness (also consider offering these items for sale at a reduced cost to other employees).

All of these techniques will help your employees become more motivated to achieve. It's always important to keep in mind that motivation will emerge only in an environment where employees feel they belong, that they are critical members of the corporate team.

Maximizing Your Profits

Launching and running a business, even with all of its pressures, can be an intoxicating experience. However, in the midst of this giddy experience you must always remember that you are in business to make a profit. Never lose sight of the fact that your financiers (whether bankers or equity investors) also expect to make a profit on their investment in your company. Since their profit will come from your profit, you had better manage the business in a conservative, frugal manner, so that your company starts to show a profit as soon as possible.

Here are some tips on maximizing profits as your business grows:

Capital Equipment

One way to maximize profits at an early stage of your business is to purchase only necessary capital equipment. For every equipment purchase over $1,000, I recommend you do a brief written analysis to determine how soon the equipment will save enough money to pay for itself. Then, consider the source of the money you will need in order to purchase this equipment, and ask yourself the following questions:

"If I plan to use equity capital, I will have to give up company ownership to purchase the equipment. Is it worth it?"

"If I plan to finance the equipment using debt capital, what is the cost of borrowing the money when I compute the equipment's payback period?"

"Financing equipment out of profits is the best strategy, but will I miss those dollars when I have a cash flow crunch because of an unforeseen development a few months from now?"

To make sure you don't go overboard in buying equipment rather than leasing it, establish a fixed yearly capital equipment budget and stick to it, no matter how good a deal the salesperson offers you.

People Costs

Another way to maximize early profits is to hire the right people. When you launched your company, you were able to hire people whom you knew or had checked out carefully. As your company continues to grow, you will find yourself hiring more staff people, and most of them will be total strangers.

You cannot afford to have any unproductive workers on the payroll. Furthermore, the trauma of having to fire employees if they don't work out (not to mention the trauma of doling out unemployment insurance) should be considered in developing your hiring strategy.

I suggest that you bypass these problems by hiring additional staff through temporary employment services to get you through peak periods in the early, volatile times of your company. You'll pay a little more on an hourly basis, but you will have no tax records to maintain, no withholding to worry about, no company benefit costs, and no unemployment costs. Furthermore, if the employee doesn't work out, you just call the employment company and ask for another candidate tomorrow.

And if the temporary does work out, then you can usually hire him or her permanently from the agency after a preset period (and the possible payment of several weeks' commission). Check out the agency's policy beforehand. If one temporary agency won't work with you on this full-time transfer, then find another agency that will.

All of your labor costs should be studied carefully, to ensure that you are maximizing profits. You must have an opening for a full-time job before you hire a full-time person. This may sound obvious, but many companies waste money by hiring someone they want on staff without having a solid position for that employee. No young company can afford to spend such unproductive dollars.

Another way to keep down labor costs in the early stages of your business is by taking advantage of state job service agencies. Some of these agencies offer programs that pay 50% or more of a new employee's wages during a training period that may last for six months or longer. If your company could use part-time people, an excellent source of workers may be those experienced women who left the work force to raise a family. If they have young children, you could consider offering them a 9 A.M. to 3 P.M. shift, so they can pick up their children after school. With part-time workers you don't have to offer additional benefits; this can be particularly useful when your company is young and still struggling to get on its feet. If you anticipate laying off part-time people periodically, you may also want to consider hiring them through temporary services, to avoid having to pay unemployment compensation.

For other part-time jobs in your company, such as a bookkeeper, consider hiring experienced retirees for two to three hours per day, so they don't lose their social security benefits. That way both of you win.*

Overhead Costs

Investigate each of your significant overhead expense categories. Focus on the most costly categories to determine how expenses could be reduced in them.

For example, is it more cost effective to have your leads screened by an outside telemarketing firm? Could you reduce telephone costs with a WATS line?

As you look at your in-house processes, carefully evaluate each area in terms of "make or buy." Perhaps some of the things you are now doing in-house could be farmed out more inexpensively. For example, if you are presently assembling products by hand, could you save money subcontracting this activity to an assembly house equipped with

---

*For additional ideas, see *How to Choose and Use Temporary Services* in the "Recommended Reading List" at the end of this book.

automated equipment? Conversely, maybe some of the things you are now subcontracting could be done more cheaply in-house. Each activity should be evaluated in terms of its effect on your bottom line.

Tracking Your Results

The Management Progress Report

Most of us don't want to take the time to prepare written progress reports, but I maintain they are essential, no matter how small your business. I recommend you get in the habit of preparing monthly summaries of the progress of your business (even when the news isn't good) for a variety of reasons.

When your business is small and growing, things move rapidly. Having a written summary each month helps you log events that might otherwise have been forgotten. Later, during an annual planning session, you can spread out the past year's monthly progress reports and spot trends you might have otherwise overlooked. Furthermore, by periodically providing a copy of this report to your bank, you help your loan officer better understand your company, easing the way for future borrowings.

As your business grows and additional equity is required, this monthly summary will provide assurance to present and prospective investors that you have the experience required to run the business.

Figure 9-1 illustrates a memorandum format you can use for your report.

This monthly management report should be distributed with the detailed financial statements for the period. If there is nothing to report for one of the sections during a particular reporting period, enter the following statement in that section: "No significant developments during this period."

Please don't attempt to hide any negative results from your board of directors. If you failed to meet your planned forecast, don't panic. Your written management report (as well as your summary at the next board meeting) provides an excellent forum for addressing the reasons for your failure to meet the plan and for showing how you intend to

Figure 9-1. Memorandum format for monthly progress reports.

MEMORANDUM

TO: XYZ COMPANY BOARD OF DIRECTORS AND INVESTORS

FROM: J.R. JONES, PRESIDENT

RE: CEO's MONTHLY MANAGEMENT REPORT, APRIL 19XX

DATE: MAY 10, 19XX

I.   GENERAL

Summarize the company's operating performance during the last month, along with any significant developments.

II.   FINANCIAL

Summarize the month's financial results compared to your plan. For example:

	Current Month	Actuals YTD*	Forecast YTD*	Variance
Sales	$14,560	$52,210	$54,500	$(2,290)
Cost of sales	5,830	20,840	21,100	260**
Gross profit	$ 8,730	$31,370	$33,400	$(2,030)
Operating expenses	6,710	24,010	25,100	1090**
Net profit	$ 2,020	$ 7,360	$ 8,300	$ (940)

Comment on reasons for any significant deviations from your forecast. Discuss any other financial developments, such as new loans, payments coming due, etc.

*Year to Date

**Variances shown as better or worse than forecast. Variances better than forecast are positive. Note that variance in this section is for YTD forecast only.

(continues)

Figure 9-1.   (continued)

III.   SALES

Show a breakdown of sales by product line and comment on any significant developments or deviations. Include variances against both monthly and YTD forecasts. Mention any new programs or corrective action being initiated.

IV.   OPERATING EXPENSES

Show variances against both monthly and YTD forecasts. Detail any significant expense categories if they are significantly over budget (e.g., telephone, advertising, travel). State any new programs or corrective actions that will affect operating expenses.

V.   PRODUCTION (include only if appropriate for your business)

Discuss significant developments on production line (to increase volume, cut costs, improve quality, etc.).

VI.   DEVELOPMENT (include only if appropriate for your business)

If you are developing a new product or service, its status could be discussed here.

VII.   PERSONNEL

List the number of employees in various categories (management, administrative, sales, production, etc.) as well as any changes from the previous month. Comment on the reasons for any changes.

VIII.   CAPITAL EQUIPMENT

Discuss the purchase or proposed purchase of any capital equipment. Indicate whether the purchase was included in the forecast budget, and provide an indication of the payback period (How soon will this specific equipment pay for itself in improved productivity, increased sales, etc.?).

IX.   OTHER

Discuss any other significant developments affecting the business during the period, as well as any anticipated events during the next period.

improve performance. The summary should include the following points in the appropriate section.*

- Why you have deviated from plan (provide reasons, not excuses)
- What you are doing to counteract this unsatisfactory perform-ance
- What the new results will be when you implement the needed changes

The Z-Score

Whether your company is in its infancy or is well established, do not judge its performance solely on the basis of the bottom line of your income statement. For a start-up company, this figure may be negative for a number of months. Conversely, I know of established companies that showed a paper profit but were bleeding to death internally.

A better measure of a company's performance is the Z-Score. The power of the Z-Score is that no matter how large or small your com-pany, no matter what stage of growth, it provides a fair assessment of how well you are doing, because it takes into account a number of health factors.

The Z-Score was developed by Edward Altman in the mid-1960s.** It is a single number that tracks the company's performance, and it can be used to spot danger signals before they lead to major catastrophes. The conservative calculation of this number gives you a critical perspective of your financial statements. It looks upon profits as good, assets as marginally beneficial, long-term liabilities as bad, and current liabilities as horrible.

The Z-Score was originally developed to measure the likelihood of bankruptcy, but it has proved over time to be an excellent measure of the overall financial performance of a company. If a company's Z-Score

---

*For example, if the problem was low sales, address these points in Section III: SALES; if the problem was high operating expenses, address these points in Section IV: OPERATING EXPENSES; if the problem was capital equipment, address it in Section VIII: CAPITAL EQUIPMENT; etc.

**Edward I. Altman, *Corporate Financial Distress* (New York: John Wiley & Sons, 1983).

is less than 1.1, bankruptcy is probably looming ahead. If a company's score is above 2.6, the business is on solid ground.

The Z-Score is computed by calculating four ratios: X_1 is a measure of your company's liquidity; X_2 is a measure of your company's cumulative profitability; X_3 is a measure of return on assets; and X_4 is an inverse of the debt-to-equity ratio.

These four variables are calculated as follows (if necessary, refer to the balance sheet and income statement definitions from Chapter 4):

$$
\begin{aligned}
X_1 &= \text{(Current assets } - \text{ Current liabilities)} \div \text{Total assets} \\
X_2 &= \text{Retained earnings} \div \text{Total assets} \\
X_3 &= \text{Operating profit (or net profit before interest} \\
&\quad \text{and taxes)} \div \text{Total assets} \\
X_4 &= \text{Net worth } \div \text{ Total liabilities}
\end{aligned}
$$

Next, plug these variables into the Z-Score formula:

$$
\text{Z-Score} = 6.56(X_1) + 3.26(X_2) + 6.72(X_3) + 1.05(X_4)
$$

As an example, let's use the figures from the financials presented in the balance sheet and income statement examples (Figures 4-1 and 4-2) of Chapter 4:

Current assets = $554, 250   Current liabilities = $262,400
Total assets = $961,050   Total liabilities = $488,200
Retained earnings = $192,850   Operating profit = $161,780
Net worth = $107,420

$$
\begin{aligned}
X_1 &= (554,250 - 262,400) \div 961,050 \\
&= 291,850 \div 961,050 = 0.304 \\
X_2 &= 192,850 \div 961,050 = 0.201 \\
X_3 &= 161,780 \div 961,050 = 0.168 \\
X_4 &= 107,420 \div 488,200 = 0.220
\end{aligned}
$$

$$
\begin{aligned}
Z &= \text{Score} = 6.56(0.304) + 3.26(0.201) \\
&\quad + 6.72(0.168) + 1.05(0.220) = 4.009
\end{aligned}
$$

In Altman's early-1980s study of a number of companies, non-bankrupt companies had a mean Z-Score of $+7.7$, while the mean Z-Score of bankrupt companies was -4.06.

Perhaps more important than the absolute value of the Z-Score for your company is an assessment of how this number is changing on a monthly basis. Start-up companies may have a negative score initially, while established companies may have a positive score. If your Z-Score starts to fall sharply, warning bells should ring.

Failure Viruses

Some apparently healthy companies that seem to be well along the road to success suddenly come down with what I call a failure virus. Here are some of the viruses that typically affect growing businesses, along with some suggestions for preventing them:

- *Managerial apathy.* It's not uncommon for entrepreneurs to create a new company and enjoy the thrill and chaos of the early years, only to become bored and restless as their companies grow. They find the duties of everyday management far more tedious than the hectic days when they were forming their companies, and they miss those early days.

   If these people choose to remain at the helm, they can't help but communicate their lack of enthusiasm to the rest of the company. Performance is bound to flounder. If you have reached this point of apathy, the best course of action is to relegate yourself to a creative position you crave (for example, senior vice-president of development) and bring in an experienced chief executive to ensure your company's continued dynamic growth.

- *Failure to adjust to critical market shifts.* Your customers' needs change. Iceboxes, black-and-white television, phonograph records, and black rotary-dial telephones have all gone the way of the dinosaur. If you aren't sensitive to the marketplace, and if you don't modify your products and services accordingly, the skeleton of your company may also end up in the La Brea tar pits.

- *Failure to keep up with significant technology improvements.* If the competition suddenly offers performance, more bells and whistles, and/or lower price, your product sales could evaporate overnight. Constant planning for new products is essential to the continued growth of most businesses. Always have a contingency plan in case a dramatic product improvement comes onto the scene. Not many one-product companies make it in the long run.

▪ *Increased cost of borrowed money.* What if interest rates suddenly skyrocket, as they did in the early 1980s? You could be faced with some hard choices. You might be forced either to convert some of your debt to equity or to shrink the size of your business, lest you lose it. Make sure you consider this possibility in your annual planning.

▪ *Lack of managerial ability.* Sometimes companies simply outgrow certain managers. In that case, you'll be faced with the difficult but critical decision to replace these people with more suitable management talent or risk jeopardizing the growth of your company. To keep tabs on management, in my companies we have always conducted an annual management assessment. The assesssment is made by direct subordinates, and it has proved to be very effective in determining who is competent to continue managing as the company grows and who is not.

▪ *Managerial cowardice.* Sometimes, unfortunately, senior management sees that there are certain steps that need to be taken to streamline the business, but it simply isn't willing to take those steps, preferring to look the other way and hope things will improve over time. They rarely do. Perhaps a position needs to be eliminated. If it is not, the company can be slowly dragged down by the excess baggage. Furthermore, morale suffers because everyone else sees the problem and senses management's unwillingness to act.

You *must* be able to justify every dollar spent and every staff position. If you are unable to act on your own, either replace yourself or use outside consultants to justify changes to your staff. Looking the other way when a major change needs to be made has killed more than one business.

▪ *Lack of adequate cash for new products.* Companies sometimes rush to develop an exciting new product line without recognizing (or rather choosing to ignore) the barriers to entry and the dollars involved (engineering, tooling, manufacturing, and particularly marketing). Don't make an emotional decision with a new product. Understand what the true costs to achieve profitability for this new product will be.

Then either find the capital first, shelve the product idea for now, or sell the idea to another company.

▪ *Sudden unforeseen real-world developments.* Copper prices spiral, oil/plastics prices skyrocket, a patent challenge suddenly appears, or product liability insurance doubles or triples overnight. Usually you can't predict these events; therefore, the best protection is to have some diversification within your product as a hedge against catastrophic events that could ruin your business. Take a lesson from Johns-Manville, which focused almost exclusively on asbestos products.

▪ *Management conflicts.* Healthy competition among the ranks of senior management or within your board of directors is good for business, but bad blood is not. It is the CEO's responsibility to call the shots, to resolve management conflicts before they go out of control and start to drain the lifeblood of the company. If senior management cannot accomplish this, then either get outside consultant help or replace the CEO.

▪ *Expansion beyond sources of capital.* This might sound like a great problem to have, but it stymies many successful companies and fatally injures a number of them. Planning for growth and adequate cash flow are absolutely critical. You must visit your financiers long before you really need cash; otherwise you probably won't get it. If you find your company caught in the whirlpool of increasing sales and decreasing cash, raise your prices, stretch out deliveries, or raise additional equity.

▪ *Inadequate control systems.* When production volume increases without adequate quality control, when advertising leads increase without good screening control, when purchasing increases without effective cost control, when payables increase without effective payment control, you may have big problems. After establishing the control systems I discussed earlier in the chapter, review these controls and modify them periodically to keep pace with your growing company.

▪ *Dependence on a single customer.* It's not unusual for a small company to start out with a single customer, but unless you are a committed gambler, you had better bring on other customers. Any time a customer represents 30% or more of your business, you are putting your company out on a limb. You had better increase your customer base to reduce your exposure.

There are any number of other potential viruses that could strike your business. Prevention is the best cure for them. Make sure that you periodically review all of the operations of your company, plan ahead, and anticipate as much as possible all of the problems that could seriously affect your business. That's the only way to ensure immunity.

EXERCISE: The Last Look?

By now I would hope your notebook has become your silent partner, a treasure chest storing up valuable ideas you want to apply to your business.

Add to your notebook your thoughts on quality, service, staying in touch, integrity, praising, reprimanding, and motivating as you could apply them to improve productivity, sales, and profits in your business.

Then keep your notebook at your side, because this *isn't* your last look. Your book has become your secret weapon against failure.

* * *

Afterword

The Journey of a Lifetime

In this book I have shared with you some of the insights I have gained in the process of starting three small businesses. I began the book by telling you of the overwhelming odds against your success. Then I spent the rest of these pages showing you how implementing the Microgenesis system can shift the odds of achieving success in your favor. Now I challenge you to put what you have learned into action.

I asked you to make the effort to create your personal notebook during our journey through the ten Microgenesis levels so you would have a personalized strategy guide to refer to when you need it. Even though you have finished the book, make sure to continue updating your notebook as your company's needs change. Think of your notebook as a constantly updated operating manual for your business.

Entrepreneurship is addictive. You may already be hooked. Perhaps it began with your frustration with working for others, making sacrifices so they could realize their dreams. Now it's your turn. When you finally taste the thrill of creating your own business, you can never again be content to be someone else's hireling. Once you realize your full entrepreneurial potential, you'll unleash energy and achieve results that will amaze you.

Follow the Microgenesis process, and you will march to a different drumbeat. In doing so, you will leave the mainstream of our working population. You'll begin to appear different in your own eyes, and others will view you differently as well.

Old friendships might fade away and new ones form as your life is gradually transformed. Television will be ignored and never missed.

If you are like most entrepreneurs, you will become driven to achieve your goals.

But don't confuse achieving goals with finding happiness. When I first boarded the train with other entrepreneurs bound for success, I had no idea how rough the journey would be. I kept looking up the tracks, focusing all my energies on the treasure chest of happiness that I believed awaited my arrival at the station.

If you share this same feeling, when your train finally pulls into success, a surprise awaits you. Once you arrive, the baggage of new responsibilities brought on by wealth and leadership will be heavy to handle. Furthermore, you will find that the freedom you dreamed would appear at the end of the journey does not exist. If you were a shallow person when you boarded the train, then you may be a very depressed person when you arrive. No magic transformation takes place along the way. Money does not diminish your problems. On the contrary, it creates a whole new set of them.

Most of the entrepreneurs I know who envisioned happiness at the end of the journey found that when the train arrived the expected happiness did not arrive with it. Instead, these executives found disillusionment, despair, and often divorce. They learned too late that happiness was to be found along the way, not at the end of the ride. Their spouses offered it, their colleagues offered it, their friends offered it—but they chose to ignore it and focus instead on the illusion that big money would bring them great satisfaction.

I don't wish to discourage you; after all, I'm one of those addicted entrepreneurs myself, and I had to learn some of these same lessons the hard way. But you can take advantage of the earlier entrepreneurs who blazed the trail before you. I hope this book has helped you to learn from the mistakes we've made, so that your journey to success will be as smooth and as joyful as possible.

Just as others have paved the way for you, I suggest that you strive to help make the journey a little easier for those who follow you. If you only take the train partway and decide to get off, then quit with pride, meeting your commitments and clearing your debts so the route to success is clear for others. As your train is barreling along the tracks of life toward your goal, take time to look out the windows, drinking in all that is around you. Others on the journey will be there to offer help when you need it. You should be equally willing to share your experience and knowledge with your fellow travelers.

No matter what stage you have achieved with your business, I want you to leave these pages with the sense that your journey is just beginning.

I don't wish you luck. Rather I wish you hard work, plenty of challenges, a sharp competitor or two to keep you on your toes, and the ultimate realization of your dream. In other words, I wish you success!

As you concentrate on achieving your goals, don't forget to focus some of your energies on the pleasures of the journey. For when you do reach your destination, when success finally comes into view, you'll look back on the trip as the best time of your life.

Appendix

Free (and Almost Free) Sources of Help

I frequently receive calls from young entrepreneurs wanting my help in creating their business plan and developing their companies. When I ask if they have used any of the *free* sources that are available, they are usually flabbergasted. But these sources do exist, so don't pay for help you can get for free.

One of your first stops should be your nearest Small Business Development Center (SBDC). These centers are a cooperative effort between the educational community, governments (federal, state, and local), and the private sector. There are a number of SBDC offices in each state that can offer you a variety of free services, including the creation of your pro forma financial statements. SBDCs can also steer you to other sources of assistance.

To find your nearest SBDC, contact the economic development sources discussed in the next paragraph, or call your nearest U.S. Small Business Administration district office.

You might also contact your city, county, and state government economic development offices and ask for the names of area organizations (and key contact people) whose job it is to assist small businesses. Define the specific problems for which you are seeking assistance. Area and community colleges often have offices for small-business development. Ask about these as well.

If you have a manufacturing company, you might want to contact the National Association of Management and Technical Assistance

265

Centers (NAMTAC). This association is affiliated with universities throughout the country. Its purpose is to provide university-related management and technology-transfer assistance to businesses. Contact the center in your state so that its field representative will start calling on you regularly. He or she can provide counseling in a number of areas, including administration, finance, marketing, and engineering. The NAMTAC field reps will put you in touch with one of their "experts" (college professors and a few ex-businesspeople) who can assist you.

To find out if there is a NAMTAC-affiliated group in your state, contact the National Association of Management and Technical Assistance Centers, 733 15th Street NW, Suite 917, Washington, D.C. 20005, (202)347-6740.

The U.S. Small Business Administration (SBA)

Don't forget your nearest U.S. Small Business Administration (SBA) district office. There you will find business development specialists and a number of available publications with helpful ideas. Also consider asking the SBA for assistance from SCORE (the Service Corps Of Retired Executives). The SBA and SCORE may also be able to recommend some other sources of assistance.

The SBA maintains a Small Business Answer Desk in Washington, D.C., that you can reach by calling toll-free 1-800-368-5855. By dialing this number, you can quickly locate the names of the appropriate SBA staff to contact for assistance. The SBA also maintains a Small Business Institute Program (SBI). This program offers personalized management assistance to small businesses through SBI teams of senior and graduate business administration students organized into counseling teams under faculty supervision.

Finally, there is NTIS, the National Technical Information Service, headquartered at the Department of Commerce. NTIS has a passive data search service. You provide a list of key search words and approximately $100, and NTIS will provide reams of reports related to your research topic. A caution to those using this service: Make sure you narrow the focus of your search sufficiently. You'll find it far easier to search through 200 pages of printouts than 2,000.

The Center for Utilization of Federal Technology (CUFT)

Another part of the NTIS is The Center for the Utilization of Federal Technology (CUFT). CUFT provides a number of information tools designed to link businesses with appropriate technologies and resources. Some of these publications include:

The *Directory of Federal & State Business Assistance—A Guide to New & Growing Companies.* This directory describes almost 600 state and federal programs (and agencies) that specifically assist new or growing businesses, along with names, addresses, and telephone numbers for each listing.

The *Directory of Federal Laboratory & Technology Resources—A Guide to Services, Facilities & Expertise.* This directory lists the capabilities and expertise of hundreds of Federal labs and research centers, as well as more than 90 technical information centers.

The *Catalog of Government Inventions Available for Licensing.* This catalog is a complete listing of more than 1,000 government-owned inventions patented during the previous year and available for licensing to small businesses. Individual inventions are segmented into subject areas, and detailed subject and inventor indexes are included (catalogs for the past five years are usually available).

The *Federal Laboratory Technology Catalog—A Guide to New & Practical Technologies.* This is an annual compendium of more than 1,000 selected processes, instruments, materials, equipment, software, services, and techniques in one convenient volume. These key results and developments from the past year are arranged in 23 separate subject areas for easy referral, along with a detailed index (issues for the past four years are usually available).

You can order any of the above documents by telephone, by contacting the CUFT Sales Desk, NTIS, 5285 Port Royal Road, Springfield, Va. 22161, (703)487-4650. (Credit cards are accepted for telephone orders.) You might also ask for their free information brochure #PR-801.

Recommended Reading List

Ashman, David, and Adam Meyerson. *The Wall Street Journal on Management*. New York: Dow Jones & Company, 1985.

Bennis, Warren, and Burt Namus. *Leaders: The Strategies for Taking Charge*. New York: Harper & Row, 1985.

Blanchard, Kenneth, Patricia Zigarmi, and Drea Zigarmi. *Leadership and the One Minute Manager*. New York: William Morrow & Company, 1985.

Bolles, Richard Nelson. *What Color Is Your Parachute?* Berkeley, California: Ten Speed Press (soft cover), 1985 (revised annually).

Bright, Deborah. *Gearing Up for the Fast Lane*. New York: Random House, 1985.

Easton, Thomas, and Ralph Conant. *Cutting Loose: Making the Transition From Employee to Entrepreneur*. Chicago: Probus Publishing, 1985.

Gumpert, David, ed. *Growing Concerns: Building and Managing the Smaller Business*. New York: John Wiley & Sons, 1984.

Inc. Magazine. The Best of Inc. *Guide to Finding Capital*. New York: Prentice-Hall (paperback), 1988.

Lewis, William M., and Nancy H. Molloy. *How to Choose and Use Temporary Services*. New York: AMACOM Books, 1991.

Merrill, Ronald, and Henry Sedgwick. *The New Venture Handbook*. New York: AMACOM Books (paperback), 1987.

Molloy, John. *Dress for Success*. New York: Warner Books (paperback), 1975.

Molloy, John. *Live For Success*. New York: William Morrow & Company, 1981.

Peters, Tom, and Nancy Austin. *A Passion for Excellence*. New York: Random House, 1985.

Ramacitti, David. *Do-It-Yourself Publicity.* New York: AMACOM Books, 1990.

Rich, Stanley, and David Gumpert. *Business Plans That Win $$$.* New York: Harper & Row, 1985.

White, Richard. *The Entrepreneur's Manual.* Radnor, Penn.: Chilton Books, 1977.

Ziglar, Zig. *Zig Ziglar's Secrets of Closing the Sale.* New York: Berkley Books (paperback), 1982.

Index

[Italic page numbers refer to figures.]